FOR DOG'S SAKE

A guide to understanding your dog's
soul and purpose

Dedication

This book is dedicated to all the remarkable canine beings we share and have shared our lives with.

Each one of you has provided our family with wonderfully meaningful experiences, precious memories, and invaluable opportunities for learning.

It would be our profound hope that you have found your lifetimes shared with us as beneficial and enjoyable as we have found ours with you.

Although there have (and continue to be) an innumerable number of occasions on which you have all been the causes of stress, heartache, anguish, torment, frustration and grief - and basically been a colossal pain in the butt - you have all been cherished.

Alongside the difficult times you have offered us unforeseeable pleasures, riotous fun, hilarious laughter, total acceptance, unparalleled companionship, unreserved warmth, unspeakable joy, and most of all, never-ending love.

We feel blessed to have had our lives so enriched.

We have loved, and will always love you all.

In all ways, all of you are always with us.

It is a source of sadness that you will never read these words, but we hope that in your lives with us, you will have felt and known they are true.

Acknowledgements

We would like to offer our special thanks to the following people:

Verona – My oldest friend (we've known each other since we were both five). Your patience and commitment in making sure that this book reaches the reader in as comprehensible a form as possible has been outstanding. More than this, you have reignited my enthusiasm on the several occasions when I ran out of steam. Thank you. It simply wouldn't be here without your invaluable help and advice.

Christine – You unwittingly (?) provoked the decision to write it; and then rounded up all the questions; to say nothing of your excellent work on our websites. Thank you.

Colleen – You constantly and consistently demonstrate in all ways what a good friend is. Thank you.

Mona & Glen - For the compound and so, so much more. Thank you.

My parents – For your continued support of our bizarre world and keeping the wheels on the wagon. Thank you.

Laurel and Salim – For venturing out in all weathers and road conditions to keep those supplies coming. We'd all starve without you. Thank you.

Jodie and Matt – Whose enormous kindness ensures that we manage to keep everyone fed and happy. Thank you.

Tristan – You stoically continue to do all those things we couldn't ask anyone else to do, and you make life that little bit easier. Thank you.

Tracey – Words are never enough. Thank you.

M.A.H. – For your valuable and persistent(!) input. Sorry I teased you about not giving you a mention. Thank you. PS. Teagan sends his love.

T. – We are still here now because of your generosity. Thank you.

About the author and dogs

Apart from what I've learned here, I know a little bit about dogs.

I am NOT a: Scientist; Naturalist; Dog Psychologist; Animal Behaviourist; Dog Trainer; Veterinarian; Dog Groomer, Dog Walker; Pet Sitter; Animal Communicator; or any other kind of knowledge expert in the field of dogs.

But I am a channel. This basically means I can communicate with beings in the etheric. More of this later.

I am a dog lover (despite growing up disliking the creatures intensely) and over the course of the past twenty years, my wife Sharon and I, and our grown-up son, Tristan, have shared our lives with sixty-one wonderful hairy canine beings, and one equally wonderful Grey Wolf. They have come to us with a variety of backgrounds. Some we have bought; a great many have been rescue dogs; some have been born into our pack.

When I say 'shared our lives', I really do mean 'share'. Our dogs do not live outside. They hsve free access to a four acre play area, but there are no kennels or cages. We literally all live together at very close quarters.

We're often asked how so many dogs can possibly get on with each other. Having such a large a pack defies people's expectations of what is possible. The surprising answer is that they all get along just fine. Just as in a human family, there is closeness and rivalry, likes and dislikes, disagreements, and occasional spats. But generally, they're very accepting and accommodating of one another; and heartbreakingly devoted to us.

Then people ask what our lives are like as their humans, to which the response must be: the dogs take a LOT of looking after! Our average day is full of challenges, fun, frustration, and humour, It is always interesting and it can often be very rewarding.

As you read through the book, you'll see many pictures of them (although some photos are not of our dogs).

We have opened our home to a wide variety of breeds, albeit mostly giant/large ones. If you want the fine print, we have been the full-time guardians of:

15 Siberian Huskies
10 Leonbergers
4 Alaskan Malamutes
5 Mixed breeds
3 Grand Basset Griffon Vendeens
4 St Bernards
2 Great Danes
2 Standard Poodles
2 Moyen Poodles
2 Rough Collies
2 Shar Peis

1 English Pointer
1 Petit Bassett Griffon Vendeen
1 Maremma Sheepdog
1 Japanese Akita
1 Neapolitan Mastiff
1 Afghan Hound
1 Irish Wolfhound
1 Newfoundland
1 Tibetan Mastiff
1 Portuguese Water Dog
1 Bernedoodle

and the Grey Wolf.

If you're wondering how we came to have so many dogs, the answer is the subject of a trilogy of books, details of which can be found at the back of this book. It's way too complicated to explain, even in brief!

There are also several others who have come into our lives briefly for fostering or other reasons. At present, 45 dogs are still with us. We have never let a dog go, or moved one on. Once they come to us, it is for life. We couldn't bear to let them go. We're dog people!

Me with just part of the pack.

CHAPTERS

Chapter 1

FROM DOGS TO YOU

"All knowledge, the totality of all questions and all answers is contained in the dog."

Kafka

What is a dog?

It's all too easy to look at a dog and dismiss it as *just a dog*. But do we ever stop to consider what that means? We think we understand them based upon the broad and rather superficial concept we have of a dog.

It is a limited (and limiting) belief which is created by a scant assessment of them that probably goes something like this:

A dog is a being that is different from a human, therefore…
A dog lives a simpler life than a human, therefore…
A dog is less sophisticated than a human, therefore…
A dog has less intelligence than a human, therefore…
A dog is a lesser being than a human, therefore….
A dog has less worth than a human.

And everything else that follows in our estimation of them stems from these basic tenets.

I'm not saying that you've actively thought any of these things. You don't have to. We're brought up in a society that already has this mode of thinking as the accepted way of seeing *all* creatures around us. We are undisputedly at the top of the pecking order, if only in our own eyes, simply because no other species on the planet can do the things that we do. Everything else is therefore automatically inferior. Dogs just happen to get a slightly better deal than most. This is because they're one of the animals that humankind has chosen to domesticate for keeping as pets.

Sure, we love them. They provide companionship. They can be cute and funny. In fact, we can come up with a whole lot of positives about them.

But that doesn't mean that we've taken the time to ponder over what it is that they are. What is their purpose in being here? What is their experience of life really like? Why have we developed a co-dependant relationship with them above most others? What is their expectation from their lifetimes? Do they need to achieve anything?

Even though we may regard our treatment of them as benign, even munificent, the vast majority of the population would still regard dogs as those simple, lesser beings. We may have a soft spot for them, but their lives are still infinitely less important than our human ones.

This may be understandable thinking, but it's also somewhat arrogant, short-sighted and ultimately, as this book may reveal to you, plain wrong. A dog's experience of life is *no less valid* than ours.

On the other hand, we have also evolved what may be thought of as 'The dog mythology'.

This is basically a construct of our imaginations that would have us believe that a dog is in some way sainted. It is a paragon of virtues that include loyalty, faithfulness, and a wholly benign and selfless nature. Dogs, above all other creatures, are 'man's best friend'.

Numerous learned and highly regarded writers have passed comment upon their wondrous attributes, almost to the point where we could be forgiven for believing that their name is a misspelling.

Sadly, the mythology has been created in ignorance of their motivations and needs whilst they are here. We tend to assume that they're here to benefit us and it's a convenient belief to hold.

But it's not just our attitude to dogs that is misguided.

Unfortunately, our mindset regarding them is indicative of our belief system regarding all the creatures around us.

So whilst this book is about the true nature and purpose of dogs, and the answers to the questions posed only seem to apply to dogs, many of the principles discussed here apply to *all* sentient beings upon the planet.

The purpose of this book

This book has been written not so much for your benefit but for your dog's.

As the author of three previous books (ostensibly) about dogs, I get asked a lot of questions. This one contains the answers to as comprehensive a list of questions about dogs that I could muster from the many contributors who have wanted or needed responses to the issues raised within.

As such, you may well find that it provides some interesting departures from commonly held wisdoms about dogs. It may fly in the face of the current state of scientific knowledge. Depending upon your perspective, you might find it challenging or enlightening. It may ask you to think about things you have not considered before. Hopefully, it will assist you not only in your comprehension of your pets, but everything around you.

Before you dive into the pages that follow, and as a backdrop for everything that's written here, there are some fundamental concepts you need to be aware of.

Some of you will already be fully conscious of them, whilst others may find them new and unusual. Whether you accept or reject them is, of course, entirely up to you.

The concepts relate to all of our lives, not just those of dogs, so they're quite useful to understand from any perspective.

Some thoughts to ponder

Although we may prefer constancy and the assuredness of established knowledge, our realities change throughout our lives as our level of understanding and wisdom increases. It's the way things are meant to be.

In some matters, such as pure science, we are already the recipients of data that we are taught to regard as definitive, even though it is regularly updated, revised and altered. In other areas, there seems to be precious little room for speculation or advancement.

In the dog world, issues such as how to most effectively groom a dog or what are the best training techniques to use have been experimented with and refined to a point of total satisfaction for most.

As for dog behaviour and psychology, we accept certain data as normative, at least to the point where we will use conventionally accepted wisdom to describe what we see in our pets.

Yet particularly in this latter area, even those who profess expertise in all matters 'dog' are unable to transcend the barrier of dealing with a species with which we are (apparently) unable to fully communicate.

Many of the findings we accept as categorical can only ever result from a process of extrapolation and conclusion, which is based upon unproven conjecture and assumption.

We tacitly accept that our existence is shrouded with a certain degree of mystery, and we may spend lifetimes searching for answers about why we are here, and what is our purpose. Yet we stop short of going beyond our rather superficial musings upon dogs.

Have we considered that perhaps, if we were to understand more about the true essence of their being, we might, in the discoveries we would make, reveal truths about ourselves?

But we do not have a window that allows us to view and explore what occurs in a dog's soul.

Or do we?

Chapter 2

INFANCY

"Whenever I want to laugh, I read a wonderful book, 'Children's Letters to God.' You can open it anywhere. One I read recently said, 'Dear God, thank you for the baby brother, but what I prayed for was a puppy."

Maya Angelou

Do dogs choose their breed?

Yes. What breed a dog incarnates as is an important decision for all sorts of reasons.

This question presupposes that we have choices about what occurs in our lives before we ever arrive here. It's not as far-fetched as it sounds.

We may all be described as 'souls' or as having a 'soul'. We, in common with all beings, are not so much bodies that have souls, as souls that have bodies. We incarnate many times over so as to undertake the learning we can glean from the vast variety of experiences, relationships, and services that lifetimes may present us with.

Before we arrive here, we will have established an agenda for ourselves This applies every bit it as much to dogs as humans, the only difference being that their agenda will contain a completely different range of experiences, relationships and services. For instance, just as we may experience different genders, ethnicities, and sexualities, a fundamental for dogs is their breed.

All dogs will incarnate as both purebreds and mongrels. It is essential for them, across their many lifetimes, to experience the range of possibilities of canine body occupancy that the species can offer. This does not mean that all dogs will experience all breeds, but they will certainly 'sample' a broad selection.

The purpose is to allow them to comparatively reference one type of life with another, since the experiences of different breeds are likely to be quite different at levels that have nothing to do with looks, size, type of coat, degree of athleticism or any other facet of a dog's physical make up.

As with all choices about an upcoming life, the choice between purebred and crossbred is made while the dog is transitioning between lifetimes. When our scheduled time here is complete, we return to where we came from. Where we exist now, Earth, is a place of

At this stage of life (less than 24 hours old) these husky puppies may have their intentions for their lives mapped out, just based upon their breed.

substance with a physical tangibility. The place we come from is a place of light, lacking substance and tangibility. It may be referred to as *the etheric*, but we commonly think of it as heaven.

The etheric is where we embark from when we begin our lives; and where we return to when we transition or pass on from this life. The etheric has a higher vibration than the usual 'bandwidth' we can see or perceive. It exists alongside our reality, separated from us only by what we may physically observe, or to a certain extent, by what we can accept.

We review the learning achieved in our recently passed lifetime, then we plan and prepare for our next one. A dog will decide, in consideration of the type of learning and experiences that it will most benefit from, which breed will present the greatest likelihood of those opportunities being available to it. This may be deduced from the probable lifestyle that a dog of that breed is likely to have because of the way it is viewed by humans.

Over the millennia that dogs have come to develop a 'preferred animal companion' status with us humans, we have attributed certain dogs with behaviours and attitudes which we now describe as 'breed characteristics'. Initially many of these would have been developed because when considering the size, build and apparent aptitudes of a dog, our ancestors would have decided that a certain breed seemed particularly suited for a purpose. This would have created consequent expectations about the breed as a whole.

Kennel Club classifications in Canada, define dogs as Sporting; Hounds; Working; Terriers; Toys; Non-sporting; Herding. In the US, an additional Miscellaneous group is added to the list. Thus, dogs are already officially classified as being of a specific 'type', implying that we believe them to be suited for a particular role or purpose in life. But even if we ignore this 'official' thinking, it's easy to see how we stereotype them, both in terms of what we believe they are, and what they are not.

For example: A Weimaraner is a great dog to go running with; Poodles are natural show dogs; a Rottweiler would seldom be considered a lap dog; a Pomeranian would not spring to mind as the ideal guard dog; a Labrador can be relied upon to be both steady and dependable; few would pick a Cane Corso as their first choice as a buddy for their young children; you can always have fun with a Boxer; it would be a rare celebrity who picked a Basset Hound as the image boosting dog they wished to carry around LA in their handbag. You get the idea?

The contemporary image of dogs goes beyond what they are physically capable of, even to the point where there is a mythology associated with many breeds that belies how they *could* be. We feel that we understand their breed characteristics to such an extent that they can be 'explained' in breed guides. We may do the same thing with humans when we attempt to typify national traits, but it tends to be humorous and life altering decisions are not based on what is written. Yet with dogs we make judgements that effectively limit the life opportunities that will be available to them because of our perceptions about how they are. Thus, a dog is often predestined to a certain sort of existence.

Ask yourself what you see when you look at this little sweetie? It's probably easier to imagine all the roles you wouldn't expect her to perform.

In truth, all dogs are the same, irrespective of their breed. They merely inhabit bodies with different appearances, which humans have come to form different associations with. Yet having identified a behavioural aptitude or tendency, it is our assumption that all dogs of that type will possess it. And it is precisely this assumption that a dog will use in deciding what breed they will incarnate as.

They cross match their personal development needs with our beliefs about breed characteristics, then inhabit the body of the appropriate type of dog that will either allow them to demonstrate their ability to deliver the expected qualities, or deal with the challenges of working against type.

A while after I wrote this section, I was amused to read that actor George Clooney and his wife had just adopted a Basset Hound called Millie from a shelter. When I wrote the line about their image, I had a female celebrity of a different ilk in mind. I have to admit that George Clooney with a Basset Hound is cool and definitely fits.

A Basset Hound. Actually, a very cool dog!

If you think my teasing comment implies any prejudice against the breed on my part, I would like to offer in my defence that at one point we fostered a very sick Basset Hound called Flash. He was a wonderful character and a lovely dog who, I am pleased to say, recovered fully before rejoining his family.

Do dogs choose the people they go to, and if so, how?

Before incarnating a dog chooses its people, most often from those it already knows, in full knowledge of the life those people will lead, and consequently, what kind of a life it will have with them.

Explained very simplistically (for the sake of not writing several chapters on this one subject alone!), a dog has two basic 'strands' of life it may choose from and plan for.

1.   A lifetime that begins with the intention to live in close quarters with humans i.e. one where it is 'owned'.

2.   A lifetime that begins with the intention to live 'rough', struggling to survive.

Both are valid in terms of the range of possible experiences open to a dog, and both experiences must be gone through, just like the purebred/mongrel choice. Of course, beginning a type 1 life may lead to type 2, or it may transpire that the lifetime becomes a combination of both.

However, when it is planning for its next life, if the dog intends to (at least at some point) live with people, it will certainly choose who those people are. It does this in conjunction with them, and they are not selected at random.

We all select the families we will be born into or live with. Most frequently we will decide to be with those who we've shared, or are destined to share, multiple lifetimes with. They're called our 'soul family' and we see them almost every time we reincarnate. Our relationships with them change each time so that we may experience different aspects of inter-relationship and learn from our experiences on a comparative or relative basis.

A soul family is *not* necessarily the same thing as a biological family. It's not even made up of other beings that are only of the same type as us, i.e. humans. A soul family can contain *any* form of life.

Most often, a dog will elect to try to go to human members of its soul family, rather than 'strangers'. The lifetime to come will be one within which they explore another possible permutation of their time together.

Here are a few examples of the way this can be:

- A dog may have been its person's protector in one lifetime; now it will be the vulnerable one in need of care and protection.
- In a previous lifetime, the dog was a companion for its person when they were old; now that same individual is a child.
- The dog was a female in its previous lifetime with their person; now it is a male.
- When they last encountered one another, their person mistreated them; now the dog is cherished and pampered without measure.

The permutations are literally endless, and each time a new one occurs, when the individual souls re-encounter one another in the etheric and review their learning, they can compare each new experience with the previous ones.

Reading this, you might conclude that there is only one key relationship in a dog's life, but this is not the case. This type of planning will incorporate all those beings (human, dog and otherwise) with whom the dog has a soul family connection, and who it will encounter in its up and coming lifetime.

Although in any one incarnation it is unlikely to meet all the members of its soul family (which is quite a large group) it will still plan for encounters with all of those with whom a connection is reasonably foreseeable.

Which specific individuals it goes to live with will be an issue of what type of life those people have decided they will be leading. For instance, if they are due to be farmers, and the dog has already had fifteen lifetimes as a farm dog, it would be better to go elsewhere and try something new with other members of the soul family.

Attitudes of their intended guardians also come into play, since these are key in determining not only what breed of dog they will select, but also how they will react to the dog. This in turn will partially define what the animal's relationship with them will be, and what its resulting life experiences will be. Attitudes and consequent actions (hopefully) evolve over time, so precisely *when* the dog joins its people during their lifetime is also a key issue.

Planning to be with particular humans does not imply that the dog must be with them as a puppy. Necessary learning may dictate that the dog join its people as a mature adult, an infirm senior, or anything in between. The connection is still planned for.

So, the choice of person to incarnate with is a combination of numerous variables, and basically involves an exploration of what different soul family members are doing in their lifetimes. There is *always* a match, and more often than not, a dazzling array of choices.

Throughout this planning process, all parties are the same. There is no distinction between humans and other life forms. It is only after incarnation takes place that the nature of the relationship may change so that the dog may now become something less than a valued equal.

Once the human element is decided upon, a great many other elements in the complex equation must be balanced. Things such as relationship with birth parents (soul family members or not etc.), and a whole gamut of circumstantial impacts must be factored in.

It is a mind-blowingly complicated process that would leave even the most skilled earthbound logistician pulling their hair out. In the etheric, it is all achieved with consummate ease.

But ironically, it does not mean that all things go per plan.

Do dogs always get to the 'right' people?

Absolutely not. There are many things that can go wrong and change everything that has been planned for in a dog's life.

From the point that a dog incarnates, it hurls itself into the void and anything can happen.

Humans, at their birth, may guarantee their initial pathways with almost complete certainty. Once birth parents are agreed upon, and the circumstances thereafter, our lives are pursued with an almost relentless and inexorability.

Dogs, despite of all the planning and agreements that have been made, are subject to the vicissitudes of human nature and the uncertainties of the ways in which we use our freewill. We have the right to choose everything once we get here, and we frequently change our minds. Typical things that go wrong include:

- We decide not to get a dog
- We select a different breed from the one planned for
- We choose the wrong puppy
- We find that the puppy that we were meant to have has already been taken (*very* common)

If you think this puts humans in a bad light, it must be understood that after we are born, we simply do not remember our commitments to a dog, or any other agreements we have made for that matter!

However, our pathways do not go completely unguided. Not all beings from the etheric incarnate. Some (often referred to as *angels*) remain to assist us while we are here. Their purposes are basically to:

- Assist us in planning for our upcoming lifetimes.
- Try to make those learning opportunities and experiences we had planned for actually happen when we are here.

- Help us to understand the nature of our learning when we return.

During our lives, we are supported by these etheric beings who will go to extraordinary lengths in their attempts to ensure that what was intended occurs. But they are by no means omnipotent and they cannot 'make' things happen. They can only attempt to influence by 'whispering' thoughts and ideas to us that we then choose whether to act upon.

They are every bit as concerned with the outcomes of all non-human lives as they are with ours. So, to ensure that dogs get to where they are mean to be, extensive efforts will be made to influence those who are intended to be their adoptive parents.

Frequently their efforts will go unrewarded. Principally this will be because much that we receive by way of their interventions, will be perceived as hunches, instincts and coincidences. We may be fascinated by the strange and unusual feelings provoked, but it is the exception rather than the rule that an individual will act upon them. This is particularly the case when they may seem to fly in the face of common sense, a need to not appear 'weird', or pressure from others. Nevertheless, this is us exercising our freewill.

When a puppy does find its way to the intended person, both the dog and the person will find themselves strongly attracted to one another for reasons which may not even be conventionally explicable. Both are likely to experience a deep-seated recognition of one another. There will be a sense of the 'rightness' in taking a certain dog, and the dog will feel perfectly content to go with that person. This does not mean that they will not experience some initial trepidation at leaving their mother and siblings; but they will leave with some confidence that in the long run, all will be well.

Our first ever dog took me and our whole family by surprise because I had grown up with a dislike for canines that persisted into my thirties.

Then one day I saw a breed I had never seen or heard of before, and to my great surprise, fell totally in love. The attraction was so intense that within a fortnight I went to visit a breeder and was introduced to a procession of the cutest wriggling puppies.

Having supposedly seen them all, the breeder awaited my decision over which one I wanted, and seemed somewhat crestfallen that I professed no preference. "Well, there is one more" she said. Apparently, it was rather "sub-standard" and not a "good quality" animal. Nonetheless she reluctantly fetched it and handed her over.

The instant she was in my arms, I knew this was the puppy we were meant to have.

During the fourteen and a half years she lived with us, she was the 'apple of my eye' and despite not being anybody's idea of an ideal dog, she was perfect for us. I have absolutely no doubt that she got to the 'right person', and that she had a lot of help to ensure that happened.

And she literally changed our lives beyond all recognition.

If a dog has chosen to be with you, it's a privilege, plain and simple.

What happens if a dog does not get to the 'right' person?

It is not all doom and gloom and this unfortunate twist of fate by no means implies that the dog will suffer as a result.

The chances of a dog finding its way to its intended home are only around 50/50 at best - a pretty 'hit-and-miss' statistic!

Consequently, many dogs spend whole lifetimes with people with whom they have no soul connection, living with unplanned experiences that do not automatically assist them in their learning and growth. All by itself, this accounts for why dogs have many more lifetimes than we do to meet their learning objectives.

Whereas planning for all lifetimes includes a vast array of contingencies to cover as many potential choices as possible, to provide for a dog *always* going to its intended home would mean that all those buying a puppy, from a particular litter, would have to come from the same soul family. This in turn would imply that they all had similar learning to acquire. And since this is never the case, the dog cannot be 'covered'.

They may still find themselves in homes where they are treasured and loved; perhaps more so than they would have been. They may even dodge harsh and unpleasant lifetimes, (albeit temporarily, since these are valid permutations of experience they must go through). And as far as their learning goes, some will get lucky and have the opportunities they intended anyway, on the basis that there is a reasonably strong likelihood that those who choose a particular breed will have similar lifestyles.

The 'danger' of a dog not getting to the intended people is so foreseeable that it is not even deemed a bad thing, and the concept of there being 'right' people simply means those intended. The 50% success rate is considered perfectly acceptable.

Neither does it mean that attempts to intervene to get the dog to the right people cease when these accidents of misplacement occur.

If the pathway the dog now finds itself upon is likely to be an unhappy one, etheric beings will try to change the outcome. Some dogs that initially find themselves with unintended people or in unfortunate circumstances may end up in the right home later in life. But if the pathway they have inadvertently come upon now shapes up to be a good one, they are left to enjoy the pleasures it offers.

Sadly, misfortunes in placing a dog may mean that some end up in bad places, and some do not end up with people at all.

Neither of these two ended up where they were supposed to be, but still found a happy ending.

Is it possible that a dog is born to a family it has already shared a lifetime with?

A dog and its people may certainly have encountered one another in previous lifetimes. Meeting repeatedly in the same lifetime is less likely.

For the reasons already alluded to, dogs have many more lifetimes than we do. Whilst certain lessons may only be learned when incarnating with its soul family members, it does not necessarily have to be the same members.

If, between the dogs passing and their reincarnation, the circumstances of their people have not altered in any significant way, for the dog to come back to them would be to repeat a lifetime with no appreciable gain. A dog (when reviewing its experiences from the objective position offered by the etheric) would not be keen to do, so they will elect to reincarnate to different members of their soul family. There are exceptions:

- If the learning opportunities that existed between the dog and its people have not yet reached the desired conclusions.

- If the dog's people are experiencing such unassuageable grief that it is considered for their highest good (what's best for them) that the dog returns to them.

- If the people still present the best opportunity for the dog based on anticipated change in their future circumstances.

Although it is possible, attempts to get back to a family are often prone to failure. Too many variables exist that can prevent success, and few dogs elect to try this option. We may like to believe that a dog would try to get back to us simply because of its great love for us. It is a slightly bitter truth that once it has returned to the etheric, the dog may still experience the intensity of the attachment, but become far more objective in its assessment of what is for the highest good of all (what's best for everybody).

How does a dog feel when it is split up from its mother and siblings?

So much is age dependent that the answer may vary from the extremes of 'nothing at all' to 'deeply upset'.

If you challenge yourself to recall what lies in your memory, you will likely struggle to give any examples of recollections before the age of three, or maybe even older. And even these are probably no more than the merest glimpses of what has been.

The reason for this is that it takes at least that long to come to terms with what we were (i.e. beings of the etheric) vs. what we have become (i.e. incarnate individuals).

There is a post birth adjustment period that in duration will be directly proportionate to the length of our lives. Although a great deal of development and nurturing takes place in this period, it is still effectively a learning dead zone from a spiritual development perspective. During this time, we are not 'human enough' to comprehend life lessons, and we certainly can't evidence our success in applying them. Our responses to the world around us are not reflective of how they will become, and our ability to process all that goes on around us is severely limited. We are learning how to be human (again) and this is all we can cope with.

It is like living within a mist that slowly clears, until one day, quite suddenly, it is gone and we are aware. Thus, there is little memory of this time in our lives.

Whereas this adjustment period may take two or three years for a human, it is at around eight weeks that a dog starts to begin to come into itself. Up until this point they are doing the same thing that we do, but from a doggy perspective. If they are removed from their mother and siblings during this period, although they may be distressed and upset in the short term, their removal is unlikely to have any detrimental long term affects, because they will quite simply fail to comprehend what is going on.

If, when the 'mist' clears, they are in their new home, it will appear that this is the way things have always been and their recollections of the family they have lost will be mercifully few. Over time, without further contact, the memories of them will disappear completely.

It has long been recognised by compassionate breeders that puppies must stay with their mothers for eight weeks to be fully weaned; but they also come to realise, if only tacitly, that if the puppies stay any longer, the risk of the 'mist' having lifted quite literally grows stronger by the day.

If it has cleared, separation is deeply distressing for the puppy and heartrending to observe. I have come across several breeders who will insist upon the dog's new people collecting their puppy on precisely the fifty sixth day, or they will simply not allow them to have the animal.

This is no bad thing. Eight weeks is a guideline figure and in some cases, the 'mist' may already have lifted.

The first hours of separation can be distressing for any dog, but may rapidly become no more than a hazy memory.

How does a mother feel having her puppies taken away from her?

It is very much an issue relating to the nature of the dog and their awareness of the purpose of the separation. At best, they may feel numb or neutral; at worst, the mother can be devastated.

Many species know innately that their lives cannot be lived together, if only for the sake of their long-term survival. In some cases, dependent youngsters will even be driven away from the family group. This is not the case with dogs. Packs of wild dogs may consist of several generations of family members living in a unit not unlike the human extended family model, still prevalent in some countries around the world.

It can be the case that if a mother has all her puppies taken from her, she will feel utterly bereft. But it is equally likely that she will be indifferent. There are a couple of reasons for this.

1. Not all dogs are natural mothers and having puppies will be the unfortunate result of indulging in sexual activity.

    Instinctively they may nurse their puppies, but may be resentful of having to do so.

    Many will be the equivalent of teenage mothers who feel that their youth and opportunity for life is being stolen from them. They do not like to have their freedom curtailed.

    Add to this the fact that puppies may rapidly become precocious and difficult to manage, and the mother may experience little, short of relief, when all the children are gone.

    In the human world, we would judge such a dog to be a bad mother. But in a wild environment, multiple animals may share the burden of child rearing and assume quasi-parental roles, with puppies even becoming pack property.

The choice of the animal to eschew motherhood is neither considered wrong nor problematic as a life choice made before incarnating.

2. Because of the in-built foresight with which we all arrive when we incarnate, a dog may well know that her puppies will not be staying with her.

    They are unlikely to be conscious of this, but at some deep level, they can accept that it is necessary for their offspring to go, in order that they progress in their learning.

    This is potentially an extremely difficult piece of learning and acceptance that they might have to come to terms with before they are at peace with having their children taken.

The truth of a mother's reaction is difficult to discern because it is dependent upon the individual dog, or even the specific litter, if there is more than one. What we may take to be canine ambivalence may well be stoicism on the part of the mother.

If questioned about such matters, breeders will usually claim that their mothers don't mind that their puppies are taken, or that they quickly adjust to being 'unburdened'. This may well be the case, but a breeder will seldom breed on a repeated basis from mothers who are not 'good' by our human standards. And good mothers *don't* like to lose their offspring.

Add to this is the fact that it is not a good thing to report to buyers that their newly acquired puppy's mother will experience depression after her offspring have gone. It will certainly spoil the pleasure of the moment, at least for the compassionate, or even change their mind about purchase.

An empathetic breeder will keep one puppy, not just because it represents potential breeding stock, but because it may be some small consolation for the mother that not all her children are lost.

A dog that is predisposed towards motherhood (which will be obvious from her endless loving ministrations towards her puppies) may suffer enormously from the removal of so much as a single dog. They may fret, whine and clearly demonstrate their misery.

Mothers used in full-time breeding operations or puppy mills repeatedly have their puppies removed. Although they are kept hidden away from the buyer's eye, if encountered, they may seem inured to the process. But nonchalance may mask despair. Many suffer severe and damaging psychological trauma, from which they seldom recover.

These two have never had to cope with the pain of separation; in fact the whole family unit remains with us.

When dogs have babies does the maternal connection ever stop?

The maternal connection between beings and their offspring is, at least from an etheric perspective, almost an illusion. Nonetheless, it is a strong bond if chosen by a dog.

It is human society's definition that the bond between a mother and child is sacrosanct. This is an almost uniquely human experience, and most other species, whilst lavish in their care and attention to their babies, ultimately realise that their children must walk their own pathways without intervention and without regret.

The learning point is more easily mastered for animals than it is for humans because their circumstances, wild or domesticated, enforce separation. Whereas human society supports the maintenance of contact and connection (and perhaps the consequent development of a more maternalistic approach than is found in many species) theirs does not. For a dog, a mother that sees their children leave may reasonably anticipate only that it is extremely unlikely that it will ever see them again.

In some, the maternal connection may be almost automatically extinguished once the parting has occurred. This can arise through unconscious acceptance, or conscious choice. They may be happy to live with their offspring throughout their entire lives, but they are equally accepting of seeing them go. This does not contradict the previous answer. The issue is one of timing.

From a mother's perspective, it is considerably easier to lose a puppy when it is fully grown. In the wild it could reasonably be anticipated that at least some youngsters would leave to form their own packs or join others upon reaching adulthood. In much the same way as humans expect their children to leave home in their late teens, and even welcome their departure(!), so it is for dogs.

A mother would face far less concerns and distress if puppies left at two years old. By this stage, their expectation of their role in parenting has been totally discharged. Their puppies are now mature adults, and can be more trouble than they are worth!

If the term maternal connection, when extended to dogs, means love and recognition, then it may never stop. But love does not mean like, and recognition does not imply a desire to reconnect as a family or live together.

One of the most heartbreaking rescues I have ever undertaken involved a young St Bernard mother who had been discovered living rough on a Native American People's reservation in New Mexico.

We had arranged her rehoming, and I made the three-day drive to collect her. But when I arrived in Albuquerque the night before I was due to pick her up, I received an email from the rescue telling me that she had a puppy, and asking me if I could take him too.

I was taken aback and totally unprepared for this revelation. Worse, circumstances did not allow me to accede to the request. I explained to the rescue that we had a great many dogs and had not planned on taking another, and they accepted this.

The next day I met the St Bernard and her year-old mixed breed son. He was a magnificent creature who was bigger than she was, and a colossal bundle of love and excitable energy.

It was explained to me that when they were found, he was the only puppy with her, although it was known that there had been many more. The others had likely starved to death or been taken by Coyotes.

Both mother and son had been in a very bad way when they were taken in, but after a great deal of loving care, were now fit and ready for new homes.

What struck me immediately was the adoration that the mother obviously felt for her son. I met her first, and then when he came out, she rushed up to him, licked his face, ran in circles around him and almost glowed with obvious pride and pleasure.

After a short while, I led her to the back of my SUV and we prepared to leave. At first she seemed to think that I was just taking her for a walk, but when I started to close the tailgate, she suddenly realised what was happening and that we were leaving her son behind.

She panicked and became quite stressed. I drove away quickly, but glancing back in the rear-view mirror, I saw that she was standing with her nose pressed against the glass, obviously desperate to catch a glimpse of him. She did not sit down for fifty miles, and then suddenly dropped to the floor and did not get up again.

Sometime later I pulled over at a rest stop. I opened the tailgate to find an utterly dejected dog, head sunk between her paws, interested in nothing and the very picture of misery. I fussed with her, but her response was half-hearted.

Throughout the course of the next three days we made many such stops, and I was pleased to note that she quickly regained her interest in the world around her; but then I realised that she only became truly engaged when she saw other canines.

Upon seeing another dog, even at a great distance, she would rush headlong towards them, dragging me comically in her wake. Then once she got to them, she would almost immediately lose interest and potter away, her head and tail hanging.

It wasn't until the third day that it finally dawned on me that she was looking for her puppies.

In the weeks that followed, I tried every possible persuasion to get the rescue to allow me to come back for her son, but they refused to even communicate. I guessed that they were put off by the revelation that we had so many dogs and thought we must be hoarders.

Somewhat cruelly from our perspective, they moved him on to another rescue. We immediately applied to get him, but we were second on a waiting list for him, and despite explaining the circumstances, they would not allow us to queue jump.

Of course, the first person on the list took him, never knowing the heartache his mother suffered.

The mother eventually got over her sadness and became a wonderful happy-go-lucky family pet.

When I see her and look into her eyes, sometimes I fancy I catch a glimpse of sadness, and I wonder how she would be if she saw her son again now.

I believe she is one dog who has not abandoned the maternal connection. But I also believe that the experience they shared together on the reservation, struggling to survive and witnessing the tragic demise of their other family members has a large part to play in that.

Throughout the whole journey, she always seemed to be on the lookout for other dogs, but not just any dogs. Her puppies.

Do dogs recognise their own offspring after they have been separated for some time (e.g. a year)?

Recognising offspring is easy because of the vibrational output that makes them instantly recognisable. That doesn't imply that they want to see them though.

Each being has a distinct and individual vibration. This is like a unique personal 'signature' that is not repeated in any other soul. Imagine each being as a totally unique musical note. We can hear the vibrations of a note, but only those within a certain frequency or bandwidth, just like a radio signal. Dogs are far more aware of, and receptive to experiencing vibrations (precisely how they can do this will be discussed more later). This means that their recognition of their offspring will be easy for them, even after years of growth and physical change have radically altered the appearance of those they maybe last saw as puppies.

However, the model of parenting that is followed in the dog world is significantly different from the human one, of necessity as much as anything else.

For all creatures, there is a hard-wired recognition of the need to reproduce. This is not just to survive, but to allow other souls who have elected to assume the same incarnate form (species) to be born or reincarnated. Practicality dictates that for many species, living as a large extended family unit is not viable and youngsters will be encouraged to leave when it is appropriate.

Dogs and their related kin are a little different. As already mentioned, a pack is often made up of related individuals, possibly of several generations, and the pack environment can be supportive of large numbers. But humans seldom allow family groups to be together. Our concept of ownership allows us to treat them as our chattels and do with them as we please. Thus, offspring are sold or given away.

The subsequent return of children may present mothers (especially) with emotional challenges that might be difficult to cope with.

If the reuniting is only temporary, more heartache may follow. If it is permanent, it may be difficult to accept that one of your own has been raised by somebody else.

Or it could be that their pathway has caused them to develop in ways that renders them incompatible with their parents.

A joyous mother waits to greet the son who she has not seen for over a year.

Is what we call a dog important?

Names are very important!

We all have within us deeply embedded soul memories, accumulated across our numerous lifetimes. We also have knowledge of the purposes and goals we have defined for ourselves in our current one.

This key data is stored in what can be described as 'soul DNA', which resides in our subconscious as a (largely) dormant feature: a component of our brain chemistry. It is available when we need to recall it (to guide our actions and choices) or will surface spontaneously to provide us with options, as and when appropriate. It is immensely unlikely that we will be aware of the origins of the wisdom it provides for us, since, like etheric intervention, it will most often strike us as our instinct or intuition. We seldom question the source.

Each and every individual being is comprised of a vibration that is utterly unique to them. Their vibration is comprised of sounds, which may be expressed as syllables, and intoned in whole, or part, as a name. In its entirety, or even as an extract from it, this name acts like a memory jogger at a soul DNA level. It brings to the fore of our consciousness aspects of what we need to know in a lifetime. The effect of this is to give us hints, or glimpses of all that we are, all that we have been, and all that we intend to be.

But only *if* we have the right name..!

Before a being incarnates, considerable effort is made to ensure their parents are presented with the 'correct' name (always a component or derivative of the complete vibration) for the impending arrival. Delivered (perhaps repeatedly) at the appropriate time, this guidance enables us to ensure newborns have this potentially helpful connection as they embark upon their lives.

Receiving this input, most human parents will apparently 'instinctively' know what is the 'right' name for their child; or at the very least, know what *feels* right. Of course, there are those who will ignore what comes to them and name a child something wholly inappropriate!

The effect of ignoring our gut feelings about names is to make that being's lifetime just a little bit harder, and reduce the likelihood of their connecting with those learnings or experiences they are meant to have. It's not uncommon, and it may not be a major issue, However in extremis, it might mean that the newborn ultimately goes through an additional lifetime to catch up on learning they have missed out on, simply because they have the wrong name. The only good news is that they'll probably never know!

But naming is not just a human thing. Many species use monikers and the memory jogging effect is identical. Dogs are given names by their parents and distinguish between litter mates on this basis. If a family stays together, the names are used much as ours.

Because of the importance of a name, when dogs are named by people, etheric beings attempt to convey to them what the pet should be called. Success in achieving this is substantially lower than is the case when trying to inform and influence parents about their children. By no means all custodians are open to influence when the matter seems as trivial as a dog's name. Consequently, very many dogs are lumbered with wholly inappropriate monikers, and the value of their true name is lost.

Most of the dog owning population are unlikely to give quite as much thought to naming their pooch as they would for a child. We do not recognise that there could be any unseen implications with that name. Provided we like the sound of it, what the hell!

Of course, not all dogs are named frivolously, but look at this list of some of the more popular dog names in North America.

Trapper, Bailey, Otto, Boomer, Hawkeye, Wrigley, Ace, Butch, Lucky, Axel, Gunner, Diesel, Delgado, Buddy, Bentley, Coco, AJ, Maximus, Rocky, CJ, Moose, Dodge, Bear, Amos, Blitzen, Blue, Grommit, Fritz, Shamus, Klaus, Huck, Biscuit, Scout, Bubba, Dante, Duke, Shadow, Rebel, Comet, Bandit, Sarge, Pepper, Bacon, Tank, Aztec, Benji, Dynamite, Marley, Taco, Byron, Milo, Hunter, Czor, Rex, Goose, Sparkey, Scrappy, Gordie, Foster, Coby, Fuzzy, Rockwell, Oreo, Auggie, Zeus, Loki, Yogi, Bamboo, Nugget, Dixie, Barkley, Riley, Buster, Izzy, Blaze, Anubis, Chewbacca, Gizmo, Snoopy, Aang, Axle, Bubbles, Azurite, Scooby, Bone, Dakota, Baba, Riptide, Tyson, Snowball, Rufus, Chip, Brady, Willaby, Gyro, Alvin, Simba, Alfie, Baxter, Angel, Jacob, Cookie, Jasper, Harley, Pepsi, Waffles, Sparky, Buzz, Avery.

Now ask yourself how many of these you would *seriously* consider to be legitimate names for a child of yours, and you'll start to see what I mean! They're not necessarily inappropriate, but...

This dog came to us with the name 'Twist' and was utterly unresponsive until renamed Valentine!

Chapter 3

FEEDING

"Owners of dogs will have noticed that, if you provide them with food and water and shelter and affection, they will think you are god."

Christopher Hitchens - *The Portable Atheist: Essential Readings for the Nonbeliever*

What is a dog's favourite food?

What can be a favourite food will always be defined by what is available; but given the opportunity, what is 'natural' to a dog will always be preferable.

Imagine the mirth (or worse?) that would be provoked if another species were to ask of humans "What is their favourite food?" The idea that there could ever be a straightforward answer, accurate and applicable for all, is plain silly.

The personal taste and preferences of our pets affect the answer to this question every bit as much as they might for humans, as you may well have experienced if you have a picky pooch. In fact, the only reason why it is possible to even begin to respond to this one is because what dogs are fed is so limited when compared with a human diet. The range of choice for what constitutes a 'favourite' food can only be correspondingly smaller. Even so, the answer must be broadly generic and encompass some other tangential issues that are involved in determining a dog's ideal dish.

A dog does not have as many taste buds as we do and therefore how they can perceive the subtleties and nuances of flavour are very different from ours. If this sounds like a raw deal for dogs, it should be borne in mind that there is a very good reason for this. By design and intention, a dog's life may be considerably harder than ours and there is far less certainty about what foods will be available for them. Although they are omnivores, there may be less leeway for them to be choosy about what they eat and what they don't. Therefore, having less awareness of flavour can act in their favour, and make things that we would consider unpalatable, at least acceptable.

However, this is a bit of a double-edged sword because it also means that their ability to enjoy flavoursome things is also impacted. Overall it has the effect of making only those things which have stronger flavours truly worthy of the term 'enjoyable'.

Beyond taste, texture can also play a part in a favourite eating experience.

Kibble is gritty and uncomfortable to swallow; sticky foods can be irritating in the mouth and difficult to get rid of; food that is mushed can only be swallowed. Bones often afford the most satisfying sensation, offering a good chew and removing other food deposits from the teeth.

However, textures are also a matter of what the dog is used to, and unless their jaw muscles have developed well and been maintained through proper use, softer products may be all they can cope with.

When all is said and done, the most satisfying meal for a dog is a *real* meat based one that has both texture and flavour.

For many dogs, there's nothing quite like a bone for pure enjoyment.

What *should* dogs be fed?

Dogs are flexible enough to eat whatever is put before them, but given the choice, they will invariably prefer a raw food diet. For the majority it's a lot healthier, it's natural and it's what was intended.

As dogs have evolved in their relationship with humans, they have moved a long way from the natural state of their truly wild Canis species cousins, to become the domesticated, dependent household pets we know them to be today.

Despite this, they (notionally) retain their hard-wired instincts and physical capability as hunters, being well able to scent, track, pursue, catch, kill and eat what then becomes their food. There's a purpose and reason for this. Irrespective of pre-incarnation planning, due to the uncertainties, inherent in all their lives, they cannot rely upon the comforts of a human household and guaranteed feeding. So, they arrive equipped to provide for themselves.

In a wild state, dogs might prey upon other animals for sustenance. But in their domesticated state, much of the dog population of the planet are in urban environments or at least in proximity to humans. Being fed, or adopting a scavenging approach to feeding is far more likely as a means of survival than a hunter/killer one. It is fortunate that their omnivorous digestive system allows them to include a wide variety of food sources into their diet.

However, there is a vast difference between what is intended/natural for them to eat, and the synthetic diets that they are so often required to feed on. Today, if a dog is born in the protective environment of a human household where they are fully provided for, ferociously relentless persuasion by corporates has 'trained' generations of dog custodians that they *should* be feeding their pets what is convenient or pleasant for them, the customer, rather than think of what is best for the dog. A major reformation in shopping habits has also greatly affected the availability of more traditional dog foods. The 'going to the butchers to get the dog a bone' mentality that was prevalent over half a century ago has long since been replaced.

There hasn't exactly been a backlash from the dogs themselves. They are grateful for whatever they get. They are blissfully unaware of dietary related ailments that may be caused by synthetic dog foods. And to make foodstuffs appealing to dogs, the pet food industry has long used additives to try and render its products attractive and edible, some even (it is rumoured) to the point of creating addiction. The notion created by the *'should feed this'* message matches with total acceptance from the dogs.

Although public demand has led to increased quality amongst higher end products, there is a great deal of clever marketing at work that preys upon our desire to give our pets the most nutritious and (apparently) appetising food possible. For our part, we are all too easily convinced of what we *should* be doing when it also happens to be so convenient for us. Since dogs are dependent, unable to vocalise, able to adapt to, and prepared to accept whatever is put in front of them, many generations of dogs have been fed on foodstuffs that, given the choice, would in no way constitute a preferred meal.

Like so many things, taste and choice of food becomes a habit. A dog reared on the artificial products manufactured by the pet food industry can become the eating equivalent of institutionalised, regarding their tastes. But more seriously, as alluded to above, their physical capability for food consumption can be compromised. Kibble and canned mush do not encourage the development of jaws capable of healthy chewing, and an animal raised on the expectation of bland pellets may experience taste overload when presented with something 'real' to eat. They can lose their ability to enjoy what is natural and intended for them – or what they really *should* be eating - which is based upon the type of beings they are.

The good news is that jaws may be strengthened and taste expectations may be altered if opportunity for restoration to 'the norm' is given. Dog people who are made aware of the choices beyond what the rather insidious (and frighteningly profitable) pet food industry creates in their name, will often realise that a change in their buying habits can radically alter both the level of pleasure their pets experience from eating, and their health. But change can be difficult once habits are established.

For our first eight years of dog guardianship, we fed kibble to all our dogs. They didn't seem to object and we only came to truly appreciate what diet meant to them when we switched to raw food and saw their reaction. They were ecstatic. Or what I should say is that five of them were. The sixth refused to touch raw. For the next three years, we would periodically present her with raw, but on every occasion, she would walk away in disgust. Finally, one day, she took a mouthful. Then the rest of the bowl disappeared in seconds. She never touched so much as a pellet of kibble after that and went from being a picky eater to a wildly enthusiastic one.

Since then I've come across many people who have tried to transition their dogs to a raw food diet, only to meet with rejection from their dogs. Yet every one has ultimately become a wholehearted convert.

We should not underestimate how easy it is for a dog's approach to food to become totally habituated. Dogs can be as resistant to change as humans. They feel they have a lot to lose.

Some dogs prefer meals they can get involved with!

Is kibble an acceptable diet for a dog?

Have you ever had a good look at your dog's teeth? Their shape and spacing alone give a rather obvious answer to this question. Although there may be extenuating circumstances, an overall answer to this question must be a definite and resounding "No!"

Consider the following about kibble:

- Imagine yourself eating the same meal, perhaps several times a day, day in, day out, for years on end.
- The meal doesn't have much taste; in fact, it's very like eating cardboard.
- The meal comes in a form that is difficult to chew with the design of your teeth.
- Even if you do manage to break it down somewhat, you end up feeling like you have a mouth full of gravel.
- The texture is coarse and uncomfortable to swallow.
- It hurts your gums.
- It grates in your throat.
- Just occasionally you might get a new variety to try.
- It's almost identical but because you're so used to the blandness, even the slightest variation can seem exciting for a while.
- Is it acceptable?
- Do you have a choice?

We have come to accept kibble as a perfectly normal thing to feed dogs, but it's very far from it, and it's an extremely long way from what could be construed as a 'natural' diet or what we *should* be feeding our pets. Kibble is a relatively recent invention that has been popularised as part of the tide of convenience culture that swept all before it in the post WWII era.

In 1964 the Pet Food Institute, a lobbying group for the pet food industry began campaigning to persuade the public of the evils of feeding anything but processed, prepackaged dog foods, and they've never stopped. The pet food industry is now worth over $11 billion annually in the United States alone. There is a great deal of vested interest in making sure that consumers continue to feed its intended target whatever products it puts out.

You may well be in awe then that vets would seem to be so supportive of something that isn't in the dog's best interests to eat. We must remember that vets are essentially scientists and from a scientific perspective, kibble, with its multiplicity of formulas and specialist dietary offerings, may well appear as the logical best offering, particularly for dogs with health issues.

It is certainly possible to encounter vets who recommend a more natural approach to feeding and only prescribe kibble when a medical condition warrants it. This is no bad thing at all. But a general recommendation that a dog should be fed kibble may be directly attributable to lobbying, and generous incentivisation by pet food manufacturers.

Naturally enough, science has little to do with the intended range of choices for a dog's incarnate physiology, spiritual journey and intended learning.

I once followed an argument printed in a local monthly newspaper, begun when a pet store placed an advertisement stating that the raw food they sold was cheaper per pound than kibble.

The next month a local veterinarian felt it necessary to write an editorial that basically proffered an explanation of why kibble was an excellent choice for dogs. It made a rather obvious and underhand jibe at the pet store.

In the months that followed, there were several letters written to the newspaper either supporting the vet's statement (with only personal justification rather than evidence) or refuting the assertions made in the editorial.

Both the pet store owners and the vet refrained from further comment, but the argument went backwards and forwards until finally the editor refused to print any more letters on the subject. The debate was concluded by the printing of a letter that pointed out that amid the heated argument, the one point that seemed to have got lost was that the contentious advertisement was wholly accurate. The raw food the pet store sold was indeed cheaper per pound than kibble.

From my perspective, it highlighted two things. Firstly, the corrupting influence of incentivised marketing; and secondly how easily people felt threatened by the introduction of ideas that challenged their established practices; and how unreceptive and defensive they could become about the notion of making change, even if it could bring benefit to those they loved.

It also demonstrated the blind acceptance of supposed science over common sense; even if that science was bought and paid for with the intentions of generating vast sums of money.

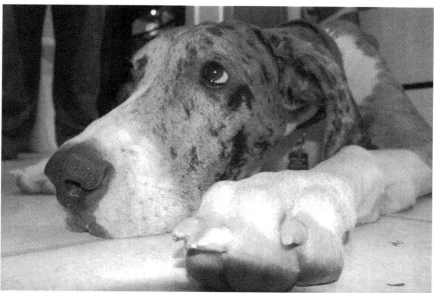

Don't I deserve more than kibble?
(In truth, she's only ever fed raw.)

Are two meals a day enough for a dog?

An adult dog neither requires nor expects two meals a day, let alone the three that some custodians feed. The quantity appropriate for the dog may be spread out across the course of a day, but repeat large meals are unnecessary.

A dog can exist quite happily on one meal per day, or when circumstances force, less. The idea that they should have two reflects the way humans tend to eat, which is closer to a grazing way of eating rather than the feast or famine experience that is the lot of so many dogs.

Wild dogs feast because grazing is a luxury a competitive feeding environment does not allow for. In the wild (which must now include living on the streets) meals may be few and far between and a feast can be a scrap of food found in a dustbin. Although it is not healthy for them and does not promote longevity, a dog can survive on very little food, provided it has water to drink.

So even having one regular meal per day is perfectly adequate to sustain a dog, and if it is the 'right' sort of food for them, they will be perfectly happy and maintain their weight.

If a grazing habit is developed in a dog by feeding multiple meals, it becomes an expectation for them and they will appear to need more than one meal per day. They will exhibit antsy behaviour and worry their person in an attempt to persuade them of their hunger.

But with complacency borne from fulfilled expectation, their digestive system can become lazy, their metabolism acting faster and doing less to extract the nutrients that are in the food. More waste is produced and hunger returns more quickly. A kind of vicious circle of phantom need is developed.

I was contacted by someone feeding their Mastiff ten pounds of food per day. She couldn't understand how a dog of ours, the same breed and weight, was only being fed two pound of food per day...

Why do dogs eat their food so quickly?

Not necessarily for the reasons you might hope.

It would be nice for us to imagine that when we see our dogs eating their food at great speed, that they are taking great pleasure in the experience and can't wait to get their next mouthful. Somewhat more unkindly, we might think that they are being greedy. Or perhaps a middle ground of supposition: that they are ravenously hungry. However, the truth is likely to be somewhat different.

Scoffing down food (almost as if it is being inhaled) is most often a learned response to being presented with a tasteless meal. Why take time to savour what lacks flavour? This way of eating can then become habitual practice. The tastiest of meals may end up being eaten in hurried gulps.

Conversely, a meal that is laboured over and picked at may also be lacking in appeal.

The habit may also come about through an instinctive need to eat food quickly to protect it from rival mouths; or from actual experience of the need to do so.

Eating quickly is not a pleasurable experience for a dog, and although they are not prone to develop indigestion in the same manner that we might, it can nonetheless cause them to feel quite uncomfortable afterwards. Although relatively few will develop comfortable eating habits from the get-go, dogs that live as solitary pets may manage to break the habits of puppyhood and eat at a reasonable pace.

Can dogs be vegetarian?

Yes, but they shouldn't be unless there are certain circumstances.

A dog that is fed only vegetables and only given the option of vegetables, will inevitably be forced to eat them to stave off hunger. Rapidly they will become quite accustomed to them and even learn to enjoy them, perhaps as much as they might acquire a taste for kibble.

A dog can certainly survive and thrive on a vegetarian diet, but it is not what is intended for their species overall, and for most of their incarnations it would be as unnatural for them as eating kibble.

Unlike humans, who (because of their absolute freedom of choice) will ultimately need to avoid any aspect of diet that results in harm to other beings, dogs may continue to eat their fellow animals with impunity.

However, as they evolve in their soul ages (as they advance through lifetimes), dogs may be progressively more inclined towards eating less meat in their diets. Although the opportunity to totally avoid the carnivorous aspect of their diet is unlikely to present itself naturally, a guardian should only make such a major choice of diet on their behalf if meat is totally refused or if their physiology demands it.

A dog on a vegetarian diet? Perhaps not.

How do dogs feel when they see us eating and they don't get anything?

It's all a matter of expectations!

It is one of a dog's hardwired instincts to pursue the acquisition of food. Consequently, any situation that seems to present the opportunity to get food is of interest to a dog, and when they see us eating, the prospect of an ad hoc snack looms large in their mind

However, how they react or feel about it when there's a dining event, be it a casual family breakfast or a large dinner party, is very much a learnt behavior. This is determined by expectations created at an early stage in their relationship with whoever is eating. From the dog's perspective, the scale of anticipated reward goes something like this.

- If with a human who has never given you something from their plate, or has scolded you for your interest in food which they seem to believe is for them only, prospects are not good. Set expectations at low to non-existent. No chance. Allow only feelings of ambivalence.

- If with a human who has a consistently good track record of feeding you from their own meals, prospects are very good. Set expectations to high. The food is yours as a matter of right. Anticipate participation in the feast and allow feelings of excitement. If they don't come up with the goods, allow disappointment (or even resentment).

- If with a human who occasionally feeds you from their meals, prospects are ambiguous. Set expectations to uncertain. Retain cautious optimism. Allow initial feelings of excitement and enthusiasm, moving to bemusement and frustration as the meal progresses, and ultimately, irritability bordering on anger if the meal ends and your tolerance of their teasing behaviour has not been rewarded. A good sulk may be necessary.

- If with a human who has no previous track record or is unknown to you, prospects are hopeful. Set expectations to positive. Allow feelings of optimism and apply strongest influencing methods to achieve desired feeding goals. Worry them!

The penultimate type of experience is a dog's least favourite and will cause the most confusion. They will not relate to the inconsistency of the behaviour. Since dogs themselves tend to be consistent in most things, unpredictable behaviour in humans is unsettling and potentially upsetting. Add to this equation the ever-present food drive, and these dogs will be the ones who are unhappiest about not getting fed. From their perspective, they have been toyed with (even if on this occasion food was not offered at all) and their confidence in their ability to trust in the human has been lessened, if only by a tiny amount. To keep the dog happy and prevent what to them is an experience of emotional turmoil, a consistent approach is a good idea.

Aside from all of this, a great deal of the food we give to dogs is bland and uninteresting. From a sensory perspective, there is very little that is exciting about kibble. Raw food, although infinitely more appealing, still does not have the potentially unusual and powerful aromatic qualities of a lot of human food, at least from a dog's perspective. Because of this, their interest is almost automatically sparked by human foods and it can become a source of great interest. This is why dogs may be interested in watching us eat in the first place.

In most general terms, a dog may experience curiosity, envy and even awe at what they perceive us to be eating. This is not always the case, since some foods are unpleasant or uninteresting to their sense of smell; and experience of that food, despite having hankered after it, can ultimately disappoint.

The intensity of interest in human food is in direct proportion to the animal's food drive and state of hunger; and how much they have taken on board the messages learned from the signs their humans have given them regarding what behaviours are or are not acceptable.

Thus, you may well find that a dog will leave familiar family members uninterrupted at meal times and behave in exact accordance with what they would wish. Yet when a guest arrives for a meal, the dog may act (seemingly) out of character and pester the visitor for food. This is simply because they have not yet had the opportunity to define the parameters of acceptability with that person, and optimism is their prevailing state of mind.

Most dogs will happily take food from you are the slightest opportunity, if you let them!.

It might be imagined that living with such a huge pack of dogs, we are constantly pestered for food. Quite the opposite is true. The dogs are fed once a day, and they know the rules. Our meal times are treated with courtesy and respect.

However, when we have guests, it's a completely different story. With totally open plan dining space, we get surrounded by a milling mass of doggy flesh, both around and under the dining table, trying a variety of approaches to persuade the strangers that what is going into human mouths should be coming their way. It's amusing only for a very short span of time, after which they have to be shooed away.

Why can otherwise perfectly nice dogs turn nasty over food?

Because it's a BIG issue for them!

I've come across many dogs who have been branded as 'bad' because of the temperamental changes that overcome them when food is involved. Otherwise sweet and gentle animals can become snarling terrorists, and the moniker 'food aggressive' is often attached to them. It's an unfortunate thing to happen to a dog, because such judgements seldom reflect their true nature, and the reasoning behind their gustatory driven transformation is perfectly simple to understand.

All you need do to 'get it' is watch a litter of puppies nursing with their mother.

If the litter is above a certain size, there aren't enough teats to go around. In this early blind stage of development, the puppies only feel one compelling urge, which is to feed. Thus begins a struggle to gain access to the food; and once you have it, to remain with it until satiated. At this stage, the infants are not equipped with either the strength or the tools to aggressively fight for what they want, so they make do with butting heads, flailing paws and rolling bodies.

As they grow older, the imperative to get what they instinctively know is keeping them alive (and happy) does not recede one iota. Weaning likely presents an increase in the challenge for getting food. Even if a litter is fed in separate bowls, if they are in proximity of one another, raids on those who have not yet finished their meals will occur. Protection of your valuable sustenance resources becomes an imperative for the growing dog.

By the time the early stages of youth have been arrived at, the once so innocent puppies have it deeply embedded in their psyche that food is both limited and precious, and worth fighting for; and that's just domestic dogs. Those living on the streets have it even worse.

Sharing food need not be a contentious thing, but if there's seemingly not enough to go around, you quickly learn to fight for it.

Then, as with all things, an element of choice then takes over. Does the dog continue to believe that it needs to fight with all-comers throughout the whole of its life (including with its own people in some cases)? Or does it accept that the 'food wars' are a thing of the past and accept that there's enough to go around? Selection will be determined by circumstances, and (to some extent) how much intelligent consideration the dog gives to its situation.

As with all things, this is a learning point for the individual animal.

In recognising and accepting this latter issue, we may find it easier to accept that the dog is merely where they are on their pathway, and not condemn them for their intolerance of interlopers, who may or may not be trying to make off with their precious rations. And again, as with all things, if we try to understand this element of their being, we might provide ourselves with a gateway to understanding *all* things, canine and otherwise.

Why do dogs eat their own excrement?

Because there is an off-chance that it might just be food...

Of all of a dog's questionable habits, this might strike we humans as the most awful and repugnant. Science has dubbed the habit 'Coprophagia' and no definitive explanation has been found for this behaviour. That's not surprising because the roots of the habit are flimsy to say the least. However, you're about to read the two reasons that explain why they do it.

As puppies, dogs will usually witness their mothers consuming their waste, almost as soon as they expel it. This immediately normalises the behaviour and gives it the seal of approval. However, this is by no means a certain cause, since the puppy's level of consciousness during this period in their lives may not be sufficient to engrain the memory. The second cause is the one of most significance

Equipped with an omnivorous digestive system that is considerably stronger than the human one, a dog's stomach can cope with some pretty horrendous things, and the dog itself has an awareness of its relative lack of sensitivity in this respect. Thus, it is prepared to try anything *if* it is food driven enough.

The smell of its own waste, that we perceive only at a rather obvious 'deeply unpleasant' level, is more multi-layered than it will ever appear to our unsophisticated noses. All of these tiers of scent are available to the dog's olfactory sense. One of those layers will contain a trace of the food that originally comprised the waste, and if needs must, the dog will eat it simply because of that trace scent.

Ironically, the more indigestible the food that has comprised the waste, the stronger the recognisable smell is likely to be. The sense of smell overrides the sense of taste, because on a relative basis in a dog, the former is so powerful and the latter so weak.

Once the first foul meal has been consumed, it is a small step to do the same thing again and again, and before you know it, a habit has been formed that has no motivation to compel it, other than habit itself. Once acquired, the habit is every bit as hard to break as smoking may be for a human.

It is also the case that dogs will often follow the 'monkey see, monkey do' principle, and copy the actions of other dogs. This is provoked by a thought pattern which goes something like:
"If they're eating it, it must be OK, so why shouldn't I?"

This can quickly lead to their own addiction.

It's not a medical condition and it does not fulfil some dietary need that we don't understand and are not meeting. It doesn't even deserve its fancy Greek originated 'Coprophagia' title.

It's just a bad habit, plain and simple.

I would love to be able to say that we've never had to experience this phenomenon, but I'd been lying if I did.

When we first came across it, we were appalled and sought every means possible to correct the behaviour. We tried to alleviate the problem by removing waste as soon as it appeared, but with five other dogs at that time, we found it was a losing battle.

We sought guidance and found that sprinkling sour apple liquid on the offending mess, before it could be consumed, seemed to be the most recommended approach; but it made not one iota of difference to our dog. Finally, going to extreme measures, we tried using extra hot habanero sauce. But the dog was greatly enthused by the introduction of the new flavour, and ate with relish!

We gave up, and after a while, fortunately, she grew out of the habit. It coincided with a change to the raw food diet...

Chapter 4

PLAY AND EXERCISE

"Yes," said Mr. Powell, "they have fun in a simpler and more joyous way than most humans do. Their pleasures seem more reliable. All you have to do is say the word 'walk' and they're wiggling from head to toe...."

Betsy Woodman, *Jana Bibi's Excellent Fortunes*

Do dogs enjoy games?

Most dogs do, most of the time. But not all dogs do, all of the time.

If you were to ask a question like this to a human, it might be phrased something like "Do you enjoy sport". Now imagine the variety of permutations of answers you could receive and the reasons behind them. As you do so you'll start to get a flavour of how it is with dogs.

When we think of their gameplay, we should consider activities that are solitary, those involving interaction with people, those which involve other dogs, and those which are a combination of both. Simplistically, some love all games, others aren't bothered at all, and some only like certain games.

The reasons why are every bit as complex as those we might relate to explain our own personal preferences.

Any of the influences below may factor into a personal perspective that ultimately results in a lack of enjoyment of games.

- Lack of aptitude
- Failure to comprehend the rules
- Bad first or early experiences of playing
- Dislike of team/solo activities
- General propensities
- Genetic predisposition
- Mood in the moment

Conversely, possessing a natural skill set, wholly positive and inspiring initial encounters with an activity, a love of being involved with a group/striking out on your own, general propensities, genetic predisposition and attitude at the outset, may well result in a lifelong love affair with an activity. So it is by no means the case that all dogs enjoy all, or even some, games.

We all too easily get into the mindset of believing that being canine automatically equates with being play-loving and game seeking, when to do so ignores the fact that dogs are every bit as much individuals as we are. This stereotyping would be frowned upon were we to try and apply it to humans, yet there are many more dog people who will expect their pets to join in activities which they may not find stimulating, than there are 'jock' fathers who will try to persuade their reluctant children of the value of football or baseball.

Some members of our extended pack enjoying a game of competitive 'fetch'.

For some it is a case of firmly believing they are doing the *right thing* by constantly having their dog indulge in play activities; whilst for others it's almost as if the dog is a plaything and therefore *should* indulge in gameplay of our choosing. Puppies especially may have activity forced upon them relentlessly, particularly when their upbringing involves young children growing up alongside them. Consequently, the dog can learn to go along with an activity even though they do not particularly enjoy it, just through a desire to keep their people happy. It is all too easy for humans to confuse willingness to please with willingness to play.

Intra-group dog play is usually rough and competitive. Like children play fighting, a dog's game can quickly degenerate into less jovial conflict and get out of hand. Nevertheless, their people should learn to distinguish between the spirited and the hurtful, since the former is a good way for dogs to find an outlet for their energy, and the latter seldom gets too serious. At a certain age, most dogs tend to stop rough and tumble type games completely. We might think they are 'growing up' when in fact, stopping results from the dawning of recognition within them that serious harm can result, and a consequent abatement of desire. Some dogs will never involve themselves in the roughest games, learning very early on to abstain and live gently. This is because this particular piece of learning is already well integrated in their mindset. Inevitably they been 'around the track' many times.

Play with humans is far less natural for dogs than playing with each other and only those without age compatible playmates of their own kind tend to prefer person focused games. Alternatively, if other doggy chums are available who have no interest in playing, the human must be the substitute. (This often happens when a second dog is brought into a home where the older incumbent has been an only dog. It is not uncommon for that dog to avoid inter-dog play completely.)

When there is more than one dog playing with a human, the dogs may try to show off to their person, and these games are likely to be the most competitive of all.

Only as an unreasonably broad generalisation could it be said that *all* dogs love games; but it may certainly be said that *most* dogs, for at least some part of their lives, like to play. The trick is to recognise which give them pleasure due to the intrinsic nature of the activity itself, and which they are merely 'going along with' to please you. Games should be experimented with to see if they genuinely do bring happiness. If they don't, they should not be forced upon the animal.

However, if a dog genuinely loves gameplay of any sort, it is a minor tragedy in their lives if they are not afforded the opportunity to express themselves through that activity, in just the same way as it would be a grievous thing for a potential tennis prodigy never to be allowed to hold a racket and hit a ball.

As a matter of interest, only about two or three of our entire pack have no interest in games at all. These are the eldest. But of the remainder, less than a dozen are interested in playing with humans.

Do dogs ever stop enjoying games?

Assuming that they enjoy them to begin with, a love of playing may not be as perpetual as it may appear.

Whereas inter-dog play may have stopped relatively early on in life, seniors may still appear to be enjoying themselves playing with their person. This can be symptomatic of the desire to please rather than actual enjoyment, since pain from aching joints, that is exacerbated by rigorous play (even though we may not detect it), often besets a dog at a far younger age than we might imagine.

A dog's desire to indulge its people will often be without measure. You may read crushingly sad stories of guardians repeatedly throwing sticks into the ocean for their dogs to retrieve. The story always ends tragically with the dog disappearing on one of their retrievals, caught up by the tide, swept out to sea, and drowned. Their grief-stricken people are left relating how much their dog enjoyed the activity and just kept on doing it, never wanting them to stop.

A devoted pet will indulge their guardian in repeated gameplay until the point of exhaustion if we do not protect them from themselves. It is not just in this type of activity where this response is typical. In any game, the pleasure may not be just in the activity itself but in keeping their people happy and doing what their human wanted them to do.

When no humans are around, a group of social dogs will quite happily play their own games.

Do dogs need to be entertained?

There is quite a difference between 'need to be' and 'like to be'. Dogs do like to be entertained, but quite what they will find entertaining is anybody's guess.

A lack of stimulus in their day-to-day living experiences can result in a variety of issues effecting a dog's personality and behaviour. But entertainment should not be thought of as a counter for boredom. For canines, it is something that brings an amusement outside of the parameters of their normal life and expectations, by introducing something which is unanticipated or unusual. Going by these criteria, all dogs *like* to be entertained; none necessarily *need* to be entertained.

It is not anthropomorphising to recognise that animals:

- have a sense a humour
- can and do experience amusement
- do derive enjoyment from aspects of the world around them
- do have an emotional response of pleasure to the experience of enjoyment.

It would be a greater act of foolishness to assume that:

- what we think is amusing is also entertaining for them
- because we do not see or hear them laugh that nothing strikes them as funny
- because we do not see them smile they are not entertained
- because they do not give us a warm critical appreciation of an experience they have had, they did not enjoy it.

It is also true that what strikes them as entertaining, amusing or enjoyable may bear no resemblance to our appreciation of such things. This should come as no surprise. If you are a Westerner, have you ever tried to share a joke with a Korean, or watched a Chinese soap opera? It is not merely a language issue that may affect your level of enjoyment. The precepts of our cultural background form the context within which we find an experience entertaining or otherwise.

Anyone wondering about this particular question is perhaps wishing to understand not the spiritual or even psychological aspect of entertaining a dog, but whether or not there is an onus upon their people to provide it. Is there something more we should be doing?

On the one hand, we may console ourselves with the universal panacea that a dog knows what it is getting into when it comes to us. If we don't provide entertainment, it's something they have already accepted. On the other hand, we may wish to make our pet's lives as fun as possible by providing them with entertainment. But since providing fulfilment is not necessarily within our control, what can we do?

Is it your role, in addition to your guardianship, to be your dog's entertainer? Frankly, even if you could be, it's negligible whether they'd like your act! Choices about what is found entertaining are as unique to dogs as they are to humans. Nonetheless, this should not deter the caring custodian from attempting to provide as many stimulating activities as possible for their dog, in the hope that some may provide them with entertainment.

Some things that humans find amusing are just NOT funny!

How much exercise should dogs get?

The simple answer is that a dog will generally take what it can get and any exercise is better than none at all. However, the response must be extended to cover both physical and mental exercise.

At a physical level the need for exercise of some kind is fundamental and essential, and those that do not get it will experience some degree of atrophying of their muscles and consequent affects upon their ability to keep fit. Lack of workout also carries with it the potential for psychological repercussions affecting temperament and behaviour.

Depending upon the breed, the impact of lack of activity might not be as negative as this might suggest, since even the most basic level of exercise, such as walking around the home, might keep the body functional.

It is also true to say that the implications for state of mind could be more an issue of the challenges the dog wishes to face and the mastery they wish to achieve in a lifetime, than it is about what their human is doing.

This is such an important issue for a dog's wellbeing that it needs to be understood with crystal clarity:

- It does NOT imply that a dog need not be exercised.
- It does NOT infer that it's OK not to walk your pet.
- It does NOT suggest that you should not do everything you can to make your dog's life as stimulating as possible.

The mere fact that you are reading this probably demonstrates that you have your pet's best interests at heart, and that this shouldn't be a concern.

But it is acknowledging a rather uncomfortable truth for any true dog lover to face.

In their choice of at least one lifetime, dogs must elect to go through an experience wherein they receive very limited exercise, and learn to cope with it.

It is a sad fact that some dogs live rather tragic lives chained to a deck, kept in a garage, or caged indoors for the majority, or even all of the day. In all likelihood, upsetting though this is, it may be what they must go through.

As with so many things, expectations are key. A dog will adapt to the circumstances in which it finds itself and adjust its expectations accordingly. Its psychological needs will rapidly be in direct proportion to what it believes it can reasonably anticipate, based upon its previous experience.

Where fit young Huskies are concerned, the more exercise they get, the better it is.

Do dogs need humans to exercise them?

Physically, no. Psychologically, yes.

A treadmill may provide physical exercise for a dog, and a dog park is a fabulous opportunity for gregarious canines to romp, but dogs take unusual pleasure in being accompanied on walks by their person.

For a dog, exercise that is taken alone is like visiting somewhere special for a human. It's great, but if you don't share the experience with someone else who you love and care about, it's just not the same. And oddly enough, even if there's another dog with you, it just won't do.

Ironically, unleashed, a dog will seldom spend a walk at its person's heel. Running ahead, plunging into bushes, sniffing amongst undergrowth and disappearing for periods of time are all characteristics of dog walking we can relate to with familiarity. The exercise can hardly be said to be a shared experience. But from the dog's perspective, not only have you been together, you have entered their world. And the thrill they experience at this is considerable.

Sharing the snow together. What could be better?

Why do some dogs seem to prefer one walker over another?

Whilst the walker's selection of route, distances covered and duration are important factors, the vibrational output from the walker is ultimately more significant from the dog's perspective.

For a dog out walking with a human, the level of enjoyment they receive because of the companionship of that person can be measured in much the same way as we might assess our pleasure in an outing with a human companion. Irrespective of how you feel about them as individuals, some people are quite fun to be with; some you can have an absolute blast with; and some just drag the whole thing down!

Although somebody is better than nobody, canines are affected by a whole host of walker-related factors that can all too easily alter their experience of the outing. These will include the human's:

- Mood and mindset (being relaxed and happy is best).
- Attitude to the walk (the more enthused the better).
- Level of anxiety experienced (not worrying about encounters with other dogs or losing their charge).
- Amount of communication (regular, positive and excited is preferred).
- Need to control what the dog is doing (the less the better).
- Energy level (matching theirs if possible).

How the walker feels about what they are doing (and the dog itself) exudes from them in vibrational form, since the emanations thoughts create may not be contained. These are totally perceptible to a dog.

Humans who can experience empathy and care about the experiences of their fellow beings may go to considerable lengths to 'manage themselves' when they are with others of their own kind, but they may neither mask, nor deceive a dog about their deepest feelings. Dogs are wholly aware of what is going on with their walker, and more than anything, they want that individual to take as much pleasure as they do, simply because if they don't, the dog's innate ability to empathise will inevitably impact their own feelings of satisfaction. In other words, to maximise the overall enjoyment for the dog, the human must take as much delight in the excursion as they do.

Of course, circumstances and attitudes often prohibit this. Custodians can all too often arrive at a point where walking is a chore. Anxieties (well-founded ones) too often override any chance of relaxation. Some people just don't bother to talk to their dogs in a public setting. (Uttering commands doesn't count.) And if the custodian is intent on making their control/domination of the dog of paramount importance during the walk...

As a consequence of all that is written above, it is not uncommon for a dog to develop preferences about who they walk with. "Any port in a storm" may well apply; but they would prefer to spend this important time with someone with whom they may share a common experience.

NB. Interestingly, a preferred walking companion may assume a totally different positon in preferential rankings when considered in regard to other aspects of the dog's relationship with their humans.

A few dogs and their walker.

Why is chasing a ball repeatedly so rewarding.

Quite simply, there's joy in repetition!

If you know anything about chanting as it is practiced by monks or others as part of a spiritual routine, you will be aware that it has purpose aside from the actual significance of the words or sounds used in the incantation. It is believed that the cumulative effect of the repetition causes the mantra or sounds to embed within the subconscious and continue repeating, bringing overwhelming joy to the individual even when they are amid their everyday lives.

And so it is with chasing balls! Well, something like that anyway...

If you have a dog that *really* loves to chase a ball, the fun that they have while playing is a combination of:

- the thrill of the chase (and the physicality of the exercise)
- the challenge of catching the ball (which is akin to pinning down prey)
- the satisfaction of retrieval (which would be considered an act of keeping their person happy)

Since each experience is the same, yet entirely dissimilar with each throw, as the ball bounces differently or is thrown to different places, the game is seldom tired of, at least mentally, and as such it can be endlessly rewarding.

Whilst the dog is going through what may appear to us to be an almost mindless routine, the unending reiteration of the experience is being anchored in muscle memory, as well as subconscious memory. The result for the dog is that they are left in a euphoric state which may continue long after the game has ended, replayed in dream as well as awakened states. And if that's not a reason to chase, what is?

Although sticks can never mimic the uncertainty of prey dodging and darting to avoid capture that balls can, they may be more exciting to some dogs than round bouncy things. If so, the pleasure is derived from the joy of engaging in play with their person, and the happiness they think they are bringing by retrieving such important items!

The thrill of the chase! (Can you spot the ball?)

On land or in water, it doesn't matter if there's fetching to be done.

🐾 Why do dogs chase cats, rabbits, squirrels and deer?

Prey drive is latent in all dogs unless they have already achieved a certain soul age.

Chasing potential prey is an obvious throwback to the hardwired mindset that dogs are born with. They're chasing food.

What is interesting to note is the reason relatively few dogs manage to catch the things they chase. Deep within the soul memories they carry around with them there is perhaps the knowledge that in this lifetime, they don't have to catch their own food. There have certainly been lifetimes where this has been essential for survival, but if they are living as domesticated pets, then this time around it's neither necessary nor desirable.

As we progress through lifetimes, we gain understanding of key learning points. These are too numerous to mention, but one of these is about adopting a 'no harm' mentality. This is basically attaining and acting upon a realisation that the harm that we do to other beings harms ourselves, and that we do not need to bring about injury, suffering or death.

At this point, there is a bit of a divergence between human and dog learning. For humans, the no harm philosophy extends all the way to the realisation that we do not need to (and should not) be eating the flesh of other beings, or tacitly be complicit in allowing the slaughter of other beings. For dogs, it means that taking the life of another is only necessary when killing for food is required for survival. It may take both humans and animals many, many lifetimes to arrive at this conclusion, but not 'getting it' is a major road block in a soul's progression.

A well fed domesticated pet has no need of food that it catches after a pursuit, and it is often the case that during a hunt, the inappropriateness of what they are doing dawns upon them. It rises from the depths of their subconscious where the soul DNA resides, and produces a glimmer of doubt in the conscious that prevents them from killing.

From an observer's perspective, it may appear that the dog is too slow, or the prey too cunning in their evasion tactics; but it should be thought of as a situation comparable with a man who believes he wants to kill, points the gun at his intended target but is unable to pull the trigger.

When a dog does catch and kill whatever it pursues, it is (almost) a guarantee that the dog is a younger soul who is still coming to terms with some of the many lessons its multiple lifetimes will provide for it. And it is irrefutable evidence that it will be coming around again.

Dogs that do seek to relinquish their carnivore eating habits often run into difficulty since, if they are with humans, their diet is a by-product of their people's feeding. Were human society to be vegan, because of their relationship with us (living synergistic and dependent lives), dogs would also evolve into vegans, as their omnivore physicality allows them to, and even intends them to.

We have had several dogs that have been relentless pursuers of squirrels and other small creatures.

It may be imagined that with so many canines, we have witnessed numerous kills, but in truth, only three squirrels and several mice have ever met their ends at the paws and jaws of the pack (that we know of).

We have (thankfully) seen chases and hunts stopped short on many occasions, but we have never intervened, since to do so would potentially disallow the dog's choice and consequent learning opportunity.

Many of the dogs never chase at all, creating some amusing situations whilst out hiking.

One dog had a squirrel run out in front of him on a hiking trail, only three feet away. The squirrel paused briefly, looked at the dog, and then continued. In return, the dog looked at the tiny rodent but didn't so much as move a muscle.

On another occasion the same dog ignored a large (and obvious) toad who hopped right between his front paws when he was lying down outside our front door. The toad remained for at least five minutes whilst the dog turned his head and quite literally tried not to look at it.

On yet another occasion, the same dog suddenly stopped mid trail on a hike and refused to move another inch. After a few moments of futile coaxing, my attention was caught by the appearance of the most enormous porcupine, about fifty metres ahead. It shuffled around for a few minutes, and then disappeared into the brush. Only then would the dog move on. Having never encountered one before, he did not know to be wary, and although it was the most colossal porcupine I have ever seen, our dog still had size advantage.

Many of our other dogs would have needed restraining for their own protection. I believe this one quite clearly knew that no creatures should be harmed.

Just being on a squirrel hunt can be every bit as exciting as catching one.

What is it dogs enjoy so much about going for a walk?

Going for a walk affects a dog in several different ways.

Pleasure taken from a walk operates at different levels. Most obviously, there are factors such as:

- The opportunity for physical exercise.
- A change of environment.
- The possibility of new experiences.
- A whole world of interesting scents to savour.

At a completely different level, to be in the outdoors is a far more 'natural' experience for a dog and is far more rewarding for them at both a psychological and spiritual level.

Deep within their subconscious, dogs feel a connection to the outdoors which is 'fed' when they are in it. This is not to say that they are not capable of living whole lifetimes without seeing so much as a blade of grass or a ray of sunshine (as circumstances may force). And as with all things, if you have not experienced it, you never know what you are missing.

But the experience of nature and a world that no longer seems 'contained' speaks volumes to the mind of endless possibilities of, and a link to, something much larger than what they commonly experience. It's no aggrandisement to say that a greater sense of self and an awakening of purpose may be achieved.

The easiest way to understand a dog's experience of going for a walk is to imagine yourself going outdoors and feeling a tingling sensation all over your body, as if billions of minuscule elements within you are bursting to connect with what is outside. The sensation is a very pleasant one and you feel as if you are getting bigger. You are most aware of the feeling in your spine which seems to almost vibrate, producing in you a sense of euphoria which, if you are lucky, may last for a considerable amount of time.

The outdoors is so awesome for a dog that a puppy experiencing the natural world for the first time may well register wonder, and even fear (on a scale that may range from caution through to absolute terror). Then once they become accepting of and comfortable with the sense of there being a 'world at large', an adjusted mindset follows very quickly. Fear is most usually replaced with relish and a seemingly endless appetite for more.

Whilst walking, most guardians cannot fail to notice the transformation in their dog's state of being, typified by a heightened level of interest, alertness and vibrancy. And of course, their level of anticipation when there is the prospect of experiencing it again never seems to go away.

A walk can be magical. And if you can share the experience with friends...

Where do dogs enjoy going for a walk?

Almost anywhere doesn't cut it. There are definite preferences.

How long the euphoria of the outdoors lasts for is directly related to where the dog is taken for a walk. The basic rule is that the more urban the environment, the quicker it will be dispelled.

Here, from a dog's perspective, is the amount of pleasure various walk venues may bring, explained with human experiential equivalents:

The usual walk in the town/city - reading a copy of the National Enquirer when the content is mostly ads and the biggest stars in it are reality TV 'celebrities', most of whom you've never heard of and don't care about. The cover promises a great deal but the pictures are all in black and white and the apparently interesting stories are already known to you in advance when you get to them.

Walking in a familiar neighbourhood with front yards - thumbing through a copy of HELLO! magazine whilst sitting on a bench facing a pleasant but familiar view, getting an insight into the lives of celebrities you have watched and whose lives interest you, with glossy colour photos.

An unexpected walk in an unknown location - whilst out driving you came across the quaintest little town with fascinating narrow streets to explore. The unique stores hint that they may contain exciting unknown treasures, all at bargain prices. You have no pressure to do anything else but browse at leisure and see what you find.

A visit to a local park - going to Six Flags amusement park when there are no queues and there is a good chance you'll be able to hook up with friends and share the pleasure of the rides together. You have free coupons for the concession stands and the aroma of cotton candy and popcorn fills the air.

A run on the beach - a friend invited you onto their luxury yacht. The waters are calm and tranquil, there's plenty of liquid refreshment flowing and food is superb. You might take a dip later if you fancy it and you haven't a care in the world.

A long hike on a forest trail - going away for an impromptu weekend with someone you love. You're staying in a fully stocked, secluded and cozy cabin where there's a fire to warm you, wonderful food and drink in the refrigerator and a host of exciting things to do.

A day long hike up a mountain - someone gave you tickets for an all-inclusive luxury vacation in a dream destination where you can spend a week indulging yourself to your heart's desire. The possibilities are endless.

Being taken on family vacation with new walks everyday - OMG! You're doing the three-month Grand Tour, plain and simple. Unbridled excitement 24/7.

Get the idea?

Of course, personal circumstances invariably mean that people are not able to provide their dog with the variety and level of excitement afforded by some of these walking opportunities, and that's not necessarily a problem for the dog on face value. However, dogs can arrive at a point where they become so habituated to the urban environment that they lose their connection with the 'natural' world and start to fear it. In humans, this is referred to as 'natural world deficit disorder' and it's quite prevalent. Having a dog is one of the easiest ways to help humans overcome this odd disconnection and realign themselves with nature and the outdoors.

Bearing in mind just what these expeditions mean to a pet, it is easy to see how to bring them pleasure and at least occasionally pander to their needs. Be aware that too much of a good thing becomes routine. So, a daily walk that always follows the same route is like reading the same issue of the magazine. And even going on the yacht can become passé if the yacht is always in the same waters. Variations in routine can double the excitement and refresh a dog's perspective.

Do we put dogs under stress by taking them to things like off leash dog parks?

If you have an introverted dog, yes. And I'm not being funny!

On the above scale of outings, a dog park is the equivalent of a mystery day trip.

You may end up going somewhere where you have an absolute blast. Perhaps you get to visit somewhere you'll love, where the scenery is beautiful, you'll meet great new people, make new friends, do exciting things, and come home feeling you've had the most wonderful day.

Or you could end up somewhere that has already become so familiar it's boring, the landscape seems dull, it's the same old faces, there are some positively hostile characters around, you do the same old things you always do, and when you get home, you wish you'd never left.

Fortunately, there are very few days a dog would describe in the latter terms, and when they do have a bad experience, it is almost always down to the behaviours of those whom they encounter at the dog park.

Depending upon the nature of the dog, this can indeed turn the experience into a highly stressful nightmare. To fully understand this, we need to draw another human comparison: There are those who are the life and soul of a party, those who head straight for the kitchen, and those who simply don't go to parties. Why would we imagine that dogs would be any different?

The signs of reluctance or discomfort with multiple (and sometimes) invasive contacts from other dogs should be pretty evident in your own pet. Stress is of one of the non-verbal cues that dogs communicate with consummate ease, and it is only total insensitivity on the part of their people that misses it.

We may be caught up in the notion that despite how things appear, they're enjoying it really; or that being with other dogs and having the freedom of the dog park is 'good for them'.

Don't be deceived.

Whilst the outdoors *is* good for them, for all the reasons previously outlined, they may prefer their dose of the outdoors to be taken as a solitary activity with only their person for companionship. And they may prefer their interactions with their kind to be limited to manageable numbers. After all, a dog may just as easily be a quiet dinner party type, rather than a full-blown party animal.

To force a dog to do anything it does not enjoy is cruel and unnecessary, and we should never assume they will enjoy an activity just because they are a dog; and certainly, not just because *we* think it's good for them.

Not a dog park, but a few members of our pack (who are very familiar with each other) relaxing in the outdoors together.

Chapter 5

SLEEP AND RELAXATION

*"Is your dog in a coma?" Quinn asked when the dog didn't move a muscle.
"No. Lump leads an active and demanding internal life that requires long periods of rest."*

Nora Roberts, *Blood Brothers*

Why do dogs sleep so much?

Despite the appearance of boundless energy, being a dog is an exhausting thing at many different levels.

Whatever the physical activity level of a dog, a dog is far more aware of and influenced by the energies around it, than we humans are. Whereas we (of necessity) become inured to their impacts, dogs do not. Consequently, they often find themselves in a state of fatigue without apparent reason.

The air and space that is all around us (the ether) seems like an empty void. It is actually a maelstrom of chaotic energies, some natural, some man made, since they emanate from all living things. The vibrational emissions of trees, plants and other beings are supplemented by waves from colossal telecommunications masts, sounds of all kinds, and of course, the thoughts of all of those who exist within the space. The higher our level of sensitivity to energies, the more wearisome they may become. Because dogs are considerably more sensitive than us, they far more easily fall prey to being affected by them.

The experience of vibrational energies upon a dog may be likened to standing in the pathway of a fan that is blowing full in your face. It is not necessarily unpleasant, but it can become tiring after a time. In parallel with a fan's speed settings, certain environments can be the equivalent of a fan operating at a higher and more irritating setting. Urban situations, with their increasing proximity to communications masts, will have far more vibrational 'static' than rural settings. But even within a house, the energy emissions from (for instance) turning on a television are like turning up the fan. The subsequent soporific effect upon a dog may be quite noticeable.

The easiest way to combat this kind of wearying onslaught is to be physically active. Ironically, expending physical energy creates much more energy; whereas conserving energy through inactivity can engender tiredness. This explains why dogs have such apparently boundless energy (although age does take its toll upon this self-generating ability); but also, why long periods of sleep can lead to even more extended periods of slumber.

If the opportunity for activity is not likely to present itself any time soon, a dog will instinctively seek to reduce the 'buffeting' effects of the vibrational 'fan' by reducing their energetic state to the point of least resistance, i.e. sleep.

Seldom does a dog's sedentariness have anything to do with a slothful approach to living; and if it does, it is likely to stem from having its expectations for life reduced to a point where it has lost the will, or enthusiasm, for pretty much anything.

The one exception to this is, of course, age. The relentless onslaught of the aging process will eventually slow even the most energetic of canines to a pace that allows them a modicum of comfort, and assuages the effects of aching bones. The closer a dog comes to passing, the more likely it is to take pleasure in reflection upon its glory days, often experienced through the review facility provided by a state of dreaming.

Age can turn even the most active former sled dogs into couch potatoes.

Do dogs dream in pictures, and if so, are the dreams in black and white or colour?

A dog's dreams are nothing short of being akin to a technicolour movie reel.

The canine dream state is on a parallel with our own. Dogs go through every bit as vivid an experience as we do, and their dreams appear equally real, incorporating the entire colour spectrum that they see when awake. As for the dreams themselves, the dogs are not so much seeing pictures as having things happen to them that seem as real in the moment as anything that they would go through when they were awake.

Like all sentient beings, a dog's mind is comprised of both conscious and subconscious elements. Their capacity for data storage (memory) and recall is not dissimilar from our own. The imagery which is available to them may not be as complex and varied as a human's, because of the relatively limited opportunities that their lives, current and previous, may have afforded them. Nonetheless, the range of available pictures from which to create dreamscapes and roles within them is still broad and diverse.

What dreams may come...

What do dogs dream about?

What don't they dream about?

It is a rather patronising idea to imagine that the substance of doggie dreaming consists of scenarios relating to chasing rabbits or getting bones, as we popularly caricature them. The question could equally be asked of humans "What do you dream about?" to which the most apposite answer would probably be, "What don't I dream about?" The same applies to dogs.

Because of the rather superficial way in which we view their lives, it can be difficult for us to imagine the complex array of subject matter available to them, yet they too can live, or relive, emotions, encounters and situations, go through the unimaginable, the bizarre, the frightening, the pleasurable and the humorous, just as we may.

Our dream activities may be divided into several components that describe the reasons for the dreaming, any of which could affect us during a nighttime. These include, but are not limited to:

- Review of learning points from previous lifetimes that are stored subconsciously, and only become accessible when the conscious mind is switched off.
- Re-examination of troubling circumstances that we have (recently) faced, presented in the form of allegory.
- Suggestive etheric input intended to forewarn, caution or stimulate.
- Conjecture, regarding choices to be made that is unrestricted by convention or a limitation of belief about what is possible.
- Abstract 'play time', within which the mind is unencumbered by boundaries and exploring reality.
- Astral travel, wherein the consciousness leaves the body and experiences other realities.
- Meetings with the 'higher selves' of others (a part of a soul that remains in the etheric) we know, to reconcile issues between our physically incarnate states.

All the above is possible for a dog.

Why do dogs never seem to have scary dreams?

It might seem that way, but that's certainly not the way it is.

On the contrary, dogs can have dreams which, for them, are every bit as scary as ours may be for us. They have bad dreams and full blown nightmares.

These may most easily be recognised if your pet twitches frantically, accompanying their motion with whimpering, yelping or other peculiar noises. Even troubled sounds that are not accompanied by movement are likely to indicate that the dog is not enjoying their dreamtime. Although these things are not necessarily cast iron guarantees that the dog is having a bad dream, it's usually a sign that there's something a lot more disturbing going on than the reliving of the day's activities.

Dogs do not enjoy bad dreams any more than we do. They are just as likely to forget them upon awakening as we are, but there are the occasional ones that will leave them feeling as if they are still amid the bad experience the dream has plunged them in to. This can result in them being unsettled and upset.

Waking a dog from a dream that is obviously distressing them is a kind thing to do, but it should be done softly and sensitively. A 'rude awakening' is much more likely to leave them feeling partially (if temporarily) trapped in an unpleasant netherworld. Gentle shaking followed by soothing talk and affection will restore them to a settled state much more quickly, and be a lot nicer way of reconnecting them to the 'real' world. However, it should be noted that whispering, which may be comforting during the daytime when the animal is fully awake, is disturbing and surreal when they are coming out of a dream.

All this said, dogs are less likely to be impacted upon by many of the things that can cause a human to have bad dreams. In part this is because their sentience doesn't incorporate the vast array of activities and experiences that a human's might have done. But it is also an issue of what preoccupies their lives. In general terms, dogs are not nearly as concerned or troubled by the immense range of issues that we are.

It is sometimes suggested that dogs do not have bad dreams because they 'live in the moment'. Irrespective of whether this is true (it is discussed later in the book) such a state of being can only be said to apply to those times when we are consciously in control of our thought processes. As soon as we are asleep, our conscious mind turns off, and our subconscious takes over.

Sleeping companions

Do dogs like to be stroked and petted?

Yes, but surprisingly, it takes some getting used to.

It may come as a big surprise to you that for new born puppies, touch by a human can be alarming. It takes time for them to learn that the contact being made is not threatening or harmful, so despite our fondness for believing that puppies are instant cuddle bundles, relishing our loving touch, it's not the case. If nothing else, human contact is a very different experience from what they are used to, which is their mother's tongue and coat. And even for older dogs who have not become accustomed to the sensation, petting can be surprisingly scary.

The reason for this lies in the sensitivity of their coats. Contact can feel a little like the equivalent of an electric shock since energy transfers from the human to the dog via the individual hairs. Whilst the strength of the shock is not uncomfortable, it is certainly something they are acutely aware of. It happens through any sort of coat (although curly and wire coats are slightly less sensitive) and although they become accustomed to it and can quickly grow to like it, the sensitivity never goes away. It is possible to observe dogs jumping at the slightest touch; and to find dogs that are ambivalent to being stroked.

More than anything else, liking of being stroked and petted is an issue of trust. Over time and with frequent contact, a dog will learn to understand if the touch is carried out with genuine affection, and begin to derive pleasure from the experience.

Nowhere is this more pleasurable for them than on their stomachs, hence their rolling over behaviour. This is conventionally thought of as submissive behaviour. In fact, when this display is done to a human, it is an attempt by the dog to demonstrate its desire to form or maintain a connection with that individual. The exposure of a very vulnerable area demonstrates great trust, and when a dog does this, the person should feel quite honoured.

Some dogs like to be petted more than others.

Since they are so aware of intentions and the widely differing energies of the variety of humans they may encounter, the touch of some will inevitably be preferred over the touch of others. Dogs can tell if stroking is perfunctory, or if there is genuine affection behind it. They will also actively dislike the energies of some individuals and not relish their touch at all. With loved humans, a vibrational compatibility will develop that makes contact seem quite normal and no longer register as shock. And some dogs get handled so much that they can become completely inured to the sensation.

When a dog is taken by surprise or they do not like the energies of the person touching them, there is always the potential for an aggressive response. This applies to any dog, no matter how uncharacteristic this may be. Imagine your response if a creepy stranger came up and touched you(!); or ask yourself what your reaction is if you are touched suddenly and unexpectedly; then you'll start to understand how the dog feels.

Dogs have sensitive areas are around the middle of the back to the base of the tail. The nose, which is the most sensitive part of the whole of a dog's body, has more focus in the tip rather than around the muzzle, as if all the energy receptors have been pointed in one direction. Dogs rarely like their noses being touched because it temporarily throws their sensory array into total confusion and even blurs their vision (this will be explained later); yet they can be quite comfortable with having their muzzles touched. The most neutral place to pet a dog is on the side of the neck and under the ears, or on the flanks.

Stroking the head can be unwelcome for two reasons. Dogs are often referred to as 'head shy' when they duck to avoid contact in this area, and it is assumed that they have received blows at some point in their past which cause them to be fearful now. This may well be the case, but it does not automatically mean that this is so. When a dog's head is covered by a human palm, the 'crown' chakra is blocked.

This is one of the energy centres within a dog's body that keep the dog's vibrations in balance (humans generally have seven). Blocking the crown chakra impacts their use of it and affects their receptivity to all that is around them. The effect is a bit like having your ears covered, suddenly and forcibly by someone else. Initially, this is a very unwelcome sensation and takes some getting used to. Again, it is an issue of trust and a dog may allow some people to touch their heads and not others.

Many humans seem to feel it appropriate to give dogs a hearty and heavy slap on their side or flanks, often repeated several times and accompanied by "Who's a good boy then" or some such phrase. Why on earth they imagine that being thumped in this way would be a pleasurable experience for the dog is anybody's guess. It can hurt them, and it is *not* enjoyable.

How often do dogs like to be petted?

This depends upon the preferences of the dog and what petting technique you're using!

Some dogs will gratefully and happily be the recipients of unending strokes and fussing, whilst others must be in the mood before they'll let you anywhere near them.

It is possible for dogs to become quite needy and constantly attention seeking, which is neither a good thing for them, or convenient for their people. The reason it is not such a good idea to encourage this type of behaviour is because it smacks of extreme dependence and is not a balanced need in relationship terms.

If you draw the parallel with human relationships, an overly demanding partner can be stifling and create a claustrophobic atmosphere in a relationship. The needs of both partners must have balance for the relationship to succeed.

Both our energies, and those of other living beings, flow freely around us. (They may even be photographed as an aura, or 'auric field', like an electrical field.) Petting your dog inevitably involves an energy exchange that occurs just because of the physical contact, which causes the two fields to meet and intermingle. However, the two fields meeting may or may not be of equal strengths. Sometimes a dog will come for attention when it feels you need it, or vice versa. If the energies are mutually compatible to begin with (or of equal strengths), the meeting is balanced. However, the weaker may increase its power by draining the other. Our fields will seldom be as strong as those of a dog, so (although it is such), this should not be thought of as a physical energy transfer so much as an emotional or spiritual one. The dog is aware of what will happen.

When it has developed a bond with their person, the dog will give freely. Connecting with them physically at least once per day is a reassuring and confidence boosting event for them.

However, need for constant attention can be upsetting. If denied what they seek, the dog can feel rejected, despite this not being the case, and their humans get distressed because they are unable to fulfill this aspect of their pet's need. Sadly, there is no easy solution, since this is invariably a learning issue for the dog.

One of our more aloof dogs. Yes, really! (NB. I do other things apart from sleep.)

Our extended pack consists of members with widely differing needs, but each will make a point of connecting daily, and if one misses out, it's a cause for concern.

We have also had several dogs who have almost completely eschewed any physical contact. Frequently, these have been dogs from the most awful rescue situations where they have been abused. They have learned to live without being petted and have no expectation of it. Only occasionally do they feel the need to connect.

However, one dog raised with us since puppyhood also resisted all attempts at petting, and was hyper sensitive to touch. Occasionally she would seek out contact, often with no evident reason other than she seem to require some sort of reassurance, which we were only too happy to give.

Why do dogs enjoy having a 'good old scratch' so much?

They don't!

To me it is one of life's great mysteries that humans assume that when a dog is scratching, it is finding it a deeply gratifying experience.

It is strange that we should have arrived at this thoughtless assumption when we know that scratching is often symptomatic of skin irritation and discomfort, which is *not* a good experience. If it brings momentary pleasure, it is only because to gets rid of another sensation that is uncomfortable.

If scratching were so enjoyable for them, why wouldn't all dogs spend considerable amounts of time in this activity?

Thus, it is a source of personal irritation to me when I see a dog's custodian who has found a spot on their dog's body that, when rubbed, causes a sensation elsewhere that the dog then needs to try and scratch with their hind legs.

I have watched people do this to their dogs repeatedly, aghast. The funny thing is that they always imagine that they are bringing the dog immense satisfaction.

All they have managed to do is find a place on the dog's body, where a connection in the subcutaneous nervous system causes stimulation at one point, that provokes an irritating response elsewhere in the body, that can only be alleviated by scratching. The autonomic response is abrasive and easily damages the skin.

I have often wondered how these people would like it if it were done to them.

I'll get off my soapbox!

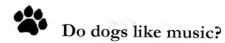 # Do dogs like music?

Yes, but don't assume that your tastes and theirs are compatible!

Music can be enormously soothing or totally discombobulating to a dog's ears, so this question warrants a 'yes and no' answer. Their appreciation of music does not register in the same way that ours does. We would describe a liking for a tune, melody, harmony or lyric. A dog is interested in the effect that the vibrational qualities of the sound have upon them. And music is full of very obvious vibrations!.

In fairness, much of what we listen to sounds plain discordant to them. Certain types of music, most especially those with pulsating beats are unpleasant for their acute auditory senses. Some instruments, like the electric guitar or clarinet, may be as grating to their ears as chalk on a blackboard. Of necessity, those living in households where they are relentlessly exposed to heavy metal, gangsta rap, techno or trance music (to name but four) learn to turn a deaf ear. Nonetheless they will find what they are subjected to quite discomforting. If a dog's people claim that their dogs like it, they are unfortunately deceiving themselves and misinterpreting the reactions they see from their pets.

Humans may well regard a dog's taste in music as being quite sophisticated, since most will find classical music very appealing. Gentler music overall would be a strong preference, and the incorporation of natural sounds such as surf, streams or rainfall is quite listenable for them. Instrumental is much better the vocal.

Some dogs may evolve very specific tastes resulting in a variety of responses. I have known people who have variously claimed that their dogs howl in derision at Barry Manilow, or bark with joy when Bruce Springsteen is singing. But such claims (which I have no particular reason to doubt the veracity of) are few and far between.

The effect of music upon a dog is usually quite subtle and you must be very observant to see anything more than apparent indifference. Mostly, it results in a calming effect.

As I write this, I am surrounded by thirteen dogs who are all crashed out, mid-afternoon, when they would normally be outside playing. They are all totally chilled out by a slightly soporific Dan Gibson 'Solitudes Series' album. They're a great favourite with our pack.

There are those who have taken the study of the effects of music upon dogs to a whole other level of science and produced CDs specifically intended for various aspects of stress reduction. Amongst these, we highly recommend Lisa Spector and her 'Through A Dog's Ear' series.

They are in regular use in our household, not because of high stress levels, but because we find it helps the dogs sleep. We play them all night long.

Volume 1 of Lisa Spector's excellent 'Through A Dog's Ear' series.

Do dogs like to have music in the house when their people are not there?

It can be very helpful if what is put on is to the dog's liking.

If it is the right sort of music, a dog that is left alone can certainly take some solace in music being played.

It should be calming, and ideally, of the sort mentioned above.

However, it is not a guaranteed cure for separation anxiety, which may only be dealt with by the presence of other pack members.

There is even a case for arguing that in the absence of something suitable, it is better to play music that dogs may dislike if it is familiar and reminds them of their absent humans...

But it's a pretty flimsy excuse for offending their ears!

Music is good, but it's never a substitute for companionship.

Do dogs get bored?

They certainly do, but their response to it is a matter of soul age.

A dog's experience of boredom is very like ours and the causes almost identical: A lack of interesting events, contact or stimuli that would otherwise occupy the mind. The only real difference is what constitutes events, contact or stimuli for a dog, since the parameters or standards of requirement are substantially different. These are based in part upon expectations, in part upon general level of sentience.

To understand this, it is necessary to get to grips with the way sentience (the capacity to respond to, or be aware of, those impressions which we get from our senses) evolves in all things:

- All beings begin their incarnations equipped with a variety of modes via which they may experience their existence. i.e. visual, auditory, kinesthetic, olfactory and gustatory.
- The senses feed consciousness, notionally on an ever-expanding basis, constantly raising our level of awareness of the world we occupy.
- When coupled with consideration and reflection, understanding is heightened.
- The combination of the physical experience, awareness and understanding shapes the level of our sentience.

When a being is deprived of the opportunity to increase their level of sentience, it remains at whatever level has thus far been achieved.

A wild animal that is born in captivity will have a very limited degree of sentience when compared with one born in its natural environment.

The opportunities afforded to a human are very different from those available to a dog. From the outset, a dog's general experience of life is likely to be somewhat 'smaller' or more limited than a human's; but the mere fact of an existence as a domesticated pet living alongside humans is a limiting factor. You may well be able to imagine why a street dog's experience of life would be considerably more 'colourful' than a lap dog's, even if is not necessarily as easy or comfortable.

It is an unfortunate truth that for most domestic dogs, their lives are lived on the margins of their people's existence, regulated by human comings and goings, what activities they are allowed to participate in, and what the duration of those activities is. Their opportunities for excitement may be limited to minutes rather than hours within a day, and everything else is merely an opportunity for boredom to thrive.

Not bored, but definitely relaxed.

But you don't miss what you've never had. The less activity and opportunity for experience a dog is afforded, the lower its level of expectation. If a dog has a familiar and repetitive routine, they experience a lower level of sentience; but they're easier to please, and they experience less boredom.

In some dogs, the expectation for developing sentience is pegged to the home in which they find themselves or the role they will perform. In other words, they plan to go to homes where they know their lives will be rife with opportunity. Not arriving with their intended people could therefore mean that their whole lifetime is spent with dashed expectations and a feeling of boredom.

For many, this is a foreseeable and anticipated issue, and merely another aspect of experience which they must learn to deal with. Thus, many dogs can and do accept very low levels of stimulus in their lives.

A human response to boredom is to find ways to overcome it by creating stimuli. This can be difficult for dogs since they control so little about their lives. Their opportunities are limited by their environment and what other beings are around them. Lone dogs may respond with destructive behaviour (although boredom is by no means the only cause of havoc wreaking).

A dog that has had many lifetimes is far more likely to be accepting of their lot. They do not feel the same drive to experience that younger souls do. Their response is a *choice* to feel no rancour and be uncomplainingly tolerant. It will be acceptable to them that pleasures must be taken when and wherever they may be found. They will know that agitation for more is futile. Consequently, they do not experience boredom per se; merely periods of neutrality and periods of stimulus.

Unfortunately, older souls represent a relatively small component of the overall global dog population, so boredom is rife. The caring pet person, when reading this, may find themselves overcome with feelings of pity and guilt. The only way to resolve this is to provide your dog with stimuli. But to provide stimuli is to create expectation, and to then dash expectation is a sure-fire way to generate boredom. Sorry!

Companionship of any kind is one way to brush away boredom

What can we do to help dogs have a more fulfilling life?

This is a reasonably complex question, requiring a multi-part answer.

Fulfilment may be achieved at a physical, emotional, intellectual or spiritual level. Fulfillment, in this context, may be defined as leaving the individual with a sense of having done something worthwhile.

We should not assume that it is any different for a dog. However, since their intended experiences and perspective upon life are radically different from ours, precisely what allows them to arrive at a sense of personal satisfaction or fulfillment may bear very little resemblance to any human criteria!

What works for us may not work for our dogs!

Physical

At a physical level a dog has a great level of awareness of the chemical elements affecting its body and the impact of intake upon its overall wellbeing.

This may strike you as ironic considering the dreadful things dogs are prepared to eat, but what this means is that they are possessed of a heightened awareness of the extent to which their bodies need physical exercise to effectively utilise or purge those things which they have ingested.

Adventuring in the snow. For some - totally fulfilling!

A 'good' run is therefore not merely an issue of hedonistic pursuit. The evident pleasure you may observe in your dog following an intense and apparently exhausting hike has as much to do with their instinctive realisation that they have successfully detoxified their systems, as it does from the sheer joy of the exercise. The former is physical fulfilment; the latter is liking or pleasure.

That said, many dogs do enjoy experimenting with the physical potential of their bodies and discovering precisely what they are capable of. This can also be fulfilling.

Emotional

Emotional fulfilment for a dog may stem from experiences with its own kind, with humans, both, or even another species. Here it is a little more difficult to be specific about precisely what may lead to fulfilment, since the criteria are as unique for canines as they are for humans.

For some, intimate connection with a single human to the exclusion of all others will be the epitome of fulfillment; for others, belonging to a pack will be the definitive aspect of their lives. Of course, these are only two examples of the parameters of possible relationships.

What is important to understand in this context is that in our relationships with them, what we attempt to do is of far less significance than things they will create for themselves. Our actions cannot bring about fulfillment for them unless they are synergistic with their own individual needs. These in turn, have more of their origin in the spiritual aspect of their being than anything else, or what they had planned for prior to incarnating.

Intellectual

At an intellectual level, fulfilment for a dog revolves around their opportunities to use their senses and consequently, to enhance and extend both their awareness and comprehension.

Primarily this is about being in an environment where they can fully utilise their senses to experience things which are new or different for them. Their learning and understanding about the world around them comes largely from relatively limited chunks of data 'input', which are most often the product of (and therefore dependent upon) the number of walks they have.

However, this is not to suggest that a walk is automatically fulfilling. Repetitious walks along a familiar route provide a chance to pick up the latest news and may certainly give pleasure; but they are not in themselves fulfilling because they do not add anything new to the dog's perspective upon the world.

New environments, experiences and (possibly) encounters are far more suited to this. A dog that regularly gets to visit previously unknown places, walk a wide variety of routes and observe wholly unusual (for them at least) things (including species that are new to them) is far more likely to experience intellectual fulfillment.

Now you may understand the answers given in the section '*Where do dogs enjoy going for a walk*' in a new light!

Spiritual

That leaves us with spiritual fulfilment, which is possibly the most important, but also the most difficult to understand.

All beings arrive hard wired with the knowledge of what they're here to do, and dogs are no exception. We usually describe it as 'having a purpose', but we often corrupt our understanding of this by aggrandising what we are here for, imagining that by its very nature, a 'purpose' must be something of major and evident significance to the world at large.

In truth, our purpose in every lifetime (most often through a series of small and seemingly insignificant steps) is to:

- Encounter or embark upon experiences.
- Recognise the learning opportunities in them.
- Integrate the consequent knowledge and understanding into our consciousness.
- Apply it through our actions.

It may be that along the way, rising to meet the challenge of some great and good task will fuel our purpose and provide the opportunity to demonstrate our mastery of a learning point; but in general terms, a 'purpose' may be defined as a need to evidence our success in learning by converting acquired wisdom into action.

When we do what feels *right*, we may experience a sense of fulfilment at the deepest level, sometimes so deep that we may not be able to explain the satisfaction it brings to us. But it stems from the fact that we are ticking off an item on our spiritual 'to do' list, without even recognising that this is what is happening.

Of course, this is no less the case for dogs. They just have a learning agenda (specific to the type of being they are) which is very different from ours.

So, in summary, you may indirectly assist your dog in finding fulfilment in some aspects of their lives (mostly through the creation of opportunity) but probably not all.

The coincidence of what you can provide versus what they need may be somewhat limited, but if you are prepared to put yourself out, some comfortable overlaps may be found.

Even the most apparently mundane experiences may be fulfilling for a dog.

Why do some dogs watch TV?

Basically, because it flickers and moves, and they're trying to work out what they're seeing. It's rarely because they're enjoying the program!

For most dogs, their apparent watching of a television screen is caused by a momentary attraction to the dancing images, which usually lasts for a very limited time. Whilst it is amusing to watch as their heads cock to one side or suddenly dart around in response to what is happening on the screen, why they give up is perhaps more interesting than why they begin in the first place.

Their (possibly intense) curiosity is sparked by motion or recognition of what it is that they are seeing. Sounds are also a great attractant, particularly barking. But they are likely to rapidly realise that what they are seeing or hearing is not 'real'. A bark being used on the programme is unlikely to be situationally inappropriate for them, so they give up wondering at it. Moreover, they are unable to perceive any vibration from the image that is meaningful or consistent with their first expectations. They simply cannot relate to it.

There is very little place in a dog's reality for manufactured fantasy and escapism. Other than in their dreams, they have no comprehensible prior experience of it, and no need for it, so they ignore it.

Because of the effects of the energetic and vibrational outputs from a television, a dog is far more inclined to sleep through some scintillating drama than it is to be glued to the screen.

There are of course, exceptions. A very limited number of dogs will continue watching TV even when they know it is not real and worthless to them. When this is observed, on very rare occasions it is symptomatic of a dog that has a high level of focus in trying to relate to the human world it occupies, more than any attempt to alleviate boredom.

One evening I visited a house and passed through a room where two dogs, reclining on couches, were apparently watching a TV soap opera.

They were all alone in the room and I got the impression that the television was on purely for their benefit. Curiously, when I blocked the view of one of them, it jumped down from its couch and took up a position in an armchair that afforded an unrestricted view. I was fascinated and moderately amused, but said nothing.

Some weeks later I returned to the house at a completely different time of day. Passing through the same room, was taken aback to note that the dogs were in the same positions, seemingly enamoured of a different program. This time it was a daytime melodrama.

I could hold my tongue no longer and asked their person, jokingly, if the television was on for them.

"Yes" she replied, "They like soap operas and they won't go outside until they're finished."

Sure enough, when we passed back through the room sometime later, a cookery program was being aired and the dogs were nowhere to be seen!

One of our dogs finds Disney's 'Bolt' momentarily distracting, but fails to appreciate the finer points of the story.

Do dogs enjoy being groomed?

Grooming may be enjoyable or a nightmare. What's most important is who's doing the grooming.

When we endow dogs with the desire to be clean and neatly presented, we are anthropomorphising. Concern for appearance is a uniquely human perspective.

From our standpoint, it would certainly appear that for many breeds of dog, regular grooming is a necessity if uncomfortable and unsightly matting is to be avoided. Yet whilst coats can become so tangled and knotted as to be painful, many dogs do have some proficiency in their own ablutions (if not the obsession possessed by cats), or at least enough to keep themselves happy. Nonetheless, since we coexist with them, a bathing regimen may be something they must endure, and despite themselves, it should be acknowledged that being (from our perspective) clean and tidy can bring considerable advantage to a dog's overall comfort.

Whether a dog can enjoy the experience of being groomed is a complicated equation of:

- The dog's coat type.
- The dog's predisposition towards water.
- The grooming tools used.
- The grooming technique used.
- The person doing the grooming.

Whereas most issues within the equation may be overcome by a skilled and empathetic groomer, they must work considerably harder at the task if the dog has had previous bad experiences that have become ingrained in their conscious. Here are some very broad general rules.

Coat Type

Simply categorized, for a dog with a single coat, being groomed is a lot easier than it is for a dog with one of the several types of double coat. The single coat offers far less resistance to the tools, and the grooming experience may be something akin to being stroked, and quite pleasant.

A double coat not only requires more time for grooming to keep tidy, the removal of the dead hairs of the undercoat can be painful for the dog. The tools used unavoidably pull at, and even remove live hairs as well as dead ones, resulting in an unpleasant pin-prick type sensation on the skin. Even the dead ones can be highly resistant to removal, causing further tugging at the skin. Ask yourself if you like having so much as a single hair pulled out, and you'll understand their reaction.

Palpable sensation is a feature of every hair in a dog's coat, just as it is for hairs on the human body. But unlike humans, who can become fairly desensitized to contact with their bodily hair (head hair is more sensitive, but intense coiffuring methods often result in near irreparable damage to sensation on the head) dogs maintain a very high level of sensitivity as part of their sensory receptivity to the world around them. To relate to this, lightly brush the hairs on your arm with your finger without making contact with the skin. You should experience the sensation of the touch. Now imagine that amplified by a factor of four and you will understand what a dog can receive through its coat.

Water

It is by no means the case that all dogs love water. Some breeds do have a genetic predisposition to favour it; others simply hate it, be it rain or the water being used to wash their coats.

In a natural state, dogs would not use water to cleanse their coats. They would (ironically) rely upon rolling in dust and dirt. This would eventually dry and soak up any over-abundance of the oils that are present in their coat, and could then be shaken out. This is particularly effective for single coated dogs; but some coats inevitably get snags when things get caught up in them, seriously reducing the effectiveness of this 'dry bathing' method.

Water alone is not a detangler, or a medium they would naturally rely upon; so immersion in it, or even limited exposure to it from a shower head, can make for a shocking experience. The water-resistant dog will either decide it is not that bad, or it will loathe it. Of course, water temperature plays a part in this; and how they are first introduced to it.

And it is by no means the case that all dog shampoos are equal. Some will greatly ease the effect of the water upon the dog's coat, whilst others can exacerbate discomfort and cause irritation. Cheap, thin and watery shampoos may be so full of chemicals as to cause damage to the dog's skin at a level we may not even be aware of.

Sodium laureth sulphate (in all its many guises), which has been found to be potentially harmful when used in toiletries intended for humans, is equally impactful upon a dog's skin. Shampoos that contain it should be avoided at all costs.

Not all dogs are water babies, and some may dislike it as much as cats.

Grooming Tools

Dog grooming tools are now a highly developed and sophisticated branch of the dog product industry, and there is a very wide variety of brushes and combs which are specifically designed for different types of coat and grooming requirements.

A random and uninformed approach to using them can easily result in huge discomfort for the dog and a consequent dislike of the grooming experience.

Techniques

The tools employed are of little value without the correct use of them; and the techniques required for grooming a dog may be even more complex than those required for human hairdressing.

Well intended but inept guardians can create problems for themselves if they attempt to deal with their dog's coats without adequate knowledge and preparation; and whilst skills can be learned as they go along, memories created during early, maladroit efforts, may be scarring for the animal.

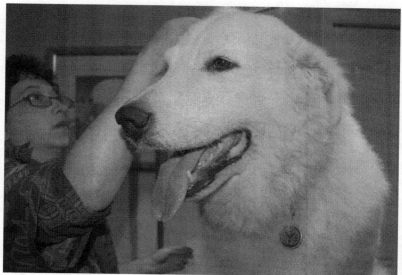

Grooming is never going to be popular unless it's a painless and pleasant experience.

The Groomer

Trumping all other considerations is the person doing the grooming. A dog will readily perceive their state of mind. Thus, if the individual is relaxed, calm, and confident, the dog will have good reason to mirror these emotions regarding what it is about to go through. But even more importantly, the dog will sense the attitude of the groomer to them as an individual, and this becomes particularly relevant when it is not the dog's person carrying out the session.

Prerequisites for a dog to feel comfortable being handled by a stranger are that the individual:

- Emanates love for dogs generally.
- Makes the dog feel liked and accepted by them.
- Genuinely cares about their wellbeing.

All this the dog will pick up in an instant. It leaves the groomer as a vibration they pick up on.

Unfortunately, for some, grooming is merely a job and not a vocation that allows them to work with creatures they adore. Their neutrality (or worse) about their clients will be quite palpable to the dogs and, particularly for more sensitive individuals, be a cause for considerable stress. Outward appearances of amiability and faux concern that keep an animal's person happy will not fool a dog for an instant.

The true measure of a professional groomer is to be found in the reaction of a dog to repeat visits and in how they greet the groomer, *not* how the groomer greets them. Evident stress at a visit to the pet spa may initially be a response to the newness of the experience, or a visit that was particularly difficult due to the condition that the coat had been allowed to get in to. But if after visits become 'normal', the groomer is not greeted with acceptance, something is likely to be amiss.

For most dogs, grooming is something they learn to put up with, and is not in itself enjoyable. They simply do not value cleanliness and a smart appearance in the way that we do, much as we may like to imagine they do. While having burdensome matts and tangles removed may make life a little easier and provide a certain short term gratification (and it will certainly enhance the sensitivity of their coats if not repeated overly frequently), it is ultimately of little consequence to them. It is therefore of far greater importance to them that when they go through this process, which is only necessary from our perspective, that they feel as loved as possible.

We used to have a dog with a coarse haired coat that per common practice for the breed required 'hand stripping'. This involves literally pulling out the dead hairs by hand. The breeder recommended an adept to us, and when it became necessary, we took the dog along.

She was a confident, feisty dog, and greeted the groomer with some enthusiasm, responding to the cooing and clucking and fussing that was bestowed upon her. But when we retrieved her a couple of hours later, she seemed somewhat shell-shocked. Nonetheless, she looked great, so we turned a blind eye to her possible distress.

Some months later we took her for another session, but when we arrived her reaction to the groomer was one of fear. She whined and fidgeted and made it clear she did not wish to be left. For her part, the groomer was a little tight lipped in her greeting, and infinitely less effusive than she had been previously. This time when we came to collect our pet, she was positively traumatised.

We never took her back.

What I believe happened was that during the first session, she found the hand stripping painful and became restive and awkward. In response, the groomer likely became angry and was rough, if not cruel with her. The groomer's second visit response was based upon knowing that she was going to have a difficult time, and the dog's trauma upon collection was in response to an abusive and punitive approach being used during the session.

I regret that we put her through the experience, and I can only be grateful that we weren't stupid enough to ignore the signs after the second visit.

Why do dogs hate having their nails trimmed?

It's all a matter of sensitivity.

There are many dogs that mistrust having any part of their physical form interfered with. Imagine if somebody grabbed a hold of you and tried to cut parts off you! From their perspective, their bodies are quite satisfactory as they are and there is no reason why they should accept or appreciate that what is being done to them is for their own benefit.

Even when something so advantageous as the removal of overly long and uncomfortable claws has been achieved, they will often fail to connect the advantage of the new physical experience with the action that has been performed upon them. As much as anything else, their reaction is caused by feelings of effrontery.

With nails, there is the additional problem of the extreme sensitivity of the nerve ending that terminates just before the nail tip. This makes the nails potentially very sensitive to the touch; and if during the clipping process the nerve is accidentally severed, a sensation like an unpleasant electric shock will course up the whole of the dog's leg. This of course will immediately put them in fear of future repetition.

Only when a dog has been made used to frequent handling, which has resulted in no unpleasant surprises, will they feel blasé about having nails clipped. The memory of positive experiences may eventually override negative ones, but memories become habituated and it may take considerable work to alter them permanently.

Nails can be tricky!

Chapter 6

COMMUNICATION

"Dogs do speak, but only to those who know how to listen."

Orhan Pamuk, *My Name is Red*

How dogs do communicate with one another?

The methods by which a dog may communicate are more numerous than those available to humans.

Dogs use three distinct active methods of communication. To us, the most obvious will be barking and the use of their tails, both of which will be discussed separately. But their primary mode of communication is telepathic. Thoughts, at their inception, have no language. Language is something that we have developed and learned to give voice to our thoughts. Prior to our use of language, we would have communicated almost exclusively via what we now think of as telepathy. It is an ability we still retain, but cannot use because of lack of practice, coupled with the fact that we are unintentionally (but actively) taught not to use it from the earliest age, by substituting spoken language instead.

If you conclude from this that humans are more sophisticated because we have a vocalised language, think again. Here are some of the problems of using a vocalised form of communication:

- We have had to create words to describe and explain our thoughts. This effectively means that we encode our thoughts within those words before we transmit them.

- Our personal encoding may be flawed because our vocabulary lacks sophistication, or we may simply lack eloquence and are unclear precisely how to say what it is that we are thinking.

- Transmission in language may be interfered with by environmental factors such as loud noises, music, simultaneous conversations or lack of appropriate volume from the deliverer.

- The pace at which a message is delivered may be too fast or too slow for the receiver, and the pitch too high or too low to make hearing clear or easy.

- The tone with which the message is delivered may fail to support or even contradict the emotion the deliverer seeks to convey.

- Factors such as the cadence and intonation used by the deliverer may add additional confusion.

- The body language used by the deliverer when making their communication may be incongruous with the content.

- When the message is received, it is immediately subject to the listening skills of the receiver, which may or may not be effective.

- The receiver must decode the message that has been delivered to them, which they do using their own version of the decryption key, which involves:

  o Their own interpretation of the vocabulary used.
  o Their own interpretation of the nuances associated with the tone in which it was delivered.
  o The added filter of their own beliefs about the deliverer at a personal level.
  o Beliefs about what the deliverer would want to convey under the circumstances.
  o Their predetermined expectations for what the deliverer may bring as a (possibly) hidden agenda.

- There is the possibility that deliverer and receiver have different first languages.

It is little wonder that so much communication is fraught with misrepresentation, misinterpretation, misunderstanding, misdirection and misleading. Not so for dogs. Telepathy allows for an extremely rapid conveyance of thoughts, ideas and intentions.

However, despite all of this, we should not assume that dogs hold conversations that are anything like as elaborate as our own.

How does telepathy work for dogs?

In much the same manner as it does for all telepaths.

Telepathic communication involves the collecting of information or messages that are sent out in vibrational form from the brain. It requires the use of a chakra (energy centre) to both transmit and receive thought vibrations. This chakra is automatically present in dogs, but it must be 'drawn down' for humans to utilise it. We have lost the use of it, as if it were a muscle gone to waste. It resides outside of our physical bodies within our auric field. (However, there are slowly increasing numbers of those who can use it to great effect.)

Any thought created by a brain is not contained by the cerebra or the skull. Neither does the auric field which surrounds all bodies keep our musings in. Inevitably, whatever is being thought 'leaks out' and becomes a presence in the ether (the space/air/atmosphere that is all around us).

Anyone using their latent telepathic abilities may 'hear' the thoughts of others if they focus upon what is being emitted by others. This may be understood as 'reading the mind' of the one who has originated the thought vibration. This is what psychics do, although this type of communication should not be described as telepathy, because it is without specific intention on the part of the sender.

Using the same principle, if the originator of the thought intends it as a message for somebody specific (rather than as a randomly generated idea) and they focus upon that person, the vibration can be targeted at them like a telephone signal from one cell phone to another. The facility to do this is not limited by distances.

The difference between random and intended messages comes from the way they are prefixed. If another's unique individual vibration (which is effectively their all-important 'real' name) is known, a message can be prefixed with that 'address' and conveyed to that individual.

Because random thoughts in the ether contain no prefix, telepaths learn to ignore them completely and filter them out of their consciousness. If they did not, they would be constantly barraged with endless chatter.

However, a prefixed message is like someone knocking on your door. It will be received in a form that has an impact equivalent to someone saying "Hello *(whatever the name is)*. This is a message for you". But even then, the recipient can choose to open the door, or leave it closed. The method may work over extended, (but not totally unlimited) distances. Knowledge of where the intended recipient is can help a great deal.

A whole conversation can be going on without so much as a sound, and we'd never know about it.

If there is a reasonably close physical proximity, a message to a being whose vibrational uniqueness is unknown is still possible. A message may be focused to make it clear that it is intended for a specific individual, without their name being tagged to it. This type of message will be received in a form which is something like someone saying "Oi you. Yes, I'm talking to you!" It is much more likely to be ignored. This method does not work over extended distances. In this, there are many parallels with the way social media messaging works!

A telepath is more likely to accept receipt of a message from another with whom they have already established a communication link (explained later).

This description of telepathy relates to humans, dogs and a plethora of other creatures, domestic and wild, who rely upon telepathy. As a communication method, it is subtle and there is no visual evidence that it is taking place. It may be conducted one to one, one to many, or many to many. Private individual/group discussions are easily possible.

Creating, addressing and delivering a message via telepathy is no more complex for a telepath than speaking a sentence might be for a human. Accessing the vibration of another, once it is known is instantaneous. It is only with old age and a slowing of the mind that the process becomes increasingly difficult.

Having a telepathic facility does not guarantee contact. Two dogs living in a home together, in close proximity, may decide that they will never speak to one another; and although they are perfectly capable of hearing one another's thoughts, they may never extend each other the courtesy of direct address.

Telepathy does not offer direct access into the mind of another as some science fiction would have us believe. Our natural thought wave emissions may be 'guarded' to stop their unintended dispersal, although to do so requires considerable effort. It takes a lot of hard work to maintain control over one's thoughts for long periods of time. Fortunately, for the most part, it is completely unnecessary. Telepathy is a relatively courteous method of communication and individuals may choose to make themselves available or unavailable as needs must.

Some dogs are much more powerful telepaths than others. This is usually a factor related to soul age. However, as they age, all dogs may eventually end up the equivalent of telepathically deaf, unable to receive incoming messages effectively.

Secondary and tertiary methods of communication may still be available, unless something in their life has robbed them of these delivery and receiving mechanisms. (Both are discussed below.)

Is body language an important part of the way dogs communicate?

It is, but it's every bit as spontaneous and unintentional as that used by a human.

The use of body language in human communication is said to account for 55% of the way in which the message impacts upon the receiver. It is something we are very good at interpreting and understanding, yet not necessarily that good at utilising as part of our own personal delivery mechanisms. This is because it tends to be natural, spontaneous, and largely unconscious.

When dogs are studied, much is made of their body language and it appears to be a very important part of their communications mix. But it only appears this way to us because we can see it and recognise its affect.

Aspects of physicality such as an arched back, raised hackles, flattened ears and curled lips send out powerful and obvious messages that are fully comprehensible to canines and humans alike. Yet by the assessments we make, were dogs to be conferring body language with the same significance that we do, almost all their communications could be regarded as negative and threatening.

There are some extremely overt examples of body language that can be conscious, but these are few and far between. Most notable would be a dog rolling on its back. This is often seen and (sometimes rightly) interpreted as a display of deference. But even here, all conclusions that we draw from body language should be made in consideration of certain rules that may alter its meaning. In discussing human body language, we talk about context, culture and cluster. And even in the world of dogs, there are overlaps:

> **Context:** The circumstances wherein you see a piece of body language occurring e.g. at the dog park; when the dog is alone with you; when there is a cat nearby.

Culture: Whilst national cultural differences have no meaning for dogs, appreciable 'cultural' differences do develop between dogs that have been heavily 'trained' and those that have not; dogs that are 'owned' by humans and those that are not; dogs that live in pack environments, and those that do not.

Cluster: The other ancillary or apparently unrelated signs a dog's body is betraying, that taken as a 'cluster' or grouped together, change the meaning of the message.

This is no display of deference, but simply raw pleasure being taken in a roll in the grass.

Overall, from a dog's perspective, their body language is largely peripheral and delivered as an automatic, unconsidered add-on response to circumstances. Things like raising of the hackles are every bit as spontaneous as the hairs rising on the back of our necks. A curled lip on a dog is no more than an intense expression on the face of a human. As we have already seen, the largest part of their communication involves no body language whatsoever.

All of this seems to take no account of the tail, which is surely a major piece of body language? However, we tend to incorporate the tail in our thinking simply because the tail is a bodily appendage, without recognising that it is a mode of communication all by itself. It is used with purpose, whereas the rest of their body language is not.

Why do dogs wag their tail?

A tail is both a main, and an extraordinary ancillary communication technique, used by a dog to meet the demands of the situation.

A tail is a device used by a dog in the same way that humans might use semaphore - to literally telegraph to others information the sender requires them to have. The only real difference is that a tail transmits as both a fully conscious independent transmitter, and as a complementary adjunct to other modes of communication being used.

It is especially useful as a means of communicating in close proximity when telepathic links have not been accepted, or messages are being ignored. Moreover, dogs will often come to rely upon their tails as the only method with which they may reliably secure a positive response, when attempting to convey messages to their people.

It is not simply a spontaneous piece of body language as we might imagine. It is far more sophisticated than a bark and more meaningful from a dog's perspective than eye contact (which dogs will most often avoid because of its relative imprecision in communicating intention). Its use is quite deliberate and (if the tail is undamaged), will always be totally congruent with the messages being transmitted via the main means of communication.

In this, dogs are quite unlike humans, whose combination of message, tone of voice and body language are often totally at odds with one another. We intentionally set out to mask the true nature of what we are saying, whether because of a need to be tactful and sensitive, or to mask our hidden agendas. Dogs are infinitely more straightforward and frankly, honest.

On its own, a tail can communicate a wide range of meanings. They do so without any nuance or subtlety. Interpretation of a tail message is deliberately unequivocal and perfectly straightforward. Just like a semaphore flag, it is clear and concise. It lets other parties know exactly what's going on without the need to get into detail. Its use simplifies canine interaction and allows complete avoidance of all the 'mis' problems referred to earlier. As an accompaniment to telepathy, the tail may be thought of as the equivalent of an unambiguous tone of voice.

Observations made by humans regarding the meaning of tail movements are often accurate, and guidelines published in books may be broadly correct. Nonetheless, we are not nearly as adept at reading their telegraphed messages as they are. Factors which we can barely perceive, such as angle of the tail from the body, amount of curl, speed of movement and how much of the tail is in motion, change the nature of a message entirely.

The way in which a dog will use its tail with humans is quite different from the way it will use it with other dogs. They recognise that we cannot understand the sophisticated range of messages that their own kind interpret so straightforwardly. With us, they stick to the basics like "Hello, I'm pleased to see you".

Even the shortest and curliest of tails are effective 'semaphore flags'.

You may be forgiven for thinking this tail information must inevitably be affected by the fact that some dogs have tails that are wildly different from others. However, this is not the case. Only those dogs that have had their tails maimed, deliberately or otherwise, will have difficulty with their tail messages.

We had a wonderful rescue dog that used his tail effusively to demonstrate his pleasure at connecting with us. He would thump it on floors with an energy suggesting he fancied himself to be Phil Collins or Stewart Copeland (but never Keith Moon or Alex Van Halen). The action was repeated each and every time he saw us, or at the mere mention of his name. It was joyous.

In those days, having only six dogs, we still took holidays and would unthinkingly put them all into boarding kennels. On one occasion, upon our returned from a two-week absence we immediately went to collect the canine members of our family.

We were deeply upset to learn that during the period of our absence, this particular dog had remained largely immobile in his kennel and never once wagged his tail. Now it hung dejectedly as if it was broken, and it was quite heartbreaking to see.

He was obviously overcome with excitement to see us, and showed his pleasure in other ways, standing on his hind legs and giving us big smiley grins with his tongue hanging out; but the tail simply would not move.

It took several days before he could even begin to wag it again, and a full week before his marvelous and cheering drumming skills returned.

That was the last time we ever took a holiday and left the dogs behind.

If a tail is important, what about dogs that have their tails docked?

This question leads us into an area that might be controversial for a percentage of the reading this book. Nonetheless, it is quite clear and unequivocal from a dog's perspective.

Almost without exception, not only is tail docking wholly unnecessary and cruel, it is a form of mutilation that does nothing less than maim and permanently, irretrievably, damage a dog's ability to communicate.

If we were to try and draw a parallel with the human experience, it is the equivalent of a redundant, cosmetic, surgical intervention, done without anesthetic, that causes agonising pain and potential health complications. It leaves the patient with a permanent speech defect that is (at best) on a par with slurring or stuttering.

The consequent difficulties that are created cannot be fully overcome. It is difficult for any listener to understand. It makes it all the harder for the individual speaking to clearly deliver any message they intend. They are forced to rely upon telepathy, creating inevitable difficulties in certain situations. There are of course no therapists or support for docked dogs, and they are burdened with the deficiency for life.

Let's pause for a moment to think about docking, clearly and logically.

Cutting off a part of an animal at birth because other people do it and a precedent exists.

Why? WHY?

The excuses given for the continuation of such a barbaric practice are feeble and a distortion of reality that any right-thinking person should see their way around. A miniscule fraction of those undergoing docking will ever be in situations where their tails might become damaged, and so are notionally better off with having them partially removed.

Docking is perpetuated because it is fashionable and expected in a limited sector of the dog owning fraternity. Yet were we to mutilate children like this, the outcry would be unending.

No veterinarian with compassion should perform the docking procedure unless there are genuine risks that the dog will suffer pain and suffering due to likely tail damage. In contemporary society, the dog's circumstances must be quite egregious to warrant this. No individual who sees beyond the frivolous nature of what is done would wish to do this inexcusable harm to creatures they care about.

Yet the practice continues through fear.

Fear of being objective.
Fear of empathising with the dog.
Fear of making a reasoned, compassionate assessment of the act.
Fear of examining personal choices.
Fear of speaking out.
Fear of making a stand.
Fear of saying "No".
Fear of being different.
Fear of going against what a certain element declares is acceptable.
Fear of being ostracised.

As with so many wrongs in our society, to say nothing, to do nothing, stops nothing. Not until breed clubs come to their senses, the dog showing fraternity change their breed standards, and key influencers such as judges and individual breeders decide to take a stand against it, will this practice be abandoned. Societal change can only ever begin with individual action resulting from personal choices.

As for the docked dogs, mercifully, they may continue their lives without apparent concern or major impact after the procedure. They learn to cope and overcome, just as any handicapped individual does. But you may rest assured that the dogs *are* damaged. If you have understood all that is written in this book so far, it will be obvious why.

Amongst our extended pack, we have four Poodles. Three came to us docked, and because of the circumstances we had no choice in the matter and no way to prevent their mutilation. (One only has about two inches of unusable stub where his lengthy tail should be.) The fourth has a beautiful flowing and expressive, full length tail.

If you watch them carefully, it slowly becomes apparent that the relationship between the pack at large and the Poodle with the full tail is far easier and more relaxed than for any of the docked dogs.

After a while of knowing what you are looking for, the difference becomes quite striking. The tailed dog is more acceptable to the majority than the docked dogs. He is more integrated, more accepted, more popular.

They are all fabulous, friendly, wonderful dogs. But I wonder what unseen opportunities they are deprived of by the cruel and unnecessary choice that was made about them in their infancy.

A dog who has made the best of his evidently brutal docking, despite communication with the others being somewhat difficult.

When dogs bark are they actually saying something?

Yes, but not very much.

Barking is a dog's tertiary method of communication. It is quite crude and the sound is not comparable with what we would think of as a language. Nonetheless, it is a good substitute for telepathy when circumstances warrant, and they are most certainly saying something!

This form of 'speech' is used to communicate information with an urgency associated with it: raising an alarm, issuing threats or making distress known. The message is conveyed as one or two 'words' and they are always imperatives. Think about instructions like "Help", "Stop", "Don't", "Back off" and "Come back" and you'll be on the right track.

Different types of bark are instantaneously recognizable by other dogs and may be received by a large number at a considerable distance, without having to initiate telepathic contact. In these circumstances, mind messaging would take much longer because of the difficulty involved in connecting over extended distances, especially if they do not know the dog they are communicating with.

There are dogs that try to make more of barking and create language from it that is more on a par with what we would expect from the spoken word. They are sometimes encouraged to do this by human pack members; or they may try to emulate their humans, believing that vocalised communication might be more successful in making themselves understood by their apparently clueless persons. Amongst breeds, Siberian Huskies are renowned for doing this.

A frustrated dog will often bark in the presence of their people, because there is precious little chance that the humans will understand their telepathy. It is their equivalent of shouting at an individual who appears deaf to them.

Certain breeds of dog, particularly (but not exclusively) those who are going through lives as guardian breeds, will bark considerably more than others. The barking is a facet of a pathway they have accepted as part of their living experience. It is not intended to be annoying. For others, an incessant need to bark *is* an issue they need to overcome!

Other dog sounds such as growling and yelping are also worth noting. These additional noises convey messages in much the same way that our non-words do. Growling is quite simply a warning, and a yelp is a registration of pain. Dogs can also scream, which is a very distressing sound to hear.

Put all of this together with telepathy, tails and sundry body language, and you rapidly start to see that their range of communication modes is more varied and maybe even more sophisticated than our human ones.

One of our dogs is a livestock guardian breed. Whenever she goes outside she will begin barking loudly and continually until she is told to be quiet. There is never any reason that is apparent to us. She just seems to enjoy this ritual. Fortunately, none of the other dogs join in. Having been hushed, she will then remain peacefully outside until the desire to come indoors takes her.

However, on occasion, her barking will start again, often attracting the attention of others who *will* join in. Whenever this happens we may guarantee that some wild animal has walked within the proximity of our house; or a potentially intruding human been espied in the distance.

Of course, we have no ability to tell the difference between the barks she uses, but it seems that the first is to warn off anything that *might* be there, and since this is her accepted duty on behalf of the pack, nobody else bothers to assist. But her subsequent barks are apparently for the benefit of *actual* intruders, and upon hearing this type of bark, others rapidly come to her assistance.

We observed this behaviour for many years without realising precisely what was going on; but then another livestock guardian of a different breed came to us. Her behaviour, and the response elicited, is identical.

Guardian dog or problem barker? How can you tell which is which and behave appropriately with your dogs?

It's a very valid question, but based on the false assumption that our response to them needs to be different.

It is important to extricate ourselves from the notion that we are completely responsible for every outcome of our dog's lifetime.

Irrespective of whether barking is an aspect of guardian dog related behaviour, or simple unwarranted irascibility, it is still an issue for the dog to deal with, not their people. Whether the noise they make is an intended feature of their lifetime's experience or an annoying personality trait should not dictate the custodian's response.

If a dog finds its way to where it was intended to be, the human(s) it lives with can/should only ever respond and behave towards the dog in accordance with what has already, pre-incarnation, been known and accepted by the animal, and consequently, is expected of them. Their response to whatever behaviours the dog delivers cannot be wrong.

Whilst many custodians seek to do what is right for their pets, in this aspect of sharing a life with a dog, simply being their people, whatever you may consider your personal shortcomings, is often 'right' enough.

A (temporarily) silent livestock guardian is always on the alert for things to shout about.

Why do dogs sometimes howl and sometimes bark?

Barking and howling are two very different things, undertaken for completely different reasons.

Whereas barking is a specific mode of communication, usually only utilised in situations where it is warranted or when enthusiasm gets the better of them and they wish to convey something to their humans, howling is an activity that only has one purpose: to create a connection with others. However, participating in the activity may be a matter of pleasure, or pain.

For a dog, howling is something that is best when experienced communally. It might well be considered the doggy equivalent of a good old sing-song. When their voices are raised in unison, the sense of unification and belonging experienced by the dog is quite deep and profound for them. It becomes an expression of their collective identity.

Often a competitive element accompanies a howling session, with each dog trying to outdo the others in both duration and volume of the howl. If dogs were to have traditions (which they don't) howling would be one of them. It's fun and they enjoy it. Their understanding of it and what it means to their kind is deeply embedded in their psyche. If we could but listen past the ghastly cacophony that assaults our ears, we might hear a thing of beauty being created.

It is perhaps a sad thing that some dogs will go through their entire lives and never be involved in a howling. Pack living has long since been replaced by membership of the human nuclear family, where they are most frequently the only one of their kind. The ability to engage in this primal pastime is greatly reduced through want of opportunity, and the complete lack of enthusiasm of their people for it!

The sadder side of the reason for howling comes about when dogs are separated from the ones they love. Readers may have known their dogs to howl when left alone in the house, or when they are separated from beloved friends, doggy, human or otherwise. This is caused by feelings of aloneness and an inability to connect using telepathy; so they howl in an attempt to reach out and connect. Because of the frequency used, a howl travels further than a bark, and is instantly recognisable to other dogs as the attempt to communicate that it is. It may be thought of as sending out a message 'Where are you?' because telepathy has failed to provide a response with humans or canines. On hearing another's lone howl, a dog will be capable of discerning if that soul is calling for their own kind, or for their humans.

If they make a connection, they gain considerable solace from others joining in, and even howling on their own can make them feel a little better. But unfortunately, we as their people have failed to understand the importance of their need to connect with their fellow pack members. Since they are living solitary lives amidst human households, we become their pack members. When they howl trying to reach absent humans, they hope for a response every bit as much as they would if they were trying to connect with other dogs.

Dogs that live within a pack environment (whether it is comprised of other dogs or constantly present humans) are not subject to the anxiety caused by separation and are far less likely to howl. And when they do so, it is that ancient, dormant instinct to experience a sense of oneness that is awakening within them.

We can personally vouch for how terrible a racket a pack of howling dogs can make, and how quickly humans (me!) will try to discourage the outburst. They certainly seem to love it. We are fortunate that in our house, it only happens every few weeks.

I can also attest to the terrible distress a howl can contain.

We obtained a rescue dog for some friends who live just over a mile (as the crow flies) from us. The dog doted on her new people, and since they were an elderly couple, they did not go out much; and when they did, she usually went along for the ride. However, there were occasions on which they were forced to leave her at home, alone.

One day I was (literally) disquieted to hear a howling coming from somewhere distant. I was indoors, but the sound was anguished and so clear I was sure that it must be one of our dogs. I went outside to investigate. Finding that it was not, for some reason I became convinced that the noise was being made by our friend's dog. I got in the car and made the ten minute road journey to their house. There I was surprised to find the dog roaming around outside, deeply upset and frightened, desperately calling for her people. I was a very familiar face to her as we had travelled together for thirty-six hours during her rescue, and I was a frequent visitor to their house. She quickly calmed down and relaxed in my company. I stayed fussing with her until they returned and she was overjoyed to see them.

It transpired that for the first time ever, they had decided that she might prefer to be outside when they left her. Of course, the effect was the exact opposite from what they had intended. Instead of being pleased with her freedom, she was panicked, confused and deeply upset. After that, they made sure that she was never left behind (outside) again, and we were all left to marvel at how the cacophonous sound of her howling had travelled. To this day I wonder if, in her desperation, she had deliberately been trying to contact me?

A distraught howl can carry for miles as this beauty showed us.

Why, when hearing other dogs barking, do dogs sometimes react and join in, and at other times ignore it?

Barking is never without purpose, but some causes justify conjoining, and others don't.

This phenomenon is most likely to occur when other dogs barking are out of sight, possibly even great distances away. The reason for joining or not joining in the barking depends upon the message contained in the bark. If it is a general warning (e.g. "Coyotes in the area") that needs to be relayed, all who hear it are likely to take up the clarion call.

If it is a localised bark to scare something off that is only relevant to the dog(s) that have begun the barking (e.g. "Squirrel!"), those hearing it will most likely choose to ignore it.

Dogs are easily able to distinguish between the varieties of information contained in the sound and respond accordingly. A sound of barking can travel considerable distances, and one dog might easily offer their support to another that is over half a mile away, or further.

When the bark of one dog triggers another in a more localised area (such as your home, if you have more than one dog) a more likely reason is one dog giving a knee jerk response to the sound made by another. Instinctively they will feel the need to join in (although they may change their mind if they discover that the reason for the barking does not justify the effort). Alternatively, they may just leave the communication of a message to another dog because they consider it to be that dog's role.

This is particularly the case where one of the dogs in the household is a guardian breed dog. They can be set off by the slightest of provocations from the world they are protecting their home from; and other dogs, once they become used to this (potentially irritating) little peccadillo, may well choose to let them get on with it.

Do dogs try to communicate with us?

They constantly do, up until the point where there no longer seems to be any purpose.

Dogs make tremendous efforts to connect with us, but realise early on that their attempts at telepathy are totally futile. Their messages are sent out like CETI's (Communication with Extraterrestrial Intelligence) attempts to connect with aliens, but they disappear into a void, and disappointment quickly kills the dog's enthusiasm.

Not to be totally deterred, they may make random attempts to get in touch with our minds, often accompanying the endeavour with intense stares, or strategic placement of a paw to create a physical link that vibrationally enhances transmission capabilities. And when these efforts inevitably go unrewarded, they resort to that most obvious messaging beacon: the tail.

The irony is that we think of them as the unsophisticated ones, yet they are the ones making all the effort.

Dogs are generally more accommodating of our failings than we are of theirs, and they will (slightly ruefully) accept that from a communications perspective, our relationship with them is almost wholly one way.

However, the failure to connect is not as complete as it may seem, because although we are unable to understand their communications with us, they are very capable of understanding ours to them!

Living with so many dogs, we have often been aware of input which, in hindsight, we have recognised was telepathic communications from our pets.

One in particular was able to establish input to my wife with consummate ease, and several others have been able to make their influence felt.

Maybe I am not such a good listener, because there is only one out of all of them with whom I have experienced clear and unequivocal communication.

She was a rescue who came from a rather sad background, and it was quite obvious from the outset that there was something a little bit different about her.

The experience of communication was stunning,. It was possible to hold entire conversations with her. She was witty, funny, often sarcastic, teasing, cajoling and highly intelligent. Having her to talk to was akin to any normal inter-human friendship. Sometimes we would talk a lot. Sometimes days would go by before we spoke again. We just picked up where we left off.

But when she passed, the absence of her voice was every bit as hard to deal with as the physical loss, and I still miss her terribly.

The intensity of this stare is a clear indication of a desire to communicate something!

Is there any point talking to my dog?

Absolutely! In fact, if you don't, you are not only depriving yourself, but being cruel to them.

Dogs value communication with their humans more than we can begin to imagine. It creates a bond and even if they do not understand the words you speak to them, the likelihood of them being able to pick up on the tenor, if not the precise content of the message, is strong.

Nowhere is this more the case than in households where the dog is an only pet. This can be a very lonely experience for them, making human contact even more crucial. Talking to them will be like a lifeline preventing them from feeling isolated in a world of silence. It also creates a link between you.

It is a sorry sight indeed to see an only dog that is ignored by its human family. It is tantamount to neglect, and certainly a form of psychological abuse. The animal will feel excluded, and since a dog has the need for companionship as a fundamental component of its make-up, connecting becomes more important.

Conversations with the dog may inevitably be one sided, but this should not imply that the dog is not participating. To the best of their ability, they will try to demonstrate their involvement, and the clearer it becomes to them that the communication is intended for them, the more their efforts will be forthcoming.

The substance of the conversation is largely irrelevant, but that is no excuse to talk nonsense. Neither should the human frequently assert that "You don't understand a word I'm saying, do you?". They *can* understand a not inconsiderable amount of human language, and negativity is off putting. At worst, it can undermine their commitment to be involved and cause them to withdraw.

If there is another person in the house, it is essential *not* to use your normal speaking voice when addressing the dog. That way they will learn that the communication is intended for their ears. A slight but consistent variation in tone will suffice, although the more distinctive your 'dog voice' is, the easier it will be for them to pick up on. Guardians who won't do this because they feel stupid will have their attempts at communication filtered out as superfluous white noise and be ignored by the dog.

Believe it or not, I have forty-five quite distinct and individual methods of speaking I inject into my voice for communicating with the dogs when addressing them individually.

Their recognition of the sound goes far beyond use of their name, which I can omit and they will still know that the variation of tone/cadence/accent (yes, accent!) that I am using is a communication with them, and them alone.

I am relieved to note that almost every dog person I have ever met has a tone they use to address their pet, so I'm not the only crazy one!

If you are prepared to strike up a conversation with them, they can get quite chatty!

How much of our language can dogs understand?

Maybe some, but maybe all.

In very recent times there has been a cautious acceptance by the scientific community that dogs *may* be able to comprehend the meaning of as many as seventy words of the human language. Other more daring advocates of canine intelligence have claimed that this figure *could* be as high as an astounding two and half thousand!

The truth is even stranger. If they trouble to, a dog can understand almost every single utterance that comes out of your mouth.

This is possible because of a dog's natural telepathic ability. They can receive thoughts at their inception, communicated without language attached to them. By matching understanding of the thoughts with the words you use, they can understand it all. But there are several reasons why they don't.

The mind of the average human is hyper-active, seldom pausing and processing a thought-equivalent of approximately one thousand, two hundred and fifty words per minute. These get fired out vibrationally, unconsciously and unintentionally with no recipient in mind, making the transmission area around a human brain a confusing morass for anyone seeking to interpret what is spilling out.

As previously discussed, messages that we intend to be sent become more focused and are easily distinguishable from general thoughts, despite being mixed in with the other things going on inside your head. But humans seldom *intentionally* transmit thoughts, so to find messages, a dog must wade through a thought bog to find any meaningful output.

When they do discover outgoing messages, they tend not to be for them or about them. It's hard work to even find them, so if there's no reward at the end of it, why bother? Most dogs will give up.

A dog is unlikely to develop a full understanding of its humans if it lives with multiple persons with many agendas. It can most certainly pick up on a limited amount, and perhaps as many words as the most optimistic scientists speculate possible.

Total comprehension is most likely to come about in a household where the dog is the only pet, sharing a house with a single human. Under these circumstances, the need for companionship creates a wholly different mindset and focus for the human. Even unconsciously, they will actively maintain a dialogue with their pet and the depth of understanding that may be arrived at by the animal is without measure.

Only in having this explained to me now, do I realise why my widowed grandmother had such an intimate and personal relationship with her dog. They were utterly devoted to each other and the dog would sit at her feet, gazing up into her face, and seemingly hang on to every word she spoke. She was apparently blessed with prescience over my grandmother's actions and expectations, and was acutely sensitive to her needs.

It seems so obvious now why all this was the case. The dog could understand absolutely everything my grandmother said, whether she vocalised her thoughts or not.

I'm no animal communicator, but it's pretty obvious when attempts to communicate are being made!

Is a dog's vocabulary the same as ours?

No, it's much more limited.

An internet search will reveal to you the claim that there are currently over one million words in the English language. Although many fall into disuse (and revision of their meaning) words are constantly being created on a needs basis; or in some cases, frivolously. Likely, the figure for commonly used words is somewhere in the region of one hundred and seventy thousand. That's still a huge number. The sheer quantity and range of words is evidence of the complexity of human society and existence, if only because we apparently need so many descriptors.

However, other languages have considerably fewer words and communications made in them do not seem to suffer because of it. This could be taken as an indication that English is a richer language than others; or it could be symptomatic of a tendency towards an over indulgence in word use. Which it is depends upon your personal perspective, but an overabundance of available words probably does no harm.

From a dog's perspective, having so many descriptors is unnecessary. Whereas we might substitute any of the following to describe or explain the idea of food: nourishment, nutrition, nutriment, diet, sustenance, nutrients, foodstuff, fare, chow, victuals, grub, nosh, tucker, eats, fodder, provisions, groceries, rations, etc. etc. a dog would only have the single idea in its vocabulary. It would require no further explanation than the idea itself, and it would not be communicated other than as the thought of food.

The ideas and concepts we conjure on a day-to-day basis are broadly limited to base concepts which revolve around needs and emotions. The base concepts remain constant, but with experience and learning, the way in which we express and describe them will alter. A baby will be aware it is hungry, but will not have the vocabulary or understanding to enable it to be discursive about its experience, or to define and explain the need, other than through that fundamental thought.

That same baby, at thirty years old will be infinitely more equipped to fully expound upon its need; but if it has never been aware of the regional cuisines of the Orient, a discussion of meal choices available to them is unlikely to include any description more sophisticated than "Chinese".

In other words, our vocabulary grows in direct proportion to our experience of life, our exposure to new and complementary ideas, or our appetite for extending the range of terminology available to us.

A dog lacks the opportunity to extend its vocabulary beyond the base concepts that are the bedrock of its communication. However, it may be exposed to many more new words that it will grow to comprehend the meaning of, simply through its relationship with its person.

Although this extended learning is by no means wholly essential and dogs may struggle to incorporate new linguistic capabilities when dealing with their peers, it is another reason why talking to your dog is important.

The more you talk to a dog, the more it will understand. And the sooner you begin the better.

Is there a common language we could learn, to be able to communicate with dogs?

Yes, but learning it might require some major changes in your life!

Through the choice of using sound over telepathy, our use of vocal chords has evolved to the point where we can produce a varied and sophisticated range of sounds, which are manipulated and given structure to create language.

This development has not occurred in dogs, (or in the vast majority of other creatures) and the capacity for speech is therefore not present. So, they could not learn to speak our language.

Barking sounds can be emulated by humans with reasonable accuracy. When we do this, it is often a matter of initial concern for a dog. They may be surprised if we suddenly shout in a good approximation of their language. Imagine how you'd feel if your dog suddenly yelled something that sounded like "Help" or "Get back"! They find such outbursts curious and even amusing.

But practically speaking, barking is not a language that is functional to learn because the range of ideas which may be conveyed is way too limited. Human vocal abilities can approximate a pretty good range of barks, but the response of dogs to sounds we make, makes it clear that without coaching, our accent and pronunciation is terrible. Even with such limited grammar, we would probably tend to say the wrong thing.

Species that communicate with telepathy directly access thoughts without any of the rigmarole outlined in the answers to previous questions. Their communications are clear, succinct and not open to any of the unfortunate 'mis' occurrences.

If we want to communicate with dogs, we should learn to do so without the aid of language. This is what animal communicators do. They access the thought as it is transmitted. The communication is flawless and unadulterated. But hope for development of this ability would probably be futile for most of us. We are too well ingrained in our preference for use of spoken language. It is habituated within us and learning the radically new approach of telepathy would take time and considerable effort, with little guarantee of success.

There are various anecdotal stories regarding people's ability to learn a foreign language in environments that are completely new to them, where total lack of comprehension makes spoken communication impossible; yet after a period of months, the newcomer may become fluent in the language, almost overnight, as a result of emersion in the language. Media popularised representations of these situations might have one individual exchanging a word with another so that each might learn the meaning of each other's language.

Yet the most effective way to understand telepathically, is to say nothing.

If we shut down our habituated need to use speech, yet still actively desire to understand, after a period we naturally lose the dependence upon comprehending the spoken word and are forced to rely upon receipt of information that is passed naturally within the ether.

So, if you want to understand your dog and learn a language you can both speak, don't look for anything spoken. Lock yourself in a room with the dog for a few months and have no other communication of any kind with anyone. It may not be practical, but sure enough, after a few months, the communication between the two of you will be quite fluent!

Look deep into my eyes. Can you read my mind?

What can dogs sense of human emotions?

Everything. But that does not mean it's comprehensible.

Every emotion that we experience carries with it a specific unique vibration. Crudely speaking, positive emotions have a high and light vibration, whilst negative ones are low and heavy.

Your dog can perceive every single emotion because the vibration is quite palpable for them. Your highs and lows are like an open book to them. The slightest change of mood pulses out of you like a jungle drum, and they can become so utterly attuned to the nuances of your feelings, they may even spot a mood coming on before you can.

However, this does not mean that they can understand the implications of them, or that they experience the same thing themselves. Gaining an appreciation of the meaning of the vibration is only something they learn from the experience of being with you, and their level of comprehension is based upon matching the behaviours, facial expressions, mannerisms and sounds you make, with the accompanying vibration that you are unconsciously emitting. Their skill and accuracy at interpreting what they see is on a par with those who study body language for a living, maybe better. But their grasp of the nuances of the emotion is nonetheless somewhat limited.

Most dog people will have noticed that their pet will seek to intervene if they are feeling low; or join with them in celebration if they are feeling euphoric. In their exhibition of empathy, they learn quickly what are and what are not appropriate responses to give their people. If a nose pushed in a face, or a lick given in response to a tear is rebuffed, they may choose to sit quietly alongside you and be content just to be there. If they get reprimanded for getting carried away in the ecstasy of their play when you are on a high, they may choose to 'tone it down'.

We do not always notice or appreciate the subtlety of their approach to our emotions, but often a dog can become a mirror for us, and in their state of being, we may observe our own with a fascinating objectivity.

Apart from hunger and bathroom breaks, do dogs give any other cues that they need something?

They do give some, but they are circumstantial and beyond classification, other than in the most general terms.

Up until the point when they finally come to accept that it is futile, dogs will constantly try to use their innate telepathic ability to communicate with us. Abandonment of this effort may occur early on in life, or never. Some dogs just will not give up.

If we consistently fail to register the messages they seek to give us mentally, a dog may try to develop other ways of letting us know not just what they want and need, but other things they wish to express.

This is principally to let us know what they're feeling, as well as have us understand that they empathise with many of our emotional states.

Many of the cues they give to us involve body language and are somewhat like those used by humans. We become adept at recognising these signs in those around us, and learning those given by a dog is no more complicated. Perhaps the most obvious to us will be those that are expressed through the eyes; but the tail is used extensively as well.

Different dogs will find different things that work with their people. It cannot be said that there are cues specific to all, because a dog will learn by trial and error what works and what does not. And some may not learn at all.

[It is worth reiterating that the use of their tail with humans should not be confused with uses to which the dog puts it when in the presence of other dogs, when it becomes an adjunct to main communication used to send non-telepathic messages.]

Are animal communicators the real deal?

Animal communication is certainly possible. But as in every walk of life, there are those who are the genuine article, and there are frauds and individuals who deceive themselves.

From everything that you have read so far in this section, it must be clear that animal communication is totally possible. Whether it is easily achievable is something else. The quietening of the mind that is necessary to not only hear the thoughts of another, but also to receive them with clarity, is a challenging discipline indeed.

I have come across a few people who have seemed to possess an awesome talent for animal communication skills. I have also noted with amusement that sometimes they are not so good with their human relationship skills.

From a personal perspective, it seems to me that if a person has this ability as their vocation, maybe there *should* be a certain detachment in their ability to relate to humans. Even though I am not an animal communicator, I will readily confess that I prefer animals to people for a whole variety of reasons. People who are destined to have a lifetime with animals surely need to have something of a different focus?

Unfortunately, I have also come across those who are merely delusional and are transposing their own thoughts and desires onto the animal. They do not relay anything from them that has any credibility whatsoever.

But in fairness, I have other sources that can reveal the truth of their actions to me!

I came across one individual who told me they had taken a class in animal communication. I hadn't realised such a thing existed and had assumed the skill was a 'gift' rather than something that could simply be learned by anyone. All those whom I had encountered previously encountered certainly took no 'qualification'. Nonetheless, this person claimed with pride they were now a fully-fledged Animal Communicator.

Unbidden, this person then proceeded to enlighten me with details of the background of one of our rescue dogs.

She gave me some gruesome details about the experience both the dog and its mother had been through. This involved the mother deliberately being set on fire and dying an agonising death. This hideous scene was witnessed by the poor pup that was with us now. The scarring effect of this (the AC explained), was the explanation for various undesirable behaviours the dog now exhibited. She needed help to overcome them.

I was greatly disturbed to hear all of this and could well imagine the terrors the dog must have gone through.

So it was fortunate that I had met the dog's mother, who was alive and well and been adopted by a great family. And I was also pleased that our dog did not (and never has) demonstrated any of the behaviours this particular 'animal communicator' described to me.

A dog's communications may be totally inaccessible to most of us humans.

Why don't dogs always come back when you're calling them?

It's a judgement call: Obey or do not obey. Often, it's because they simply don't want to. And, why should they?

Many dogs that have apparently learnt great recall skills may become selectively deaf when out walking. This should come as no surprise to their person: they are trying to stop them from doing something they want to do.

Of course, the big issue we have with this is that they are putting their agenda ahead of ours, and herein lies the real problem: for us to accept that they are unique individual beings, capable of thinking for themselves, having their owns needs and desires, and acting in total independence from us.

Domesticated dogs spend a great deal of their lives obeying our commands and trying to keep us happy. They may already subjugate a huge amount of their freewill to (what appears to them to be) our whims. This is far easier to accept in the enclosed home environment.

But it is doubly confusing for a dog when it is outdoors and its person appears to have granted its freedom, to have its pleasure summarily curtailed.

The world outside of the confines of your familiar house and yard present a veritable theme park of excitement and mystery. Enticing smells and fascinating new experiences beckon with every outing. So, when given off-leash privileges, your dog faces a choice every time you recall them: "Do I really want to do this?"

Dogs that are unfailingly reliable in their response are usually service dogs or those trained for 'sport'. Their freewill has undergone complete suppression, and although we may marvel at their obedience, something of themselves has been lost.

When your dog (who may have learned great recall skills) chooses not to respond, you are witnessing what remains of their indomitable spirit and their need to prioritize their own need for momentary pleasure, over your incomprehensible and (maybe frequently exerted) apparent control-freak nature!

Before you get too upset about it, pause for a moment to consider this: For a 'well trained' dog, this last vestige of defiance could be viewed as something to be pleased about. At least they have felt able to retain some semblance of freewill and 'attitude'.

Of course, we dog people know that when we summon our canines from their revels, there is usually something else completely different going on from what the dog may imagine. We don't wish to spoil their fun. Recall to us may represent one of several things. It may be:

- A matter of convenience because it's time to go home.
- A distraction because we need to divert the dog's attention from doing something unspeakable.
- Concern for them because we can no longer see them.
- Raw fear because we think they might be in danger.

The average custodian is unlikely to merely want to exert control or authority just to remind the dog who's boss.

All of this means nothing to them. From their perspective, our calls are unwelcome directives and there is no distinction based upon our reasons in their minds.

You may find it moderately irritating to learn that when hearing a recall, a dog is perfectly capable of recognising and distinguishing between the various tones that will accompany it. To them, a casual, and relaxed recall would sound as utterly different from a desperate exhortation as it would to us.

Yet in the moment, they have no grasp of our motivation. They cannot comprehend the reason for the variation in tone; or any added imperative to make them conclude one recall should be more important to respond to than another. In fact, a change in tone may even elicit caution in responding whilst the dog puzzles over why its person sounds different. So we can become the cause of why they will not return to us!

There is no magic method for having your dog come back to you. If you're blessed with your own 'free spirit', accepting their perspective on liberty and their zest for life may help make enjoyment of them so much easier.

Having an indomitable spirit and being responsive to recall are not necessarily qualities that go hand in hand.

We once had a dog that steadfastly refused, for her whole life, to *ever* return on command. This resulted in countless hours spent chasing and cursing her, because she was also a consummate escape artist. Eventually, reluctantly, we realised that we could never let her off leash in any area that might be unsafe. But more than this, if we wanted her to retain her freewill and identity, there was precious little that we could do about her escapades short of tethering her. This, we refused to do.

Luckily, we lived in an area where cars and passing strangers presented little threat anyway. Nevertheless, we took every possible precaution to protect her from herself and the world of predatory beasts outside our fence line. Although she always seemed to find a way out of our 'impenetrable' enclosure, mercifully, she always came back.

Ultimately she lived a long and happy life, and we can forget that during its course, she caused us more stress than almost any other dog we've shared our lives with to date. But in so many ways, she lived!

Are dogs able to communicate with other species of animal?

Yes, but it should not be assumed that they do.

Our over-arching view of the species of this planet is based upon the countless opportunities that exist for us to see everything that there is to see. Coloured picture books and animal encyclopaedias have been replaced by the instantaneous knowledge base the Internet provides as a source for animal identification. And although we may by no means have heard of all the wondrous beings that are out there, and certainly not have had face-to-face encounters with the majority, we can easily get to see what they look like.

This is not so for our canine companions. A dog can live its whole life seeing only a handful of other types of animal. It can live in total ignorance even of the species fed to it daily. So, when dogs encounter other creatures, it is not uncommon for them to go into moderate shock.

Upon seeing a cow for the first time, a dog may be so consumed with wondering "What the heck is that?!" that they miss out completely on the opportunity to connect and communicate, despite all animals having the necessary telepathic 'hardware' to do so.

If the opportunity is sustained and they can get over their initial surprise at whatever strange beast is before them, they may open a dialogue. A little initial difficulty may be experienced because different species may have what we could describe as something akin to different accents, but we all ultimately speak the same language.

If they choose to take it, the possibility to communicate is there: A cow may appear to speak 'moo', and a dog 'bark', but as we have throughout this chapter, they can both speak 'thoughts'.

Inter-species relationships of any kind are possible given the right opportunity to develop. But chances may be few and far between.

In my experience, there are few things more fascinating or pleasurable than seeing different species come to terms with one another.

As is explained elsewhere, the automatic antipathy that is assumed to exist between so many species is merely a thing of our imagination, and the harmonious relationships that may be created between non-human species are an example to us all.

I still treasure the memory of seeing one of our dogs very obviously being introduced to two moose calves by their mother; and on another occasion watching the same dog playing tirelessly with a red fox whilst both were on opposite sides of a wire fence.

Chapter 7

THE PACK

"For the strength of the Pack is the Wolf.

For the strength of the Wolf is the Pack"

Rudyard Kipling

How important is the pack to dogs?

It is one of the most complex features of their existence, and in many ways, one of the most significant.

Of the living experiences which may be undertaken whilst incarnating, perhaps one of the most obvious for any being is the choice to live solitary lives, or as members of some form of community or social grouping. Whilst these represent opposites, or the extremes of the opportunity, there are countless permutations in between. Some lifeforms, generically, are intended to experience most of their lives within a society. Dogs are one such group.

Whereas we humans are faced with a multiplicity of choice about how we live out our lives on the social-solitary scale, the range of options is much more limited for canines. Certainly, for domestic dogs, a great deal of their opportunity is dependent upon what humans decide for them. But whatever the circumstances of their living, dogs are hardwired to create, at least in their own minds, some form of pack.

A pack is essentially whoever a dog is living with: An extended family that need not be made up of blood relatives. Since so many dogs do not live in like-species environments, the concept of 'the pack' extends to humans and even other animals who are in their living environment. In their more natural state, such association would be less likely to be the norm. However, cohabiting, or at least living in close proximity with humans, is of advantage to both their learning and ours.

Being part of a pack fulfils a psychological and emotional need for belonging, innate within all dogs. Ironically, although dogs may appear to be naturally gregarious, canines may be as introverted and private as humans, yet still feel the need to be part of a pack.

Aside from companionship, being in a pack can provide physical support, structure, safety, and protection. Instinctively, all those beings with a strong social drive are aware of the underlying imperative that there is strength in numbers, which is precisely what belonging to a pack, however it is made up, implicitly offers. It's a big thing for dogs!

Do dogs really have a pack hierarchy; and if so, how is placement decided upon, and are we part of it?

When we observe canine society and interactions, we almost automatically endow what we see with a crudeness or lack of sophistication. We fail to see the similarities with our own societal behaviours, or recognise that from their perspective at least, the hierarchy defines them.

A great deal has been written about the importance of pack hierarchy and alpha dominance amongst canines. Many of the conclusions drawn about its importance to them have been because of studies made of wolves. Resulting assumptions stood as fact for decades. Yet theories once held as definitive and enthusiastically endorsed, have now been refuted. Those who extrapolated and conjectured have contradicted their own findings. Those who subscribe to, and popularized the theories, have almost been demonised for advocating what are now unpopular modes of thinking. In fact, our knowledge regarding this aspect of dogs' lives has become a classic example of the constantly shifting inferences and speculation referred to in the first chapter. So, what is the truth?

Below the accepted leader or pack alpha, pack members fit into a structure which may correctly be described as a hierarchy. However, it is informal, and totally fluid. Position within this framework is a matter of great importance to members, because it defines not only their social standing, but to some degree, their self-respect. Thus, pack members vie for position, and favour with the alpha. However, placement is a transient thing. Members may find themselves highly positioned one day, and spurned the next.

Pack relationships have a lot more in common with traditional human societal structures than we might imagine. The hierarchy is formed, like informal human ones, as much from the dog's views of themselves as anything else. We humans look for evidence of personal power, which is basically the ability to influence others within a group, or the impact one individual has upon others. We are all subject to an awareness of this phenomenon at point in our lives, even if we do not subscribe to it, or are unprepared to admit to it. It usually begins at High School, when we start to get a more sophisticated or conscious awareness of our interpersonal relationships, and adjudge ourselves relative to everyone else. Later in life, in a broader societal context, we add to this assessment material elements that denote positional power (house, car, job title etc.). These things start to play a role in our perceptions of one another and ourselves, and we may consider ourselves 'better' or 'lesser' than others because of them.

Although at some stage we may all hopefully arrive at a place where we realise that this type of positioning is wholly superficial and a matter of no consequence, those who do not join in the 'power play' are often identified by society as lacking motivation or 'drive', and may even become outcasts due their lack of conformity.

Dogs are not wholly dissimilar, although their motivations are somewhat different; and needless to say, material or tangible status symbols have no bearing whatsoever. They adjudge one another, just as humans do, with their own criterion. Stack ranking (the order in which they perceive one another) is by no means wholly dependent upon physicality. Although aggressive dogs 'thugs' may maintain a certain status due to their ability to instill fear, this is not a primary reason for achieving seniority.

Instead, position in the pack is almost entirely determined by levels of self-confidence, and consequent deportment and reinforcing behaviour. Lack of fear, boldness in all situations, an ability to entertain pack mates, effective communication skills, an amenable nature and behaving assertively are all attributes that may stand a dog in good stead for rising within the hierarchy. Conversely, evidencing worry, avoiding all risk, having little impact upon others, being withdrawn, acting unsociably and behaving passively, are all downers from the pack position perspective.

Even if there is only one dog in the pack, a 'pecking order' will be established in the dog's mind, with *all* other pack members being weighed and measured for their status. Thus, it is entirely possible for humans to find themselves placed low in the pack order.

Humans respond to their societal positioning 'aspirationally' (constantly striving to improve their standing/change their status level). So do many dogs. Humans are motivated by the belief that having 'more' will make them happier, or in some way 'better'. For dogs is about the security and protection imperative. Notionally, the closer you are to the alpha, the safer you are likely to be; and dogs have a constant awareness of the vulnerability that is inherent in all of their lifetimes.

Self-perception about placement within the pack will have a significant impact upon the way dogs view themselves. Like us, dogs need to feel valued, respected and important. The higher up the pack order they are, the higher their self-esteem.

In deciding pack order, size is not necessarily an issue. In this case, the giant is the alpha, but the little one runs a close second as far as the rest of the pack is concerned.

How is the alpha selected?

An alpha is not so much selected as assumed.

Pack leadership is not something that is overtly decided upon by the other members. When the position becomes vacant, no nominations are made or elections held. Those with potential for preeminence demonstrate their candidacy either spontaneously, or purposefully. Subsequent acquiescence to a particular individual's seniority is a personal choice for each and every pack member.

Within a wild pack environment, preeminence often accompanies a powerful physicality and the ability to dominate, since these are seen as key in fulfilling the needs of the role. The most suitable candidate will inevitably rise to the fore in response to events that occur, and the others will simply follow them, literally and figuratively. However, it should be noted that bullies and unnecessarily aggressive dogs that provoke only fear, are not accepted as leaders.

In the domestic environment, without the immediately obvious relevance hunting prowess, fighting skills and other aspects of brute force, issues of a dog's suitability for being alpha become a lot subtler. Certainly, if a dog has the muscle to back up their attitude, they are well placed for pack seniority. Nevertheless, a dog possessed of a great deal of 'chutzpah', irrespective of size or form, is just as likely to be accepted as an alpha as a big bruiser.

Contrary to popular mythology, although alpha male control is the norm, it is not necessary that either sex take precedence. Depending upon the circumstances (and what behavioural or physical traits are required in the moment) either sex may be the dominant force. Seniority of age is also an irrelevance.

Once selected, 'alpha' is not a fluid position. Established leadership of the pack is maintained until it is successfully challenged by another. Non-serious (i.e. those not accompanied by violence) challenges may be a constant feature of pack life. Some alphas retain their position until they pass on, when the remaining pack members may be left in an awkward and untenable situation which must be resolved.

Whereas wild circumstances tend to force acquiescence, domestic dogs will exercise more freedom of choice about whether to accept another as a leader, or not. Positive responses are demonstrated by both overt actions (such as licking and other behavioural 'tells'), and tacit acceptance (not responding to leadership with aggression or resistance).

Since it is not a given that pack members will automatically accept the alpha most favour, a leader may face positional challenges throughout their tenure, perhaps repeatedly. Some members will never accept a particular leader, yet still live uneasily within the pack structure. Challenge is permissible behaviour, but not without limits. The alpha will always retain their ultimate right to control, and sanction, others.

By no means all dogs desire to be the leader of a pack. Whether they will pursue alpha status is a matter of what learning has been predetermined for their lives; although a responsibility for controlling or influencing the lives of others is something that all beings go through, irrespective of form or species.

Our first male pack member seemingly took great pleasure in the harem he inherited: the incumbents were three females. He was immediately accepted by all as the alpha, and by the time we took another male into our midst some years later, he was undisputed leader of five ladies and two cats, in the animal section of the pack.

Although joining as a puppy, the new male grew quickly and soon outsized his rival by over a foot in height. His manner made it obvious that he viewed himself as the new alpha, and the ladies seemed to accept it too. The older dog would have none of it and they maintained a barely contained contempt for one another throughout the many years they spent together, neither accepting the other's preeminence, despite the fact that the rest of the rapidly growing pack wholeheartedly accepted the younger dog as boss.

They ultimately reached a form of rapprochement, but it was always an uneasy one.

What does the alpha position mean to the pack?

More than you might imagine.

The alpha's notional role is to provide safety and protection. As a by-product of their (benevolent) authority, comes order. This is as important for dogs as it is for humans, since without it, their world would be as chaotic as we may imagine an anarchistic society to be.

The alpha position is the dominant, benevolent, patriarchal role within the pack. It is one to which other members will naturally defer. For dogs, the root of this behaviour is a hard-wired belief in the need to pay obeisance to a single animal for leadership and guidance, trusting that to do so will ensure their security and protection. The role is as necessary to dogs, as having somebody fulfil a leadership role is in any aspect of human society. However, the alpha's consequent behaviour towards the pack must be understood on a situational basis.

When times are good and things are relaxed, an alpha may behave playfully and lovingly, like the father figure they are expected to be. Their impact may not be obvious, and their dominance, low key. From a human perspective, they may not even be recognizable as the dominant pack member, although from the canine perspective, it will be obvious. But if circumstances become more challenging, or the pack is threatened, the alpha is no longer the father, but the General, and obeisance is demanded. Primary roles and responsibilities for guarding and protecting now come into play, and are taken very seriously. A crisis may be momentary, or on-going, but irrespective of the situation, the pack *must* have a leader to look to.

In a domestic environment, the alpha position would seem unnecessary from any practical perspective. Yet dogs will still look for alpha leadership within their pack (however it is comprised), and submit themselves to what becomes a nominal position; or assume the role themselves. If the alpha is absent, the rest of the pack will become restless and uneasy. If they are missing for too long, infighting may begin to establish a new pack order.

How does a dog decide whether or not their human is the alpha; and does it matter if they're not?

You would think that since humans provide their dogs with shelter and food that they would conform to the standard of requirement for offering safety and protection for the pack. But a dog's thinking doesn't work quite like that...

In the absence of a being that behaves like an alpha (which could even be a cat!), any dog will feel compelled to assume the role themselves. Dogs expect their humans to be alphas, but are frequently let down, causing confusion and even bahavioural issues.

In deciding whether or not their humans are suitable to be followable alphas, the most important criteria from the dog's perspective is that they exhibit a lack of fear. It doesn't have to be a complete and perpetual absence, since dogs experience fear too. But it has to be of a level that is significantly lower than their own for the dog to be comfortable with them as alphas. Their conclusions are reached from the vibrations emitted by their humans, which are quite palpable to the dog. It is of no consequence what the fear is about, it is the sense of it, (or rather lack of it) that matters.

Of course, most of us are riddled with both major and minor concerns about aspects of our lives: relationships, jobs, children, health, being late for an appointment, or even missing a favourite TV show. These things will cause a vibrational response within us that dogs experience as fear, even though we do not think of them as such. Whilst many of us may like to regard ourselves as being fear free and supremely confident in most aspects of our lives, dogs can sense what is below the surface. They know what we suppress or actively manage. They are aware of the impact the little things that we regard as inconsequential have upon our being, even when we don't realise they are fear based.

Ironically, it is also the dogs themselves that can be a cause of our fears. We may fear for them because we love them so much and worry about their illness, their moods or when they are out of sorts. Or we may be fearful of them as a species, tacitly aware that they are powerful and potentially dangerous, unpredictable creatures. When we chose to live alongside them, we assume a risk of physical harm to ourselves; or understand the damage they could do to others.

So if on balance, a person is experiencing more fear than the robust levels of confidence (and the consequent vibration of peace) required for leadership, the dog will adjudge them as an inappropriate alpha. Relatively few people have the assuredness that dogs need before they will commit to following them.

At the outset of a relationship, a dog will automatically assume that their humans will be alphas for them; but in the absence of alpha behaviour from them, most will automatically feel that they must take on the onus. Dogs that find themselves being rehomed may have previous experience that has taught them not to expect humans to be alphas, and having assumed alpha status with other custodians (and possibly been rejected for it) will be reluctant abdicate the role.

Since so much of the alpha's job is about protecting, this is precisely what the dog must do. It's judgement and choices are now – from its perspective – of more consequence than its human's, and it therefore has right of precedence in all things. The fact that it is still, essentially, a dependent, is neither here nor there. It bears the burden of assessing threats (in whatever form they may manifest themselves) and warding off unwanted intrusion. In their eyes, they deserve the respect that any alpha warrants, and if not treated in accordance with custom, at best will feel aggrieved. At worst, they may react in a very 'high handed' manner in their interactions with their humans, making their disdain for their 'weakness' obvious. Usually, this is described as the dog having 'behavioural issues'. It's not. It's a problem of our own making.

Perhaps fortunately, we humans may not see or recognise any of these issues. We may blithely ignore the signs they give us, and fondly imagine ourselves to be worthy pack leaders. From our perspective, it doesn't really matter. From theirs it does. It does not cause them to withhold affection for us, or be any less loving or devoted. But the love they give us is not the same as respect, and the angst caused to them may detract from other more important purposes they otherwise had in mind for their lifetime.

When dogs join other dogs in a household, how do they determine who leads and who follows?

A great deal depends upon what they discover when they arrive in their new environment.

When joining a pack, a dog will immediately want to understand who is the leader.

The ideal for them is to join a household where the role is firmly filled by the humans, or another incumbent. It relieves them of responsibility and allows them to feel a sense of security in their new surroundings.

A young dog joining a household will (almost always) initially defer to the incumbents. Almost immediately, they will start to assess the strength of persona of all those around them, and decide which amongst them is preeminent. To achieve this, they will most likely undertake behaviours specifically intended as 'tests' for their fellow pack members, gauging their responses, and seeking to explore boundaries of acceptability. As their own confidence grows, so will the nature of the challenge they offer to the control and authority that others might respond with. If none is forthcoming, or if it is weak or inconsistent, they will conclude that the leadership is not effective. From their perspective, failure to exert authority is a form of weakness, stemming from fear of the consequences.

If the dog perceives no effective leadership, they may well assume the role themselves, albeit reluctantly. This may lead to issues with incumbents (of any species) who do not agree with their assessment. If the ranking of their positions is disputed, position may be asserted with coercion, or even violently, until one concedes. Some rankings are never resolved, with both individual dogs and/or other species believing themselves to be dominant.

If the dog is fortunate enough to find that there is a worthy leader, a pack newcomer will still need to understand where they fit in the hierarchy, relative to any (and all) other beings present in the household.

Do dogs prefer living with a pack or are they happy to be with just humans?

What is natural for a dog can be subverted by circumstance and nurture can truly take over from nature.

Although pack living is the natural state for dogs, the vast majority do not live in packs as we might define them.

A dog's closest cousin is Canis Lupus, the wolf. Wolves live in packs with an average size of six members. However, the number is largely a feature of food availability. The more plentiful the supply, the larger the pack may be. They have been recorded as having as many as thirty-six members and as few as two; but smaller units, or even the eponymous 'lone wolf' is seldom that way through choice. Deeply embedded within the psyche of almost all canines is that instinct to be part of a pack.

Canis lupus familiaris, the domesticated dog, is no exception. We can attest through our own experience that as many as forty-six canines may live together happily and in reasonable harmony.

Dogs arrive with a hard-wired awareness that their role here is not as solo units. As they go through their lives, they do not lose this instinct and will always prefer company over isolation. Being alone causes them to feel disconnected in some way, and this inevitably results in stress and a search for companionship.

Choices made for a lifetime will seldom be devoid of the need to interact with others of their own kind. If nothing else, lack of canine companionship may make for a very lonely existence because of the lack of two-way dialogue and shared experiences. For many dogs, a trip to the dog park may be appealing simply for the opportunities it affords to 'talk'.

Lack of connection with other dogs can cause a kind of isolation that results in the equivalent of 'Stockholm Syndrome': the state of mind wherein a kidnap victim starts to identify with the objectives of their kidnappers, even to the point where they become complicit in the crime against themselves. In other words, dogs may become so institutionalised in their human dwellings that they lose the ability to relate to others of their species and may even become hostile to them. It is by no means uncommon. And what's more, the dog in this situation is quite content.

As with so many aspects of a dog's being, the type of life they will have selected for themselves is dependent upon their learning needs, which will include the size and type of pack they will be a part of.

So, would they prefer living in a pack? Judge for yourself!

Irrespective of their backgrounds, dogs can happily co-exist together and become immersed and content in a pack lifestyle.

The only dog we have ever taken in that did not respond wholly positively to the pack environment, was a very old lady who had lived rough on the streets for at least twelve years of her life. Her existence had been a solitary one in a rural community where she was constantly chased away by other dogs and spurned by humans. She could hardly be blamed that she was less than enthusiastic at suddenly finding herself amongst a large and boisterous pack. She was with us for over three years before she passed, and her diffidence gradually became a kind of grudging acceptance, wherein she could appreciate her housemates in limited doses. She was a 'crusty' but very dignified dog.

Is having a single dog a kind thing to do?

It depends on how 'single' is defined.

For a puppy leaving its mother and siblings, and going to a new home, becoming a single dog may initially be an isolating shock. For dogs with experience of only dog living, coming from rescue situations, a home is their salvation, irrespective of whether or not they are the sole canine. But whilst a dog may compensate for being the solitary member of its species in a pack by embracing humans or other pets as part of their group, there is only value in this situation if these other beings are physically there to provide companionship.

Because of their dislike of being alone, unkindness is introducing dogs to situations where they will be left unaccompanied for extended periods of time. It is cruel because of the distress and misery it will inevitably cause them. But even a custodian who is present will be of little help if they don't communicate with the dog.

Introducing another dog into the equation is not automatically a solution. Dogs can face compatibility issues with one another, just as much as we do. But nonetheless, the presence of another being is quite crucial for their happiness and wellbeing.

This dog was a miserable single pet who relished becoming a pack member.

How do dogs feel if another dog is introduced to their home?

It could be wonderful for them, or it could be their worst nightmare.

For a young dog, being joined by a similarly aged companion of their own kind can be manna from heaven. The newcomer will likely be welcomed with excitement and anticipation, and a firm friendship may be struck that can last throughout their lives. In their youth, dogs are highly predisposed towards an open and welcoming mentality, devoid of prejudices, judgements and jealousies.

For an old dog, a new companion can be like a breath of fresh air that invigorates and revitalises them. However, as they age, and particularly when a dog has been an only dog for some time, there is a danger that the type of institutionalisation referred to in the previous sections begins to set in. Over time and by force of circumstance, dogs may have little choice but to ignore their instincts towards their own kind and abandon their aspirations to connect, effectively becoming the habituated 'lone wolf'. A dog can become totally accustomed to its available company, and be accepting of it to the exclusion of others. An on-going lack of positive canine interaction can result in a psychological withdrawal from, and reluctance to participate in, the wider doggie community. And the older the dog becomes, the more 'institutionalised' it may grow to be. The concomitant effect is that a pet may become unwilling to accept another dog in its house, on its territory, with its people.

Quite how powerfully they are affected and how 'far gone' they become will be a matter of the strength of pack orientation that existed within them at the outset. This in turn is a feature of the learning they have planned for their lifetime.

Even if a dog has not become institutionalised, it should be recognised that dogs are every bit as subject to personal likes and dislikes as humans are. They are choosy about their friends, protective of their space, experience jealousy as one of their prevalent emotions, and can be resentful of interlopers. They do not automatically have an "I love everybody' mentality, can dislike with a passion bordering on hatred, be insulting and refuse to speak to one another.

There is an extra dimension in a dog's psyche about its chosen companions that is absent from our human one. As they age, dogs become increasingly experienced in, and adept at, recognising vibrational compatibilities, or lack of them. They see little point in developing relationships with those whose learning and purpose has no connection with their own. They would prefer to eschew their company from the outset and avoid interpersonal entanglements that serve no purpose. In this way, their lives are less complicated and they do not need to waste time, effort and energy upon those that they find draining.

This may be contrasted with humans who may spend years, or even a lifetime, immersed in complicated and fruitless associations that are neither nurturing nor supportive. Many of us are unable or unwilling to extricate ourselves from negative relationships, or even face the fact that our friendships can be damaging or draining to us. Perhaps if we had a dog's perspective, we would be more clinical in the decisions we make about those we seek to connect with.

One of the effects of a canine's crystal cut clarity over who they do and do not like, is that if their people introduce another dog (on the assumption that companionship may be a positive and desirable thing) there is only a 50/50 chance that the result will be positive. The dogs are as likely to not relate to one another, as they are to bond.

If the kindly introduction of a companion is met with disapproval, this can be a matter of 'planned' learning too. As with so many things (in all of our lives), a dog often needs to accept, adapt and move on.

Although they may possess the ability to recognise their compatibility with one another, the need to compromise may be forced upon them by the circumstances we create for them. It may take them years (or never happen at all) but dogs can get used to one another if they so choose. Only where there is a zero-bandwidth compatibility will detente be impossible. For the most part, dogs will learn to at least tolerate a companion, and this often leads to (at least grudging) appreciation of them and the company they provide.

Dogs can accept new pack members easily and with gladness; but only if they choose to and find each other vibrationally compatible

Our very first dog had 1½ years living with us before we got another dog, and 3 years more before a third arrived. She was indifferent to the new ones; although when (a further two years later) a fourth (male) arrived, she was quite enthusiastic about his presence.

By the time she passed on, she had to cope with the arrival of a staggering 35 dogs coming into a home that had once been hers and hers alone. There are times when this troubles me, because she was happy being the only dog. Although she knew she was always the 'apple of my eye', I do wonder how she felt about the influx. She was always accepting and tolerant of them, and the more that came, the more she seemed to be welcoming of them. If it hadn't been for her, we would never have begun what we do today.

Chapter 8

RELATING TO OTHER DOGS

"To be sure, the dog is loyal. But why, on that account should we take him as an example? He is loyal to men, not to other dogs."

Karl Kraus

Why do certain dogs become bonded pairs and not others?

Bonding goes way beyond simple chemistry and liking. It is an intense love that few are meant to experience. This is no bad thing.

The term bonded pair is most frequently seen in rescue situations where two dogs have been living together, possibly for years, and the group they are with wants to rehome them together to avoid emotional hardship. It does not suggest a romantic attachment of any kind, although the dogs may also be 'mates' in the strictest sense of the term.

The dogs become bonded because they find each other acceptable on several levels, the most obvious of which is that they get on very well with each other. Just like humans may be with other humans, there is a total comfort in their dog/dog relationship, and they fit together like hand in glove.

This goes far beyond attraction at the vibrational level, at which they mutually sense their compatibility. There is a very strong likelihood that they are members of the same soul family who have shared lifetimes and reincarnated together many times previously. They experience a deep recognition of one another, and take great comfort in one another's presence.

Most dogs are not intended to experience the intensity of this kind of relationship and such pairings are relatively rare. When dogs do become bonded, both great joy and great suffering may result. While the companions are together, their connection is fulfilling and nurturing for them both. But if they are separated by circumstances or death, they may never recover, quickly losing all interest in life and never managing to come to terms with the absence of their partner.

Of course, separation may be the reason they were thrown together in the first place. Being forced into a situation where it must learn to cope with the loss of a cherished other is just as likely to be dog's life choice, as one where it has the experience of spending its days happily together with a cherished other.

Bonded pairs may have a greater level of focus upon each other than they do upon their humans, making them somewhat different to be custodians of, than other dogs; although they may also be so ecstatic in their affection for one another, that their unbridled joy incorporates their people too. And this type of bonding is not exclusively between dogs: a pet can become bonded to its human. More about this later.

In many respects, those that do not form ties of this depth are the lucky ones. The intensity of the experience is something that all dogs must go through in at least one lifetime, where the parties in the relationship are not separated. But in others, they will be, and they must then go through as many lifetimes as it takes to learn to cope with being apart. The process can be agonising.

Although I can accept that parting may be a means to an end, we have had the misfortune to witness the tragic consequences of separation.

We took one half of an elderly bonded pair (involved in a complex rescue of many senior dogs, under tragic circumstances), without being made aware of their connection.

We quickly discovered it when it became obvious that the dog we had welcomed into our home was seriously pining.

We went back to the rescue group and told them that we wanted to adopt whoever it was that was that could alleviate the cause of the sadness.

They then revealed that she had been bonded to her male mate, who had already been adopted to another home. They also told us that soon after being rehomed, he had begun to refuse his food and became depressed and inconsolable.

When we learned of his plight, we immediately offered to take him from his new family; so as to reunite them. But it was too late. He had already died.

The female who came to us spent many weeks searching for her missing companion. Although we believe she never truly recovered from his loss, eventually she seemed consoled by being part of a pack, and took to flirting with a much younger male. She was the lucky one.

Since that time, we have come across many bonded pairs in rescue and followed their situations with concern. I am always pleased when the group they are with refuse to adopt out one without the other, although sadly, this often involves them being in rescue for substantially longer than they might be as individuals.

All too often, I read profiles of one member of a bonded pair whose companion has already been adopted.

Invariably, the rescue organisation reports something to the effect that the remaining member is "very sad and needs to get out soon."

Flirting with a handsome younger male may have saved this old lady's life, but sadly, her heartbroken mate was not so lucky.

When they come across each other as strangers what are dogs thinking?

It depends upon their overall demeanor, which may be broadly classified to assist in understanding.

An encounter with a strange dog is seldom the complicated process of posturing, masking and game playing that humans go through. They will perceive the vibration of another dog at a considerable distance and be aware of their compatibility and the intentions of the other dog whilst still several metres apart.

What then transpires, and what thoughts are experienced, is an issue best explained using a basic passive/aggressive/assertive scale, which for humans would read something like this.

- Passive: fails to stand up for their own rights and subjugates them to the needs of others.
- Aggressive: stands up for their own rights in a way that ignores the rights of others.
- Assertive: stands up for their own rights in a way that is respectful of the rights of others.

Dogs may also be seen to exhibit behaviours on this scale. Not all are balanced and able to manage their contact with others amiably.

A passive dog seeing another canine approaching will be preoccupied with the potential for being met with aggressive behaviour. Their thoughts will be filled with concern and uncertainty, until the vibration of the other animal becomes clear. If the on-coming dog is amiable, the passive canine will experience relief and pleasure that their fears are not realised. Their thinking and attitude will then mirror that of a more assertive dog. However, if the approaching animal is threatening, the passive dog's behaviour will verge upon the obsequious, and their manner will become cowed in the hope that the potential aggressor will not give vent to their baser tendencies. Their primary thought will be a mantra-like "Leave me alone".

The thoughts of an aggressive dog seeing another canine approaching will be filled with attempts to size up the rival and the development of attack strategies to be used if the animal does not submit to their superiority. Their body will become palpably tense and go to a state of 'high alert'. Even if the on-coming canine presents no threat or challenge, their response will be based upon their desire to dominate and their primary thought will be "I'm going to get the better of you".

A passive dog will not be interested in allowing a telepathic link with another dog. An aggressive dog will wish to create a link to verbally proclaim status. They will rely upon their tail (specifically speed of motion and angle) to telegraph their intentions. The aggressive dog's will be raised, curled inward and thrashing in full transmission mode; the passive's will be lowered and even tucked in to block demands for communication. The more aggressive of the two will likely become quite insistent on trying to use the 'butt telegraph' to connect (see below); the more passive dog will be quite unwilling to let this happen.

Of course, both descriptions are intentionally extreme. The passive/aggressive/assertive scale is simply one upon which any being may be assessed relative to others.

In the case of dogs, breed and size is by no means an automatic or clear indicator of likely placement on the scale. Neither does the scale (or understanding of the thoughts that underlie a position) give any indication of what the outcome of an encounter between two dogs will be.

Just because a dog is passive in its approach to others, does not mean that it is not capable of doing damage to an aggressive dog, or that it is incapable of using size (large or small) to its advantage. When pushed, a passive dog that is intimidated by a more aggressive one is just as likely to lash out as it is to withdraw further into its passivity.

The only meeting with any certainty attached to it, is where assertive meets assertive, because neither feels the need to get the upper hand or feel themselves to be the proverbial underdog.

For the average, well balanced dog, their thoughts about impending contact will reflect their openness to initiating a dialogue and being friendly and welcoming. They will be relaxed about the opportunity to briefly 'chat' with one of their own kind. Even a momentary encounter can result in an extensive exchange of data, if both parties are prepared to allow access to their experiences via their telepathic link.

Their curiosities about one another will not be extensive, but will be comprehensive enough for their needs, and cover such details as

- What kind of life the other leads.
- What they are fed.
- Where they have been walking.
- An assessment of where that dog is in a pack order relative to themselves.

If you feel this is inconsequential data to be concerned with, ask yourself what more there would be to discover about a dog's life? And then look at the parallels with human interactions.

Upon meeting for the first-time humans invariably size one another up, looking for clues that will enable them to understand such things as another's background (including origins and education) and circumstances (including family, employment and wealth), which will allow them to determine the other's status relative to their own. We need this information to give us clues as to how we should feel about, and behave towards another person.

Dogs are no different, and their seemingly simple criterion of 'need to know' information reflects their world relative to ours.

I was once out hiking with one of our largest dogs, the pack alpha who was used to accompanying me everywhere. He was very big and imposing, but possessed of a mild disposition and normally amiable temperament.

Despite his exalted pack position he was quite leery of strangers, intimidated by children and deeply unsure of new dogs outside of his familiar environment. But he was your classic gentle giant in most respects, and adored by many who met him.

On this particular hike, we saw a couple coming towards us with a non-descript mid-sized dog, off-leash. As we drew closer, our dog grew tense and I took hold of his leash collar (an all-in-one product ideal for such hiking trips) because I knew that he was becoming unsettled and anxious.

The couple did nothing to restrain their dog despite seeing us approaching. Theirs was obviously an assertive dog, excited to be making a connection, and he bounded towards us.

It was equally clear that my hiking companion was unhappy, but he was very tolerant as the other dog did some classic butt sniffing. I could feel him relax when the dog had finished and trotted away.

Then as the gap between us and the couple shortened, their dog suddenly decided to come back for another round. This time our alpha was in no mood for it and as the other dog approached, he snapped at it, nearly pulling me over and sending it yelping and scampering back to its people, who were obviously none too impressed.

First time meetings can be occasions of great curiosity.

Are domestic dogs territorial?

Only where claims to space seem to be fair and reasonable to them.

In the wild, territory has the sole purpose of providing for the needs of a pack. It will relate to a fairly extensive area of land from which the pack may catch enough food, sleep safely and raise young. The need to protect your territory is hard wired to ensure the survival of all members. It is demarked 'scenting' the boundaries with chemical messages, establishing the claim to ownership, and instructing others to keep their distance. Their warnings may or may not be heeded, and dogs may resort to aggression and violence to keep their place safe.

For domesticated canines, their home environment is their territory. The imperative to protect it may not be felt so greatly, but most dogs will still scent the boundaries of their custodian's property, or at least what they come to think of as their space! This can present problems for dogs living in apartment buildings, or without their own yard. Their ability to mark what is 'theirs' will be limited by their custodian's indignation or the encroachment of other dogs in what may inevitably become communal areas. Under these circumstances, a dog may feel itself to be 'stateless', or at least impoverished as far as territory goes.

In protecting their territorial rights, some dogs will spontaneously send out warning barks when strangers approach. Those trying to deal with mastering extreme behaviours during their lifetime, may even feel the need to attack interlopers. However, the strength of the need to protect is also partly dependent upon where they consider themselves to be in the pack order. Those who are alphas will defend far more vociferously then those lower in the order; and in the absence of the alpha, others will assume the protective guardian role.

Territorial behaviours should not be confused with those of livestock guardian breeds. Their protective natures are about their belief in the need to defend other beings, even though they may appear to be space related.

Why do dogs pee so often on a walk?

They don't. They're 'scenting' which is not the same thing. It is not because of a need to pee.

Scenting is a form of chemical communication that dogs use in addition to their already impressive array of techniques. Although the scenting action appears the same as urination, it is much briefer and may be repeated many times, releasing appropriate chemical output to give the desired information, but having little to do with the need to relieve the bladder.

Adding to the scents of others whilst on a walk may be thought of as a friendly greeting and it is not an act of dominance or an attempt to establish territory. (The 'outdoors' for domesticated dogs is neutral, no-dogs land) Some designated places may be thought of as the equivalent of internet chat rooms, where messages are regularly posted and updated, but it is seldom the case that two people are in the room at the same time.

Not all dogs share an obsession with this type of communication, and their behaviour will involve neither scenting nor sniffing. This simply indicates that their preoccupations are not based upon fellow members of their species.

Indoors, males use scenting as a technique not so much to mark and define territory as a cat would, but to indicate their presence and either approval or disapproval of whatever they are marking.

In a pack environment, it is also used to denote association. This may be both an exhibition of dominance and an assertion of belonging. Particularly when an alpha has been leaving its scent in its territory, males contesting the authority of the alpha will add their scent as a slight; whereas other females will claim association by adding their scents. Whether their claim is justified through reciprocal feelings is neither here nor there. It is the equivalent of claiming to be dating someone on Facebook when their page may or may not reflect the truth of the statement.

What can dogs determine from the scents of other dogs that they pick up?

A surprising amount of information that is left quite intentionally.

Dogs scenting activities act in the same way that they might were they to be a calling card left by a human, or a scrawling on a wall with chalk that declares "Kilroy was here". Chemical communication is capable of producing as vivid an image of both the dog, and (limited) aspects of their being, as might be delivered in a face-to-face encounter.

The most obviously intended messages may incorporate simply a dog's (real) name, their sex and age. But the vibration contained within the scent will inevitably include 'subtexts' which detailed sniffing will pick up on. These will include health issues, diet and occasionally claims regarding territorial preeminence. The latter tend to be limited to places where the claim is 'legitimate' such as in the dog's own backyard, and not in public areas.

Dogs do not automatically take in all messages. Most of their sniffing consists of perfunctory passes, seeking something of greater interest. Only when their attention is caught will they bother to examine the full text of the available messages in detail. What sparks interest may be something new, unusual or familiar i.e. left by a dog in which they have an interest.

In all things, the olfactory sense is a big deal for dogs, and they are far more dependent upon it than we humans, as subsequent pages reveal. But the importance of smell for dogs goes way beyond what we may imagine. Canines experience something known as synesthesia. This is basically the production of a sense impression relating to one sense, by stimulation of another sense. In the case of dogs, a scent literally produces a visual picture in their mind without the use of eyesight!

This facility has all kinds of ancillary and related benefits for them, but in this instance, when they pick up the scent of another canine, they can tell what it looks like without ever seeing it. The imagery is not fully clear to them, but it is enough to give them an impression of it.

When dogs smell a scent outside, can they distinguish those of other dogs they know?

Yes. With consummate ease.

A dog on a walk may spend a considerable amount of time with its nose to the ground just to gain an understanding of who has passed this way, and they will instantly recognise scents left by dogs they know.

The vibrations of the scents left, and their associations with particular dogs, are stored in a canine's memory bank as if they were names written on a card index. Recall of them is easy and instantaneous because the sense of smell is the most powerful of all in assisting remembrance.

Checking out the local smells is a serious business.

What is butt sniffing all about?

Butt sniffing is one of the most widely misunderstood of all dog actions.

Here is a typical explanation pulled off the Internet.

An average dog's nose is anywhere between 10,000 to 100,000 times more sensitive than ours, and smelling each other's butts is just another example of chemical communication in the animal kingdom. It's like "speaking with chemicals," and that's how dogs ask about another dog.

Researchers studying the anal secretions of dogs and wild coyotes discovered that next to their poopers, canines have pouches called anal sacs, which house the glands that secrete chemicals they use to get to know each other. Amines and acids are the primary compounds involved, and genetics and the state of their immune system can influence the aroma as well.

*Dogs also have a secondary olfactory system in their nose called the **Jacobson's organ**, which is designed specifically for chemical communication. Its nerves lead right to the brain -- so the smell of poop doesn't overpower their sensitive senses.*

This is an accurate explanation and very typical of the way in which scientists speculate about what's going on with dogs. It certainly would seem to explain everything. However...

The chakra dogs use for telepathy is located in the tail, just shy of the base (one of the principal reasons dogs object to having their tails interfered with, as it affects their communications). To establish a link with another dog, placing your nose in its proximity is a rapid and easy way of making a strong connection. Although not strictly necessary for creating a telepathic link, it does allow the dog to pick up that individual's vibrational frequency without error and ingrain the memory of it via the olfactory sense. This will enable instant recall in the future and facilitate communication at will. It's like establishing a 'butt telegraph' link.

If that sounds a little crazy to you, consider the alternative that is proposed by the scientific explanation offered above: Dogs are only able to communicate with one another through sniffing. Their communications must therefore be rather limited and any update must require further invasive nasal contact.

If you've lived with dogs, you will have observed that this type of sniffing behaviour is not repeated regularly. It happens upon first meeting, and seldom thereafter. If it does get repeated, it is because the dogs have been separated for an extended period and they want to ensure that the returning canine is the same as the one that left. The sight of the dog alone is not sufficient evidence of this. Physical dissimilarities between dogs are not so acutely observed as to allow them to distinguish between one another on looks alone. Mistakes can occur. A vibration, on the other hand, never lies.

The secondary olfactory system posited does indeed exist, but its purpose is for assessment of residual traces left as calling cards by other dogs, as described above. It has nothing to do with the butt telegraph.

A fine nose for picking up messages!

Why are some dog breeds more aggressive than others?

This apparently simple question is one of the most complex in the book.

Across the course of our many lifetimes we seek to achieve a balanced experience between the polarities that life presents us with. One of the areas of balance relates to our experience of emotions. All emotions stem from either love of fear, since these are the two extremes on the scale.

We will all experience lifetimes when our thoughts and actions are motivated wholly by one or the other of these two, so that we may learn from the effects of them. But the majority of our lifetimes will be spent somewhere on the scale between them, experiencing both to different degrees at one time or another, and dealing with the whole gamut of experience that individual emotions inevitably produce. Some are easily mastered. Others take a great deal of effort and multiple lifetimes to come to terms with.

Aggression is an emotion that stems from fear. Living with permanent feelings of aggression and learning to gain mastery over them usually takes many lifetimes. Even though we may quickly come to understand the lessons related to the effects of aggression, applying the learning and converting it into action that will negate its negative impacts within and around us may take considerably longer.

In common with all emotionally related challenges, we bring them along with us at birth because we have elected to go through them. It is integrated into our natures and will surface at some point during our lifetime. It is a constant feature of our psychological make-up for that lifetime at least.

Despite this hardwiring, the feelings of aggression are by no means insurmountable and they may be overcome through choice. This requires constant awareness and recognition of the moments when those choices become available.

For dogs the challenge of overcoming aggression is even greater than it is for humans. For them, dealing with the trials that this mental state will engender involves not only managing their own innate feelings and desires, but coping with the expectations of those with whom they live, and human society. The former may be considerably easier than the latter. This is because some breeds, from the outset, have a bad reputation which affects the attitudes of many people who will be around them. Irrespective of efforts the dog may make to overcome human prejudices, our beliefs constantly work against them and threaten to turn their lives into human expectation fulfilling prophecies.

The origins of human attitude once again run to the ways in which we have attributed certain dogs with behaviours and attitudes. The reasons behind this develop as follows:

- A dog seeking to cope with the challenge of aggressive feelings inevitably demonstrates them prior to gaining mastery over them.

- A dog demonstrating aggression is often selected for use in aggressive purposes by humans.

- Because the behaviour is sponsored and engendered, it becomes a habituated aspect of the dog's being.

- When the behaviour becomes a habit, the dog faces a greater challenge in overcoming and gaining mastery of it.

- It continues to live its life constantly being encouraged to exhibit the very behaviours it is trying to overcome.

- Under these circumstances, it is more likely than not to fail.

- If this happens, the individual dog must undergo further lifetimes striving to meet the challenge.

- Typically, it will reincarnate as the same breed, demonstrating the same tendencies.

- In the meantime, some humans who have observed the behaviour in one representative of one breed, will have encouraged the behaviours in others of the same breed.

- Indoctrination by expectation is inculcated into a whole breed population and a perpetual cycle is created.

Alongside these things which have affected the dogs, it must be accepted that some individuals who elect to become custodians of a 'tainted breed' all too often have a major role to play in the problem. Whilst it is by no means always the case, it may accurately be observed that a percentage of those who are attracted to 'aggressive breeds' often have issues in common with their pet.

So even if the dog *is* successfully mastering their own challenges, the attitudes and expectations of their person may (quite deliberately) exacerbate or provoke a surfacing of aggression within the animal, thus continuing the (literally) vicious circle. Unfortunately, this is as it should be, since the humans may receive learning from the experience of being custodians to dogs with these issues, and vice versa.

NB. For those who feel like lynching me now for making this uncomfortable point, please be assured that this is not intended as an indictment of all those who share their lives with these souls.

I am very aware that there are large numbers of responsible and caring guardians of reputedly aggressive breeds who go to great lengths in trying to ensure that their beloved pets live happy and trouble free lifetimes. These people are most definitely NOT part of the problem, and they are correct in their assertions that the breeds are 'recoverable'.

Equally, these same people will be aware of the element to which I am referring.

All of this is not something of our current making. We merely perpetuate it. The stereotyping of breeds is centuries old, and in our era, has merely become aggravated due to the influence of mass media.

To prevent the spread of the vicious circle to all breeds, those souls needing to cope with the extremes of aggression tend to be 'funnelled' into lifetimes wherein they occupy the bodies of the breeds with the bad reputations.

Although this may seem to intensify the negativity of the situation even further, the intention is to stop us from turning dogs from being man's best friend into an enemy we seek to annihilate. Such a potential exists.

It may be observed that from a human perspective, in ignorance of how this has come about, our attitude towards aggressive breeds appears to be totally justified. This has altered our thinking to the point where for many, attempts to eradicate aggressive breeds are acceptable.

However, were the most aggressive breeds to be done away with, the countless and never ending stream of dogs that need to experience mastering the emotional balance issues stemming from aggression would still need to deal with those challenges. Of necessity, another breed would be selected for them to live those difficult lifetimes through.

In an ideal world with total foresight and appreciation of the way things work, those dogs with the greatest instincts for aggression would find themselves with people who would be the most understanding, tolerant and accepting, in environments where the least provocation and most support in facing up to their baser instincts would available.

Of course, not only is this not possible, it would be a false utopia because then the challenges to the dog to demonstrate mastery would likely never arise, and further lifetimes would be required to allow genuine opportunity for them to evidence their success in conquering those negative aspects of their being.

Why do dogs sometimes become 'leash aggressive'?

Not without good reason!

There are four main reasons for any dog becoming leash aggressive.

1. They are aware of the potentially combative nature of another dog approaching, and know that they will be unable to fully defend themselves if they are tethered to their person. They therefore become proactive in demonstrating their ability to defend themselves; an action they would probably consider unnecessary if they were unrestrained.

2. They are the combatant themselves. They do not wish to be restrained so that they may more easily or forcefully assert themselves. The dog is not so much leash aggressive, as aggressive to begin with. The leash is incidental and does not instigate the aggression.

3. The dog's custodian actively encourages hostility towards other dogs. Consciously or unconsciously, they speculate and express their thoughts about their dog's ability to 'beat' an approaching dog. This state of mind conveys itself to their animal as a form of legitimisation, or even goading. Whilst this may not impact upon a dog that is not predisposed towards aggressive behaviour, it is a positive stimulant towards one that is.

4. The dog's guardian is wary of an oncoming dog. Their trepidation is easily perceived by their tethered canine. Sensing the stress, the dog instantly feels ill at ease and goes into 'protective mode'. Their behaviour and subsequent actions now have as their raison d'etre a mindset of *"I thought it might hit me, so I hit it back first"*.

Do dogs recognise their own kind?

At species level, yes. At breed level, rarely. And what's more, it doesn't matter.

When processing other creatures that they might see around them, dogs certainly recognise other dogs. However, whether it is looking at a Great Dane, an Affenpinscher or a South Russian Ovtcharka, a dog sees simply another dog. One of its own kind.

A simple explanation for this would be that a dog does not see itself and so does not have an awareness of what it looks like. Thus, it cannot identify others of its type. However, even if a dog saw and recognised its self-image in a mirror (which they do not - see *Do dogs recognise their own reflections?*) or had grown up with siblings (beyond the usual eight weeks) and then met others unlike themselves, it would still only identify other canines as precisely that: another dog.

We humans, by choice, divide and describe ourselves based on three broad categories: race, class and religion. And within these groupings, there are any number of further distinctions. It is as if we actively look for (or even need) ways to differentiate ourselves from one another.

From a dog's perspective, a dog is a dog is a dog.

Accordingly, there is no sense of superiority (or inferiority) that a dog may feel because of its physicality or origins. Neither is a dog beset by belief systems that cause delineations between others of its kind. As such, any hierarchy that exists within their social structure is based upon practicality, and does not extend to matters of ego, prejudice or dogma (pardon the pun).

Humans seldom identify themselves as simply 'human'. In our descriptors, we include differences, not commonalities. We look at each other and do not see fellow travelers on the same pathway. Dogs do. They accept all. They will even extend their communal framework to encompass any other type of being that is 'properly' introduced, regardless of whether they are also canine. It just doesn't matter to them.

Even the most casual observer of human history, or our present state of existence, cannot fail to notice the trouble our pressing need to compartmentalise ourselves gets us into.

Dogs suffer no such plight.

Two of our four St Bernards. Since one is short coated, you might not even have realised that they're the same breed. They haven't either, and they don't really care!

Our Grey Wolf came to us after being rescued from an unpleasant and troubled background. Her mother was killed by a hunter, and she was almost destroyed herself by animal control in the US. Initially, her behaviour in most things was very un-doglike, but over the years she has been with us, she has become increasingly integrated with the pack. She is almost unrecognizable as a wolf, until she gets outside, when her whole persona and demeanor changes. We are frequently asked if she is dominant or aggressive with the rest of the pack, but she is not at all. She blends in, somewhat aloof, aligning herself very closely with the alpha, flirting shamelessly and playing raucously until he tires of her (he's much younger and tries to shake her off). However, it has always been quite clear that she *does* know that she is not a dog.

Why does so much dog interaction seem to be rough, or even aggressive?

Not everything is always quite what it appears to be!

When interacting with others of their kind, dogs frequently engage in apparently borderline violent activities, endlessly chasing, wrestling and mauling. Prevalent mostly (but not only) amongst younger dogs, these goings-on are often accompanied by growling and yelping, completing the picture that the canines are hell bent on killing one another. But it's not so.

Within their natural world, such physicality is 'training': mock presentations of pursuit of prey and fighting that keeps them prepared for battles they instinctively imagine they may face. Whether bringing down a food source or struggling for position within a pack, this sparring is essential for maintaining fitness and developing paw-to-paw combat tactics. Even though the imagined confrontations may never happen, intuitively dogs feel the need to keep in trim, agile and prepared.

This type of 'play' seldom results in serious harm to any of the participants. Even when biting, the dogs are aware of the amounts of pressure they can safely exert with their jaws without doing harm. They are also acutely aware of who they should partner with for these wargames. Vibrations telegraph the difference in intentions between dogs who will happily join them in a joust, and those that want to 'have at it'. But before commencing, telepathic agreement will have been reached about the parameters of the conflict.

Of course, as with children playing rough and tumble games, the interactions can 'end in tears' and result in actual fighting. Desire to dominate can override restraint, and retaliatory action may spark off real hostilities. And there are instances where one dog is insistent on doing battle when another is not too keen, or already worn out. Trouble follows.

As they mature, domestic dogs may come to recognise that the preconceptions they once held about how their lives would turn out were illusions. The need to practice either attack or self defence wanes.

Overall, from their perspective, this lively activity is an essential component of engaging with others. It forms a connection between the dogs, and however it may look to us, it is (mostly) fun for them.

Two ferocious dogs trying to kill each other.

Oh wait, no.

Chapter 9

DOGS IN SERVICE

"Dogs have given us their absolute all.
We are the centre of their universe.
We are the focus of their love and faith and trust.
They serve us in return for scraps.
It is without a doubt the best deal man has ever made."

Roger Caras

How are PAT dogs able to help humans, and is there any benefit for the dog?

There are two levels at which Pets as Therapy dogs help humans.

The benefits of physical contact with animals, most notably with dogs (because they are the ones most frequently used) are quite measurable. The human tactile response to animals is proven to reduce stress, have a calming effect, and produce endorphins which, by themselves, can greatly assist in any healing process.

The unseen and (currently) immeasurable benefit is that when people are in contact with animals, an energy exchange inevitably takes place which will almost certainly involve the human receiving an energy that is vibrationally higher than their own.

The lower energy from the patient will rapidly be shed by the dog as incompatible with their own (although it may have the short-term effect of making them feel fatigued and lethargic); whereas the higher energy will be integrated by the sick person, causing the vibration to be raised and the human to feel better mentally, if not actually physically.

Since so much that is physical can be affected by our thoughts, there is a knock-on effect that can only be beneficial. The more frequent the contact, the greater the likelihood of the human receiving sustainable benefit from the contact.

Whereas most human/animal relationships are defined before either party incarnates, contact with therapy dogs may be much more random and dictated by chance. This in no way detracts from the benefits that may be received, and reinforces the fact that not everything in life is planned for.

As for the dogs themselves, it may seem that being subjected to a load of low energy from sick people might be a burdensome thing. From their perspective, this is not the case. A life during which the animal gives service as a PAT dog is almost always planned for as a 'contract' (one of many agreements we make pre-incarnation, determining aspects of our forthcoming experiences, relationships and service to others) between themselves and their person. (If this is not the case, during the PAT selection process, they will inevitably be rejected as unsuitable.)

In providing the support that they can for humans, they are accelerating their own journeys by providing themselves with learning opportunities and fulfillment of contractual obligations.

By their innate nature, therapy dogs have an awareness that they are bringing help and pleasure to people. This, in return, is a source of comfort for them; and as a form of service, being a PAT dog is particularly enjoyable. Most people who are the recipients of their loving auspices return the affection and make a great deal of fuss over the animal. It is a rare dog that does not enjoy such attention, so they do get some immediate payback for their unreserved giving.

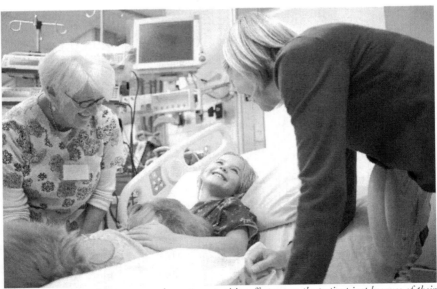

A dog that visits a sick person can have strong positive effects upon the patient just because of their physical presence and the vibrations they bring.

How can dogs sense impending epileptic fits or even cancers?

It's so obvious, they can't miss it.

A dog's unique ability to use synesthesia to experience allows them to perceive not only our physical form (i.e. our bodies) but also the auric energy field that surrounds them. We appear to almost shimmer. If that sounds uncomfortable for the eyesight, remember that dogs are totally accustomed to this and it merely appears ordinary.

An auric field surrounds and keeps contained the vibrations that emanate from our bodies, acting as if it were a kind of force field (which it is). The stronger the vibration, the further the field extends from the body. However, if we are suffering from imbalance, physical or emotional, the field can become depleted and extend no more than a few centimetres in depth.

With many physical ailments, the field is broken or contains gaps, and energy will quite literally haemorrhage from the aura. With minor ailments, such as headaches, the breach will be small and the energy leak minor.

Dogs see all of this happening in real time. When they observe it, the precise meaning will be understood by them and accepted as a natural part of life. It is not alarming to them, and is most often considered a matter of small consequence.

When they see another dog with a 'leaking' aura, they may try to repair the damage by licking the area where the energy is coming from, in an attempt to discover whether or not they may assist in healing (as they can with an open wound - see *Why do dogs lick people?*). They may also try to do this with their people. But for many complex reasons, they may not be able to assist either dog or human.

An epileptic fit does not cause a rent in the auric field. Instead what a dog may see around a head might best be described as something that looks a little like solar flares bursting from the surface of the sun.

These will be accompanied by a sound (at too high a frequency for our human ears to register) like a crackling fire. The sights and sounds do not even need to be seen; they leave vibrational traces in the air. A fit may be detected by observing these symptoms quite some while before the human succumbs to the disruptive brain activity. The 'flares' may begin several hours beforehand; but also only minutes.

Cancer on the other hand appears as a significant tear in the fabric of the aura, becoming progressively bigger, spilling out energy as the cancer takes hold. It is unmissable.

If a dog sees these things, as all can, it is a relatively straightforward process to have them indicate that they detect trouble to a human. The only limitation upon this is how attuned the dog is to understanding what the humans who are training them require of them.

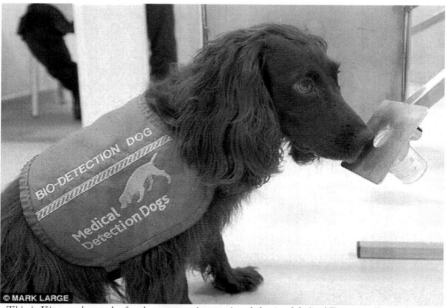

© MARK LARGE

This is Kizzy, who works for the awesome international charity, Medical Detection Dogs. She was featured in an article in the UK's Daily Mail newspaper (photographed by Mark Large) and cost around $15,000 to train. However, her success rate for detecting cancer boasts a staggering 93% degree of accuracy, compared with only 20% for PSA tests.

(see: http://www.dailymail.co.uk/health/article-3189903/Dogs-sniff-prostate-cancer-detect-tumours-93-accuracy.html)

Do Seeing Eye dogs enjoy their work?

As we would conventionally define enjoyment, no.

Almost every dog that becomes what we might term a 'service dog' will have this role defined as part of their contractual commitments before they incarnate. It is an experience they will go through and relate to by way of comparative referencing to other lifetimes where they have been completely unburdened by the onus of responsibility.

The role of a Seeing Eye dog entails the animal completely subjugating its own will and desires for the sake of the human. Involvement in the program effectively requires them to 'sign away' the best part of their lives and undertake a massive commitment (a seeing eye dog usually works for 8/10 years, sometimes longer). The nearest human parallel we may draw is probably that of an individual who takes holy orders and becomes a nun or a monk.

Even to the untrained observer, a Seeing Eye dog may appear somewhat muted in their behaviour. Their emotional range can seem stunted. They express moderate pleasure, but seldom excitement; confidence in their role, but not self-assuredness. You may catch them observing other dogs at play with a slightly wistful air, but if released to their own devices, they rarely seem inclined to connect with their own kind.

A Seeing Eye dog's training demands that they sever connections with their natural state of being. Those that are unprepared to do that are quickly filtered out in the selection process; or have their unwillingness exposed as training goes on.

Fortunately, this means that in the vast majority of cases, like medical detection dogs, only those who had elected to have the experience during their lifetime do actually become service dogs. (The same applies for other types of service dog too.) The random issues of dogs finding themselves in the wrong home with the wrong role are not problems that beset these lifetimes.

The life of a Seeing Eye dog is not what may be called an enjoyable one, if we were to compare it with the potential a more conventional lifetime holds. But dogs may have miserable lives even if they are free of any liabilities. At least as a Seeing Eye dog they are guaranteed to be fed, looked after and loved. The value that the sight challenged human places upon their dog will most usually result in them being lavished with affection, truly appreciated, and being treated with untypical care; so there is a balance and trade-off for the dog's sacrifice.

So do they enjoy being Seeing Eye dogs?

They accept it. They realise the good they are doing. They love their person with uncommon devotion, possibly to the point of the human/dog bonding referred to elsewhere. They signed up for it before they ever arrived and they have precious little choice in the certainty that they will perform the role, unless random chance alters their fate. From a spiritual perspective, it is fulfilling and the dog may find tremendous satisfaction in it.

But enjoyment? No.

This picture from Guide Dogs for the Blind, an industry-leading guide dog school that receives no Government funding, evidences the bond of love and devotion that develops between dog and handler.

Do police dogs or those who work in the military know that their work places their lives in potential danger?

No. Why would it when they are having such a good time?

In some respects, the lot of military and police dogs is very like that of Seeing Eye dogs. It's an agreed service they are performing.

The principal difference is that a lot of their activities, particularly the training, can feel like fun and in certain respects, their lives can be more 'normal'. However, it would be inconceivable to them that their lives are in danger. They do not equate the excitement inherent in what they do with anything threatening to them. (If they did, it would render them incapable of performing their roles.)

This comes down to how much trust dogs are prepared to endow their humans with. Service dogs typically bear great love and respect for their handlers and will have no concept that their person would intentionally and deliberately put them in harm's way.

It should also be noted that those police officers and servicemen who work with dogs most often love their animals without measure and would rather suffer harm themselves than have anything bad happen to their animals. The hearts of many have been irreparably broken when their beloved dogs do come to harm.

If a dog's ignorance of danger seems at odds with the implication that they knew in advance of incarnating what kind of life they were signing up for, it must be remembered that when we arrive, we forget everything.

The experience of military and police dogs is a valuable learning opportunity for dogs as they progress through their many lifetimes of learning. As with seeing eye dogs, it creates the opportunity to explore a unique relationship with humans quite unlike any other; but it is not necessarily an easy option, and certainly not a safe one.

Air Force Technical Sergeant Adam Miller carries his dog, Tina M111, to "safety" in a training session held in 114-degree heat. Dog handlers in all branches of the military have to go through intensive training sessions, and can be punished harshly if they mistreat their dogs.

Despite their potentially dangerous lives, military and police dogs are some of the most adored and adoring of all dogs in service.

Do commercial sled dogs enjoy their lives?

Pulling a sled can be physically rewarding and very exciting for a dog. But many animals used in commercial operations suffer greatly.

People who own and run sled dogs will give accounts of the innumerable pleasures their dogs take from running and pulling the sleds. It is certainly true that certain breeds of dog seem particularly predisposed towards running and pulling and may therefore enjoy being sled dogs. (Having been the guardian of fifteen Siberian Huskies, I can attest to this breed's insatiable desire to pull.).

The love of sled pulling has its origins in the love of running. When they form an attachment to their person, most dogs will absolutely prefer to run *with* that individual. Humans can rarely match a dog's speed or endurance, so bringing them along on a sled is the next best option. Hence, they enjoy pulling sleds, and the happiness of doing an activity with their person will bring them a great deal of enjoyment and satisfaction. This will be evident from their affection for their people.

Well cared for and cherished sled dogs adore what they do.

However, most people rarely get to see behind the scenes of a commercial sled dog's reality. It would be a rare exception for these dogs to experience anything but extremely cramped and unpleasant living quarters, and little by way of the kind of attention that most readers of this book would feel that their dogs warrant.

Commercial sled dogs are most definitely not pets. They are kept for one purpose only. Keeping them in cramped conditions is not without purpose. When finally let out, all they want to do is run. The fact that they must do so pulling something that is attached to them that frequently causes them to collide with other (possibly quite aggressive) dogs and constantly pulls them back, is neither here nor there.

When they are no longer useful and may no longer earn their keep, there is no happy retirement for them, unless their operators are caring enough to find adopters. By no means all are. Languishing in a small outdoor enclosure may be the most they can hope for. Or an even worse fate may await them.

Doubtless there are some commercial operations that do not subject their dogs to these conditions. I have not come across many.

Over the years we have offered a home to several ex sled dogs, both Siberian Huskies and Alaskan Malamutes. (Mixed breed dogs, 'created' especially for sledding roles, seem to find their ways into retirement homes with less frequency, perhaps because of their temperament.)

Whilst they are not always everybody's idea of an ideal pet, they seem to have profound gratitude for the simplest pleasures a 'normal' domesticated dog might take for granted:

Simply being allowed indoors is apparently such a novelty that they are initially reluctant to go outside again. None have ever adjusted to sleeping on a soft bed. Many have disliked being restrained in as simple a manner as having a leash put on them. All have initially felt a great need to be positively combative where the acquisition and protection of food is concerned.

I will leave you to draw your own conclusions.

Do sheepdogs enjoy herding as much as they seem to?

Absolutely, yes!

Being a sheepdog is one of the few service roles where a dog may be guaranteed almost endless pleasure in the form of exercise and excitement. To them it is the equivalent of making a living from playing a sport they love. And the fact that they get to spend much of their lives untethered, in the natural world, can be a major plus.

Like Seeing Eye and military or police dogs, they will most usually be highly valued by their custodians, and well fed; although they may not enjoy the intimacy of relationship they might crave with their person, because of that individual's fear of making them 'soft'. They are, after all, there to do a job.

This logic might well extend to not allowing them indoors (ever), or showing them any affection beyond the occasional word of praise and a fleeting touch. They may also be less likely to enjoy a happy retirement, since despite years of faithful service, many farmers elect to shoot dogs once they are no longer able to perform their roles. Of course, these are generalisations and their custodian's behaviour towards them may be the antithesis of what is described.

Roles for sheepdogs are becoming fewer and further between due to changes in farming practices. Unfortunately, this means that there are fewer opportunities for dogs to experience and explore the parameters of this type of relationship with humans.

So, it is the case that there are now several breeds of dog with very specific characteristics that are gradually becoming redundant; yet their popularity as breeds remains unabated. Without an outlet for their instincts and skills, they may all too easily become frustrated and troublesome. Whilst this presents a new learning opportunity for incarnating dogs, their struggles are not easily overcome. It should come as no surprise to the reader that herding dogs often register in great numbers on rescue sites.

Those that find themselves utilised for other challenging dog/human activities such as obedience, agility or Flyball are the lucky ones. Sheepdogs may love what they do, but their days of being able to do it are sadly numbered.

An increasingly rare opportunity for a lifetime of potential joy.

Flyball: Great fun, but not quite as good as herding.

How do gun dogs feel about what they must do?

At one level, being a 'sporting dog' can be fun. At another, it may become deeply disturbing.

Chasing game, whether to 'put it up' to be shot, or retrieving it in its dying throes, is the lot of gundogs. Many aspects of what they do may be as enjoyable to them as herding is for other breeds, including regular and almost uninhibited exposure to the natural world. But there are reasons why it may not be such a good thing for them.

The first and most obvious downside to this role is the utilisation of a gun. Many dogs will have a curious response to guns per se. This is because hardwired in the majority, as a result of experiences in previous lifetimes, is the knowledge of the harm and danger they represent. Early on in their incarnations, a dog is likely to have found itself the victim of a human with a gun and that experience is available to them vicariously as part of their soul memory, in all subsequent incarnations.

Thus, almost all dogs will often present an unusually instinctive response to the physicality of a gun being pointed at them. Most will shy away, despite having no experience of what a gun even is in this current lifetime. They can sense the intentions for the weapon itself, even if the person holding the gun is just 'teasing' them.

When this innate fear is coupled with the noise made by the gun (which they must be routinely subjected to), being a gun dog can be a miserable experience. Like humans, dogs are born with a fear of loud noises and their natural response to a gunshot will need to be considerably suppressed to fulfill this role.

However, the relentless physical exposure to the weaponry and the constant enduring of loud bangs in close physical proximity either results in a damaged and dysfunctional dog (which is likely to be disposed of) or an animal that has forced itself to cope with the persistent trauma. Again, this may represent a contractual lifetime challenge they have agreed to expose themselves to. However, a second tier of difficulty that might present itself to the dog lies in what it is that they are doing:

A dog may develop a conscience about their role in the 'sport' in which they are participating, either recognising that what they do is unnecessary from their perspective (since they are not hunting for their own food); or that they are complicit in harming innocents.

A retrieving dog will regularly be faced with a wounded bird, obviously suffering agonising pain. Although they may be trained to 'dispatch' them, these encounters take their toll. Any dog must, as part of its soul journey, come as near as possible to a 'no harm' philosophy, and their role in what they can easily perceive as a pointless slaughter, may cause great distress for them. Only feeding them immediately with what they have been involved in the killing of will assuage their guilt; and for obvious reasons, this seldom happens.

Eventually, for an older soul dog, their participation in the activity will only be acceptable if they bear great respect (or great fear) for their human; and even then, it might present them with the equivalent of a huge and troublesome moral dilemma every time their services are called upon.

Our second ever dog was an English Pointer, a 'gun dog', bought primarily because we believed our diffident incumbent would appreciate company.

In seeking her out we initially contacted a breeder in Scotland who (by his own account) bred dogs that were 'second to none'. When we told him that the dog would be a family pet, never used in blood sports of any kind, he was quite affronted. He expressed the opinion that people like us should not be allowed to own an animal that was so clearly only suitable for being a gun dog! Did we not realise that the instinct to 'point' was the result of centuries of selective breeding, and that to waste it on idiots like us would be a travesty?

Fortunately, we managed to find a less bombastic breeder and for the next thirteen years became the guardians of the sweetest and gentlest creature who only ever 'pointed' to one thing: A housefly on the window.

Not all 'gun dogs' want to be gun dogs. Some of them just want to be gentle and loved.

Do dogs enjoy performing in acts that are for our entertainment?

The fact that they are eager to please and malleable does not mean that they enjoy what we ask them to do for our amusement.

It is a comfortable convenience for us to believe that when we see dogs walking on their hind legs, jumping through hoops, dancing or performing (whatever) unusual acts, that they are enjoying it. Why? Because we are! We look at their apparently smiley faces and imagine that we see joy there. They're bringing us pleasure, so surely they must be taking pleasure in it?

Unfortunately, this is a misguided conceit and may be a case of what psychologists refer to as 'transference': the unconscious redirection of feelings from one person (i.e. ourselves) to another (the dog).

Dogs do enjoy keeping us happy. They do sense what brings us pleasure and try to repeat the actions that have caused it. And there are certainly physical activities they perform that entertain us that are immensely enjoyable for them, such as dog show favourites like obedience, agility and Flyball, which participants and spectators adore.

However, the physical aspects of what they are asked to do to entertain us are often unnatural and uncomfortable. Things that they are easily able to do (like walking around on their hind legs) are painful over sustained periods of time and may result in hip issues in later life. Brief moments of standing up at a kitchen counter, or begging for treats are nothing compared with what this type of act might require of them. It is not without reason that you will see your dog walking on all fours for 99.9% of the time.

Moreover, when they are used for commercial purposes and monetary gain in 'dog acts', the training behind what the audience sees, and the conditions within which they are kept, seldom match up to the lighthearted image that we would like to buy into, in the scene we see presented to us.

Since cash flow is dependent upon successful presentation, the training methods used on performing creatures are seldom based upon positive reinforcement techniques alone. Seemingly 'smiley' faces on the dogs are often relief on the part of the animal when they know that they have done what is expected of them, and will avoid reprimand; their apparent affection for their trainers is also symptomatic of the same.

As a society, when we are made aware of performing elephants or wild cats kept in captivity and made to do tricks, we are starting to feel revulsion at what is being done to them. Many countries are legislating to make animal acts of this kind illegal because of the cruelty inherent in them. Why then, do we imagine that the experience is any different for dogs?

There are limited exceptions, where the dogs genuinely do enjoy performing unusual feats. But these are extremely limited and tend only to occur where the dogs are household pets and living otherwise normal lives; where they are cherished and well cared for, and what they do is not the major source of income for their human.

Amusing for us? Perhaps. Amusing for them? Not in the slightest.

Why is it that some dog breeds are better for certain service roles than others?

In their origins, they're not, and it's only because of us that they appear to become so.

Notionally, from the qualities already ascribed to them in this book, you might well conclude that any dog can do anything. This would be an accurate conclusion; but only in the same way that any human can do anything. We all have endless potential, but our intentions for what we will experience and achieve in a lifetime are formed prior to incarnation. Even then, the circumstances of our lives may interfere with what we intended.

Correspondingly, what we see as predisposition of behaviour or apparent suitability for a role (as dictated by genetics or breed) in dogs, should not actually impact their ability to perform a service role as much as their pre-incarnation desires.

But the way in which we use certain types of dog, for certain types of work, has now developed into an association with breed characteristics.

Dogs that have service as an agenda item for their lifetime will therefore almost inevitably select a breed where there is a stronger likelihood of being for a role. They will also need to choose to incarnate in a litter wherein it may reasonably be foreseen that the puppies may be destined for a life of service.

If it needs to spend a lifetime as a service dog, coming as a German Shepherd presents infinitely more potential than a Chihuahua. If it wants to be a herding dog, a Border Collie is a safer bet than a Rottweiler etc.

Thus, we as humans have had far more impact in dictating the course of the lifetimes followed by dogs than we might imagine.

A Newfoundland, whose intelligence, strength and docile temperament make it suitable for almost any role; apart from this one who is best suited to being silly in the snow.

Chapter 10

RELATING TO HUMANS

"Dogs don't rationalize. They don't hold anything against a person. They don't see the outside of a human but the inside of a human."

Cesar Milan

If they live their lifetimes with more than one dog, why do humans always seem to get 'touched' by one dog more than the others?

The reasons are deep and may span many lifetimes.

People will often claim that they love or have loved all their pets in equal measure, but this is seldom true. It is almost an inevitability that we will love some more, and maybe not even feel very much at all for others. The chemistry that may exist between humans and their dogs is not a given by any means. Yet we will claim to view and treat all with equanimity, often through guilt or an unsettling feeling that we have in some way let down our canine companions if we do not wholeheartedly cherish their lives with us. What we don't necessarily consider is that dogs don't automatically feel that great about us either!

Although they are most certainly predisposed to approach their relationships with us with more openness, acceptance and goodwill than humans may be able to offer, their experiences with us can leave them every bit as disappointed with us as we are with them. More than this, they can end up in a home with people they are just plain incompatible with.

Humans may learn as much from people they do not 'gel' with as they do from those with whom they feel entirely comfortable. Frankly, if we did not understand what it was to dislike somebody, we could not relate to the experiencing of liking another. Like and dislike are merely examples of one the polarities we go through in life that enable us to understand all that is around us in context. They create a scale between the opposites, and the majority of our experiences with others are unlikely to be at the extremities.

It is no different for dogs. They experience their feelings for us somewhere along the scale, and they are not as inevitably predisposed to be slavishly devoted to us, as dog mythology would have it. If we were to take just the positive side of the like/dislike scale, it might incorporate an emotional response to another that included (in descending order of strength of feeling) these reactions, before it descended into the realms of dislike: WORSHIP; ADORE; CHERISH; LIKE; ADMIRE; RESPECT; APPRECIATE; ACCEPT. (The scale is intended to be illustrative and not definitive)

Naturally, those dogs that touch us most are the ones we experience at the extremity of the positive end of the scale. The reasons for us feeling this way about them have less to do with how we relate to them in this lifetime, than how we relate to them on an infinite basis.

If all goes to plan, at least some of the animals that come into our lives are soul family members. Our depth of feeling for them has developed over many lifetimes, and we become aware, at a subconscious level, that the dog that is with us shares a bond that has resulted from sharing multiple experiences, good, bad and indifferent. We sense the nurturing nature of their companionship, and we value them in a way we are often totally unable to express. Although in any one lifetime, we may encounter several members of our soul family as pets, it may be only one that we have formed a close, experienced based connection with. Other relationships may still be in their formative stages.

It is also possible that we bring into our lives those with whom we have no track record. Going through a lifetime without ever experiencing such an intimate connection with one of your pets may simply be because your animals are not part of our soul family, and were never intended to be with you. You may not experience the all-encompassing sensation of connectedness that being so 'touched' brings with it. But this is not to say that you may not still love them dearly.

The feeling is never a 'one way street' and is always reciprocated. When a human is touched by one particular canine (and vice versa), such a pet is often described as a 'heart dog'; although even this does not sum up the depth of feeling engendered. Unfortunately, the link carries with it a devastating sense of loss when one dies. Unlike the more artificial 'bonding' response described earlier, it is not a connection that is there for the sake of learning and the practice of mastery. It is a more genuine connection, and precisely because of that, it may more easily be lived with. On reflection, the one left behind who goes through the pain of the loss, may also be innately aware that they will reconnect with the one that has touched them. Soon.

A connection with a 'heart dog' is never lost.

To deny that we get touched by some pets more than others is an almost disingenuous. Sadly, the self-deception dishonours those who we did most connect with, and it in no way belittles those with whom we were not as enrapt. Perhaps acknowledging it creates the fear that we may never experience their like again? Some foreswear dog guardianship when they lose their 'heart dog' because they are afraid of not being able to get as much from another relationship, denying themselves the opportunity to forge relationships with other soul family members.

Personally, having shared my life with sixty-one dogs to date, I am quite comfortable revealing that there are only three or four that I have worshipped, many more I have adored, and several I have merely cherished; although I struggle to think of any that I have only liked. I am also sensitive enough to the dog's reactions to be able to tell that they classify me too. And that's fine.

What do dogs think of the names we give them?

Often, they will be perfectly happy with them. But occasionally, not a lot.

A dog will very quickly learn to recognise the sound of a given name and respond to it, but because of the vibrational qualities of that name, it may or may not like that it is used to address them.

Some names can completely fail to match with any aspect of the dog's true names, and so when the dog is spoken to using that sound as a prefix, although the dog has learned to respond, the name (at best) leaves the dog feeling lackadaisical or ambivalent about the need to respond. It simply feels no connection with it.

In the worst-case scenario, it experiences the equivalent of fingernails being dragged across a chalkboard, and although it is relatively rare for it to be quite this bad, carelessness at choosing a dog's name *can* have this much of a negative impact upon them.

I consider it highly unlikely that anyone who has bought this book would have been so thoughtless in their choice of monikers, but there are some colossally stupid names that people give their dogs, without a second thought to the vibration the name or the idea behind carries with it.

The unseen vibrational impact of a name may be uncomfortable for a dog, but it can also do damage them at a rather more obvious practical level. A name can create an expectation about character and temperament, and cause behaviours towards them to alter.

Nowhere is this more so the case than for ill-named rescue dogs.

I wrote a blog on our *Some Dogs Are Angels* website, about the effect of these names, an extract from which is below.

A name can present a quite significant problem for those unfortunates in rescue whose monikers are stupid and inappropriate, to the point where they border on damaging. All too regularly I find myself reflecting that some unfortunates must have been named by severely misguided individuals. It is not merely a cliché to find dogs called Fido, Pooch, Butch, Doggie or Spot. They exist in abundance, and they are the harmless ones. Consider the following, all of which I have come across. Bruiser, Scab, Monster, Thug, Devil, Beast, Wretch, Tyrant, Demon, El Diablo, Punisher, Ugli, Cujo. The list goes on... Perhaps the mindlessness that went into their naming was considered to be humorous by their one-time people, but these names now stand as hideous brandings and indictments upon their character that these poor souls have to live down.

So why, you may well ask, do the rescues simply not rename their charges? Well, that's a good point. You would think it common sense, wouldn't you? Yet I still see these stupid (and frankly awful) names on a regular basis. I always take it to imply a dearth of sensitivity on the part of the rescue staff. In fairness, more often than not these 'bad' names crop up in the urban shelters of large conurbations where the staff may well be there for a job alone, not because they love animals and want to help them. I KNOW that these individuals exist. But perhaps I'm being unkind. Perhaps the staff just feel that it would be wrong to change the name of the dog when it's used to being called in that way and responds to the moniker, however off putting it may be from the average person's human perspective. Or maybe the staff just don't realise that for humans, a name carries with it an implication about the character of the being behind the title.

Your second supposition may well be that any right thinking prospective dog person would not be put off by the ghastliness of the name. After all, they can simply change it, and therefore, it isn't really an issue. And of course, that's true. But ask yourself this simple question. Faced with two dogs of undetermined origin, similarly attractive in appearance and reported temperament, one called Bevan and the other called Destroyer. Which one would you be inclined to be more interested in? Be honest!

Now do you see the problem?

I recently came across two dogs with the appalling names 'Bugger' and 'Crappy'. Apparently, their respective owners did claim to like the dogs.

Can you hear the chalkboard? The dogs surely can.

Do dogs know when people don't like them?

Most definitely!

Although it may surface as distaste, or even revulsion, dislike of dogs often originates in humans as fear. Whatever the symptom, dogs can spot the reaction easily, since it affects the vibration of the individual in question. The response provoked in the dog is often one of curiosity, since they will be unable to comprehend what it is that they have done to cause such apparent offence. They will usually cope with this by attempting to connect with that person approaching them, sniffing them, and inadvertently, generally exacerbating the situation.

At the root of this will be an innate recognition that to eschew contact with other species is a denial of our necessary coexistence with a variety of beings. The dog is trying to put things right. The human has lessons they need to learn!

I was once returning from leading a hike to the Plain of Six Glaciers at Lake Louise, Alberta. We had brought several of our dogs along, and various members of the party were walking (or more accurately, being dragged by) different dogs.

The party included two young girls and their parents, and they had chosen to walk a dog along the final stretch of the journey, which is most populated with tourists beginning the full hike, or those simply enjoying the lake shores.

Many of the oncoming hikers were enthused by the girls with their charge and stopped to chat, pet or even photograph the dog. So, the girls were totally bemused when coming the other way was a family of Middle Eastern origin, who were seemingly horrified at the approaching dog.

Watching from some distance behind, I saw the father literally offer himself as a shield between himself and his family, wildly shouting in whatever language he spoke, and making it abundantly clear that he neither liked nor valued dogs!

What I was fully aware of, but the girls were not, was that traditionally in Islam, dogs are seen as impure, and Muslims should make no contact with them.

I didn't feel like respecting their beliefs that day, and made no intervention in what transpired.

The dog (one of our Huskies) became immediately fixated with making physical contact with the man and his family, and although the girls managed to restrain him (with a little help from their own father), the Muslim father was clearly deeply upset and made lots of noise, drawing lots of attention to himself and his family group.

I am bad. I thought it was funny.

I also felt that having chosen to bring himself and his family to a country with a very different cultural heritage, that maybe he should respect Canadian traditions and accept dogs, at least for the duration.

Later I pondered the impact of religious beliefs upon the progression of our souls, and was struck with the awareness that they seldom help.

An unlikeable dog? I don't think so!

How do I know what name to give my dog?

Listen carefully and you'll hear it.

Unfortunately, it can be the case that custodians become attached to a name long before they examine how apt the name might be for the dog.

Beings of the etheric will go to considerable lengths to communicate the name of a dog (with the same amount of enthusiasm as they will for a human baby, for reasons you may have grasped already).

All that is required is an open mind and receptivity to ideas that appear to arrive totally spontaneously. We are all totally capable of hearing the messages that are delivered from the etheric because we all retain our (crown) chakra link to it. We just don't necessarily recognise them for what they are.

Listen carefully, and you might just hear a name.

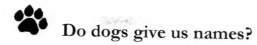 ## Do dogs give us names?

Yes, but not necessarily ones you'd recognise as names.

Dogs do not name anything other than one another, and do not recognise the need for naming just for the sake of giving a moniker. Instead their 'names' for things are basically descriptors of the way they perceive a thing at a conceptual level, and this includes people.

Although they are well equipped to perceive a person's true vibrational name, for them it does not act as an appropriate descriptor of their experience of that person, and so they do not use our 'real' names, or the ones they are aware others use when addressing us.

What they call us are summaries of how they view us or feel about us. They are conceptual titles which, because they are never actually spoken, do not require a single word to encapsulate them. The 'names' remain in their minds as a notion of a person, encompassing a range of characteristics which they perceive in an individual. Thus, they are very difficult to describe.

The nearest parallel that may be offered is with Native American names that describe the characteristics that may have been observed in the individual. Whilst it is immensely unlikely that any reader will have earned the moniker 'Dances with Wolves', a revered person might have a name that would go something like 'Cherished one who loves and provides for me'. But this would all be expressed in conceptual terms, rather than the specific words that would comprise language. As much as anything, the given name would be the unique feeling about someone that defined them, from the dog's perspective.

Dogs do not give us our given descriptions immediately. They wait to understand the relationship we have with them, and for a while, the name will be organic, changing as new facets are added to it and others subtracted. With puppies one may almost see their perceptions evolving, reflected in their attitude towards us, and the surprise they register if we are then inconsistent with the perception they were evolving. What we observe as a puppy's 'hurt' when it is reprimanded is their struggle to cope with new information about their person that contradicts the perception they had been creating.

A dog will almost always look for the good in their person and if they experience negative contradictions, they will quickly overcome the shock and continue to focus upon the good, seeking to banish the anomaly and return to consistency as soon as possible.

However, if they are only able to pick up on the negative aspects of us, they will not approach us with 'rose tinted spectacles' or naivety. They just prefer to give us the benefit of the doubt.

There will come a point when, in a dog's judgement, there is sufficient consistency in their person's behaviour for the growth of the name to be fixed, and this is how they will think of them thereafter. Positive or negative, it will take considerable repetitive action on the person's part to shift the perception and effectively change the dog's name for them.

In implication and action, this means that they will then forgive their humans any number of sins against them; and of course, this includes rank cruelty. A dog may be sorely abused by its person, yet still love them dearly for how it believes they are. This is an aspect of the 'living in the moment' phenomenon we have come to associate dogs with. The 'name' of their person stays with them in the moment, and there must be a huge number of moments to displace it once it has been fixed.

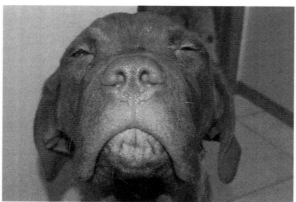

I'm deciding what to call you, right now…

Why do dogs lick people?

For all sorts of reasons. Well, at least four anyway.

There are four reasons why you may find yourself being treated to a dog's (possibly) slobbery wet tongue. Since it could be any one of them, these are in no particular order.

1. Licking does not actually allow a dog to taste a person. They do have taste buds, but since they are relatively unsophisticated, getting a taste of the flavour of somebody does not add to their perception of that person. It does allow them to explore the texture of skin with more sensitivity than the rough pads on their feet allow, giving a better understanding of a person.

2. Perspiration inevitably brings salt to the surface of a person's skin. Dogs find this appealing because it is one of the tastes more easily appreciated by their taste buds. They may decide to lick somebody just to remove the salt and enjoy a rare flavour.

3. When one dog perceives an injury in another, it will often lick the place where the wound is or was. The enzymes present in their saliva can assist in healing an open wound. If it has healed, a dog may still lick the spot where it was because they perceive a weakness in the auric field and they're attempting to restore it.

   Since dogs are also capable of perceiving health issues that are invisible to the human eye (e.g. cancer or tumours) they may lick where the invisible issue is manifesting itself in another dog. They are unlikely to lick a human for such a serious reason, but may well wish to lick a scratch or even a bruise.

4. Amongst their own species, licking is a way of demonstrating deference and fealty. Licking around the mouth of fellow pack members who are higher in the pack order is common. They also do this to dogs who they like and have respect for. If they do it to humans, it's the nearest thing we get to being stroked by them.

Being licked by a dog may not always be a welcome thing. We are subjected to a great deal of licking during a day, most of which is affection based. Some of the more slobbery dogs (particularly the St Bernards and the Newfoundland) can leave us running to the nearest tap when they're done.

Worse still, a while back I broke my hand quite badly, but wasn't quite sure what I'd done. It was a few days before I went and had it put in a cast. However, the dogs knew instantly what I'd done and were quite prepared to subject me to their brand of healing, constantly.

They would quite literally wait and take it in turns to try and lick my hand. Perhaps in response to the severity of the injury, they did this quite forcefully and it was not a pleasant experience! Since I was not prepared to be a willing participant in their ministrations, they would sneak up on me from behind and I would suddenly and painfully find a long tongue jiggling around the bones in my hand.

Three months later when the cast finally came off, their enthusiasm was unabated. I was treated to endless dog tongue physiotherapy. Unfortunately, two weeks later my hand was head butted by a well-meaning Neapolitan Mastiff. The whole process began all over again.

Being licked is almost like an occupational habit when you share your life with dogs.

What is the best way to train a dog?

The methods used by its canine parents are undoubtedly the most effective, but should not be adopted by humans.

To understand the answer to this question properly, it is first necessary to understand *precisely* what we mean when we talk about 'training' a dog.

- Dog training is about establishing behavioural expectations in the dog's mind to have them obey commands. It seeks to both impart and ingrain an awareness of how they are required to perform by their person in response to key commands.

- The anticipated outcome of training is that the dog will adhere to the commands given, without question.

- It should not be confused with a broader definition of training wherein skills are being imparted that the recipient may then exercise their freewill over, in choosing whether to apply.

However, as anyone who had attended a dog training class will know, the experience is one wherein the dog's person is trained to use methods intended to induce the dog to comply with their wishes. In other words, the human is trained, not the dog.

The dog merely learns to understand the instructions its person wishes it to comply with, and does not acquire new skills per se.

But despite the intention of the training, the dog's obedience is still a matter of choice on their part, which is in turn dependent on the desire of the animal to keep their human happy.

As with so many aspects of dog custodianship, obeisance potentially involves a great deal of compromise on the part of the dog. It is the one who must constantly subjugate its will. We seldom expect this of other pet animals such as a cat, whose willing and immediate acquiesce to our desires is not something that we would reasonably expect!

It is perhaps the apparently biddable nature of dogs that makes them so appealing to us, and so popular as pets. For many years dogs have consistently dominated the ratings for pet popularity in North America.

However, the mythology of a dog has created expectations which (in this case) belie their capacity for independent thought and action. There is a consequent assumption about exactly how compliant a dog will naturally be, and an anticipation of their subservience may all too easily cause us to disregard their intellect and right to choose.

Some may be naturally obedient without training.

Humans all too easily become frustrated if their dogs are not as willing to obey as they would wish. Historically this has engendered the use of force as a means of ensuring adherence to the rules that humans set. This is primarily because it is the quickest and easiest method of gaining compliance. Training techniques have featured varying levels of fear, even to the point of crushing freewill. And this may still be observed today as an element utilised in the training of dogs used for sport, or in certain industries where dogs are used, and absolute adherence to command is required.

Over time techniques have changed and evolved in line with societal beliefs about what is appropriate, every bit as much as in response to what is discovered to be effective. Brute force and dominance have gradually given way to kinder methods, and this is something we should surely be thankful for. The positive reinforcement techniques now favoured are a far pleasanter option for both dog and guardian to experience, since harsher alternatives can cause stress on both sides; and when used to the extreme, result in great hardship for the dog.

Yet if we were to contrast the current vogue methodology for exerting control pets, we would find it curiously different from the way in which they exert authority and discipline over one another. The canine technique for imparting requirements of one another and ensuring learning transfer is swift, and often brutal. It leaves those involved with no uncertainty over where they stand and what are the expectations of them. It is applied clearly and consistently and appears to do little damage. It requires no further correction if established rules are complied with.

It may be observed that dogs, when part of a family group or pack certainly use instantaneous (limited) physical reprimand as a method of training. Thus, a puppy that is with its family unit for the eight weeks prescribed by most breeders, will have developed the expectation of short, sharp, yet loving action being taken to clarify what is required of it; followed by an immediate restoration of its former affectionate treatment. And this, for a dog, would seem to constitute the best method of training.

However, if you interpret this as advocacy for abandoning positive reinforcement, please do not. We as humans, in size, strength and temperament are quite unlike dogs. Our use of physical reprimand can (and has historically) gone far beyond what is necessary, and we are almost certainly unable to deliver it with the same loving kindness that underpins what dogs do to each other, if only because what they would perceive from our vibration would be a poor match to what was experienced from their parents and siblings.

Whenever a dog joins a new home and moves from one set of circumstances to another, it only has the norms of its previous environment to rely upon to inform its behaviour. Puppies face enormous difficulty from not knowing what is required of them, particularly when faced with suddenly becoming an only dog. Although they learn quickly, humans often lack the tolerance to cope with their uncertainty, already setting their expectations of the dog way too high. Positive reinforcement by guardians is certainly the kindest way to help dogs adapt, and makes it easier for them to decide to accept the will of their person over their own needs and desires.

Difficulties tend to arise where no guidance is given, since this leaves the dog in a state of confusion. Dogs *do* welcome clarity and evidence that somebody is the alpha in charge. To make their lives easier, this very important need should be understood and factored into the awareness of all those who take dogs into their homes, either as puppies or as older dogs.

It is interesting to note that although it is not possible to categorically prove that dogs are any better trained now than they were 50 years ago, current thinking about method may be observed to be very much in line with our view of ourselves as becoming progressively enlightened.

As society, perhaps of necessity, seeks to regard itself (if not actually become) a kinder, more caring place, those beings on the closer peripheral edge of human relations, like dogs, are beginning to reap the benefit; whereas those on the outer rim become progressively alienated from our supposedly more compassionate auspices, and suffer more. Witness the comparison of the improved lot of pets with the rapid decline in the treatment of what we regard as merely 'food animals'. Their lives become increasingly miserable as farming methods become more efficient.

Why do dogs obey what we say (for the most part)?

Obeying commands has nothing to do with a dog's comprehension of the reasoning behind a command. It is a simple matter of their response to positive or negative motivation.

A dog is a very practical creature that quickly learns there may be benefits attached in doing what it is told. If it is rewarded for obeying, it will repeat the behaviour in the hope or expectation of the reward being repeated. Depending upon what command it is obeying, the act itself may be intrinsically rewarding, such a chasing a ball in response to a "Fetch" command, or participating in an agility course.

We should not assume that being 'rewarded' means being given food. Payback may come from having an experience that is rewarding for the dog. Whilst most dogs assuredly do have a high food motivation, a dog can achieve satisfaction from demonstrating that it has learned what its person has asked of it (it is showing off its ability to understand them); or be just be happy because it is keeping its person happy.

However, this answer would be incomplete without reference to more negative reasons for responding to commands. A dog can also learn to be fearful, and do as it is told because it has learned of the unpleasant consequences of not performing in accordance with its person's wishes.

Precisely why they choose to obey is largely the product of what type of training methodology has been employed with them.

The choice of whether or not to obey might be a simple decision of what's convenient in the moment...

Do dogs enjoy learning?

It depends upon what type of learning is meant.

We tend to assume that when we train dogs, it is inherently enjoyable for them. Yet we are not giving them the knowledge or wherewithal to do anything they are not already quite capable of doing by themselves. 'Sit', 'heel' and 'down', hardly provide the opportunities for the type of personal growth that learning the piano might for a human! What we 'teach' them is really for our benefit, not theirs. Their supposed 'learning' is limited to understanding how to respond to what we want, and precious little that adds value to them. It should be acknowledged that another phrasing of the question (in the way it was intended), could be "Do dogs enjoy subjugating their will to ours, for the sake of carrying out our commands?"

For the average dog, pleasure may be derived from the satisfaction that they are smart enough to understand what we want, and fulfilment of their desire to keep us happy. But for the caring guardian, this begs the question: 'What *do* dogs enjoy learning?'

It would be unusual for most people to recognise that there is a learning imperative present in all beings, not necessarily for skills or knowledge, but for understanding. It gives their lives purpose and meaning. We feel it in ourselves, and actively seek out answers to the 'big' questions. Yet in our regard for ourselves as the pre-eminent, and therefore most important/significant lifeforms on the planet, we ignore this in 'lesser' beings.

Learning comes in many forms. For a dog, their self-determined criteria for growth involves a myriad of experiences, encompassing encounters, relationships, exploration, and differing environments, as well as simply existing. It is a less sophisticated array of learning than we may undertake, but is no less valid for that. Everything is relative. Their learning will be experiential, and principally self-guided, occurring naturally and spontaneously. However, we unconsciously play our part in many aspects of inter-species learning, and may orchestrate events in our dogs' lives so that more opportunities for experience arise.

Often, what we interpret as their simple enthusiasm for a walk or a ride in the car, is something far more meaningful for a dog. It is a chance to embark upon a learning opportunity that they will relish, irrespective of whether anything new occurs. They realise that every experience has the potential to be enjoyable and developmental, and will be greeted with an accordingly high level of anticipation. Dogs recognise that learning comes from all experiences, good or bad. This allows them a certain fearlessness and abandon in their approach to life, that we can seldom match. It also means that in many cases, they may recover quickly when something unfortunate happens to them, leaving them relatively untroubled by their past. (Although there are, of course, exceptions.)

A human training class for dogs.

A lack of exposure to the new and interesting can lead to frustration and boredom. Although dogs certainly value routine and certainty, the thrill of exposure to the unknown, (particularly the outdoors, which is their natural habitat) overcomes the possibly conservative nature of most. The more we are able to provide for this, the more a dog will learn and the more it will enjoy its life.

It is ironic that our role as pet guardians offers dogs both the potential for learning, and a block to their growth. Just by living their lives with us, they might have their opportunities for experience severely curtailed as a direct result of our actions.

Are dogs just the product of the way they are raised by their people?

This requires a circumstantially dependent (and somewhat complex) answer...

In the canine equivalent of the 'nature vs. nurture' debate, those defending dogs branded 'vicious' or 'dangerous' (simply because of their breed), frequently use the argument that a dog's temperament is an issue of the way it is raised. It's a sympathetic argument, but not necessarily wholly accurate.

A dog, just like a human, incarnates with a specific profile for the character or persona it intends to 'inhabit' during a lifetime. That persona, which envelops the true essence of what that individual is, is referred to as 'the ego' in humans. It should come as no surprise that dogs have egos too!

The ego gives us a mask-like perspective through which we view the world around us; and it also impacts upon the way others see us. In choosing it, we decide upon the elements of emotional response we wish to explore or experiment with mastering/overcoming, during a lifetime.

Any aspect or characteristic of our ego, positive or negative, may be encouraged or exacerbated, intentionally or accidentally, by those around us, such as a dog's people, or a child's parents.

In different lifetimes, dogs, like us, experiment with many different types of ego based personality. Some will be what we would think of as generally 'good', whilst others are 'bad'. Either is valid, and both are necessary. 'Experimenting' with aspects of personality means experiencing the effects and repercussions ego based actions bring about (which may take many lifetimes); and then mastering the choices and behaviours that are the causes and effects of them (which may take many more).

If a dog arrives in the home it is meant to be in, its people will naturally, as a result of agreements made before incarnation, help the desired traits rise to the fore in the dog's character. To this extent, they may be nurturing either positive or negative, and may appear to be responsible for how the dog 'turns out'. However, this is what has been agreed between them, and the behaviours and attributes exhibited by the dog are part of the persona it has arrived with. The humans merely assist in drawing it out, and the dog is not really the product of the way it is raised at all.

If a dog arrives in a home or with people it was never intended to be with, there may be a mismatch between the dog's intentions and the circumstances in which it finds itself. The nurturing of its people may suppress the intended traits of its nature, positive or negative, or bring out other aspects of being that were not part of its envisioned learning. In this case, the dog may become the product of the way it has been raised; although if it is an older soul, its strength of character may cause it to tread its own positive path, irrespective of its people.

All this said, we assume (because of the accepted roles of responsibility) that the learning in a situation flows from the one in the position of greater control; but this is by no means always the case. A dog may arrive with a brief to exhibit certain behaviours or attitudes, specifically so that the custodian is forced to deal with them. In other words, the dog has intentionally come with issues, for their person's benefit, and the person, at least for the duration of the dog's lifetime, can become the product of the way they respond to the dog...

Who's the product of who?

What can we learn from dogs?

In general terms, lots. In specific terms, it depends upon the individual.

The typical dog-human relationship has evolved to be one of unusually intimate companionship, rather than wary co-existence. It mirrors an experience that some naturalists suggest we may once have shared with all species of the planet.

Although the idea of harmonious living alongside non-human beings is not something at the forefront of most of our minds, having a pet in the house provides us with the opportunity to catch a glimpse of the type of inter-species rapport that is possible. Most importantly, it is one that can:

- Prevent us from disappearing into our own beliefs about the innate supremacy of humanity.
- Open us up to a more compassionate outlook upon other species.
- Give us a connection with the natural world that is increasingly lost to so many.
- Remind us of our indissoluble connection to other species.
- Give us practical experience of the nature of our interdependence with other beings.

All this is key learning for humans, because it can change our perspective on all things, altering the way we see the world around us, and notionally focusing our attention upon the need to demonstrate tolerance, kindness, understanding, compassion, forbearance, selflessness, patience and unconditional acceptance.

(Note that most of this inter-species learning may be simplistically explained as taking actions, or utilising behaviours requiring 'the need to do more of' or 'the need to do less of'.)

If we don't allow ourselves close animal connections of some sort, we risk missing out, not only the opportunity for understanding them (and maybe ourselves) a little bit better, but also the chance to convert the wisdom this connection can bring, into positive personal actions. Of course, dogs are merely one type of creature that may provide such an opportunity; although because of the way they are (being essentially trusting and loving towards us), they are often our easiest option.

Unfortunately, simply having a dog in the house does not, by itself, mean that we automatically adopt or even understand whatever learning can come our way. The experience of intimately co-existing with a pet can be valuable and impactful, but taking on board the erudition in a way that produces lasting effects often requires observation, consideration and active reflection on our part.

Not everybody is ready for this. It might not be the right lifetime for them to make the leap of understanding. Whereas as some people will 'get it' with ease, many more will miss the point entirely, and pursue pet custodianship as if it were the expected thing to do, creating inconvenience in their lives, rather than benefit.

This is mainly because what has been discussed so far is a series of generic learning points. A dog's presence may provide innumerable sub-levels of learning that relate exclusively to their person's individual needs. These may range from the highly complex to the relatively simple, but will typically include the need to incorporate learning relating to aspects of attitude and behaviour.

From this, it may correctly be concluded that people *intend* to get the dogs they need for their learning. The animals themselves will have committed to providing their people with the opportunities and challenges they desired before incarnating, and if they manage to get to the right place, this is what they will do.

Many people will share their lives with numerous dogs in a single lifetime. The average custodian will typically invite three or four dogs into their home across the span of their adult years; more if their parent' dogs are included. If a pre-defined learning relationship exists, each and every one of those canines may have been intended to come primed with the same specific learning objectives to work on with their guardian, on the assumption that their predecessor might be unsuccessful in their teaching efforts.

Some dogs seem to exude calm and sagacity. Or is it just superiority?

However, it is not automatically the case that all (or any) of these dogs have learning contracts with their person, because the dogs may not be the ones intended to come to that individual (which as we have already seen, is a reasonably strong likelihood). In this case, only more generic learning is possible.

It may also be that the learning has already been successfully achieved by the person from a previous canine. Consequently, repetition of the learning is unnecessary, and the dog's agenda, or even the incarnating dog itself, may change.

It is of course possible that the human has no learning to get from the dog at all, and that the canines that they encounter during their lifetime are there to learn and benefit from being with them, rather than vice-versa.

That said, in most situations, the learning is a two-way street, and although the challenges facing human and dog may bear no resemblance to one another, they are still mutually interdependent.

What do dogs expect from humans?

If deeply embedded (and most likely forgotten) contractual commitments are set aside, a dog will have very few expectations of a human, at least not in the sense that they will feel they are owed anything.

Unlike many humans are apt to do, dogs seldom develop a sense of entitlement. Their expectations are created from their experiences, slanted heavily in favour of a belief in the innate goodness of humans.

It is one of the more curious facets of their being that they come with a predisposition to view the world around them as wholly positive and benign. It is only after multiple and repeated experiences to the contrary that they may find reason to doubt this most base of their expectations. And even then, a more negative way of thinking may quickly and easily be healed. It is one of the primary reasons why we assume that dogs live in the moment and can forgive anything. Whilst this is not strictly accurate, it is not far too from the truth.

You may have come across the phrase:

"TRY TO BE THE PERSON YOUR DOG THINKS YOU ARE"

Few of us could live up to their image of us, and there are still vast numbers amongst the population who shame our race in the way we regard and treat the beings around us.

A dog's expectations of us are not unreasonable because their acceptance of us is based upon what they recognise as the essence of our being. This may be no more than the potential that exists within each one of us, and may be something we do not even recognise in ourselves.

I am replete with stories of dogs that heartbreakingly refuse to alter their positive expectations of humans.

We were, all too briefly, the guardians of a wonderful old dog who had spent his entire life chained to a deck, uncared for and ignored by an alcoholic custodian. Perhaps through the forgetfulness of drink induced stupor, he and his similarly chained brother were systematically and slowly starved. His brother's rotting carcass finally caused neighbours to alert animal services, and barely surviving, he was taken to a humane society. There he languished for two years of painfully slow recovery before being taken in by a breed rescue group.

When he came to us another year later he was seemingly physically restored. But the starvation had taken a merciless toll upon his physical body, and we lost him after only six months. He suffered complete systematic breakdown.

Yet from the moment we collected him, he offered nothing but love and total acceptance. Having spent thirteen years either chained or caged, and despite harsh and brutal treatment, his love for life was not diminished one iota. He was supremely gentle and forgiving and he adored everybody he met.

Despite a lifetime of abuse, he never stopped loving.

Why do dogs accept so much abuse from humans?

It may be more than a simple matter of having no choice.

It is a sad fact of life that millions of dogs live torturous lifetimes where they are sorely abused by the humans they live alongside. Such instances are not limited to those with whom the dogs have no connection. Callous acts of cruelty may be perpetrated by their loved custodians, and the dogs will simply accept their lot.

On a simplistic level, dogs may be seen to have little choice but to accept the grievous harms that are done to them. Explained crudely, dependence upon humans for food and shelter may mean that they must suffer in silence or lose their livelihood.

The real reasons are somewhat more complex: Quite apart from the aspects of suffering that all beings must experience as part of their soul's journey, a great deal of the abuse that is meted out to dogs has been contractually agreed upon by both the abuser and the abused.

The permutations of the flow of learning are many and complex, but a typical example may be that the human is attempting to do no harm, and the animal has agreed to accept whatever the human dishes out to assist them in their learning.

In viewing their human, a dog will only see the positive qualities that it has endowed them with and are utilised in the name they use for that person. (You might want to refresh your memory on this by going back to the section on naming.)

Tragically, if the human falls short of their image, the dog's desperate desire for their person to become what they once were will even cause them to deny how the individual has become.

Only a dog that has known nothing but unfettered cruelty will become resentful of their mistreatment.

What do dogs see when they look at us?

Something that would appear perfectly normal to them, but very strange to us.

As you may have already concluded from earlier sections, a dog's use of synesthesia in their perception not only allows them to see a different spectrum of colour, but also an alternate view of what we look like, that incorporates our auric field and vibrational output.

Because of this, the human form they observe appears somewhat larger than we would see and contains both an inner fixed area (our body) and an outer fluid area (aura).

Changes in our emotional state register in the fluidity, and our physical wellbeing is constantly readable (if they have observed enough to enable them to draw conclusions about what is seen). The auric field may expand and contract, and bursts of energy somewhat like solar flares may occasionally burst from our surface, denoting unusual highs of positive emotional experience, or anger. (NB. These are not the same as those referred to earlier in relation to epileptic fits, which only come from the head.)

We also appear a great deal more colourful to them than we do to ourselves. The auric field is already colourful, and may incorporate many different hues at different points within its perimeter.

Moreover, our state of being will cause changes to occur in the visible spectrum, somewhat like a colour changing lamp. Transformations may be slow and almost imperceptible, or instantaneous.

Whilst the colours are somewhat muted (and certainly not primary) you would imagine that we would present an interesting spectacle for them.

But of course, it is all very ordinary for them and we are nothing special!

Can dogs interpret human body language?

Up to a point, but only if they're interested enough to study us first.

We humans can understand and interpret body language with consummate ease. From our earliest childhood days, our experiences and observations allow us to understand the nuances and subtleties of almost every aspect of the eyes, facial expressions, hand gestures, movement and posture. We don't have to study it. We learn it at an almost instinctive level, and our ability to read others is probably a lot better than even we realise.

Of course, we're most expert with people we know and see on a regular basis, and we may even share a 'mirroring' of physical responses with those we are highly attuned with.

Yet if we turn our attentions to another species, we flounder. This is because we have likely had neither the time, interest or exposure to be able to correctly assess what we see in their physical actions. But if we share our lives with them and have enough interest to be observers of their movement and form, it does not take too long before we may at least conjecture as to what we are seeing. Over an extended period of time, and with some focus, we can learn to have a full appreciation of their unique expressions and bodily movements.

It's no different for dogs when dealing with us. They are great at inferring meanings that they see in one another, but our physicality does not map out against theirs, so there are few parallels to be drawn. Only after careful study will your dog become aware of what it means if you clasp your hand to your mouth; if you yawn; if you wag a finger at them, or any one of the other dozens of gestures you unwittingly telegraph your thoughts via, every single day.

Unlike us, dogs have a strong incentive for learning about the peculiarities of the non-canines they share their lives with. Their ability to interpret us might result in reward, be that food, praise, petting; or in an unfortunate number of cases, relief from violence and persecution.

And they are quick studies. The advantage of being able to see energy fields and understand vibrational output is a great benefit to making sense of flailing arms, raised eyebrows or furrowed foreheads.

Not every dog will bother though. Engagement is based upon desire or need and there must be a motivation to begin the learning process in the first place. An uninterested dog that can see no benefit will not trouble themselves with endless study of their people. But if they feel that way, it's usually our own fault.

Instances of natural overlap in our non-verbal communications are virtually non-existent. But occasionally, if we look hard enough, we may see enough in what they do to emulate them. If we play it back to them, it may aid our communications. Baring your teeth is an obvious example (but not too useful), and others may be way too subtle, or even specific to individual dogs to be of value. Nonetheless, your dog is most likely pursuing 'kinesics' (the study of body language) so that they may have a better rapport with you; and it's probably worth reciprocating!

In observing one of our dogs, a Husky, I noticed that occasionally she would look at me and slightly lift her chin, before bringing it sharply down again. It struck me as being like the human gesture of giving a slight nod to another person as a form of acknowledgement. The action was repeated on several occasions, usually when I was watching the TV and she looked up at me from her slumbers, whilst some distance away.

Then one time, I did it back.

To my surprise, she repeated the movement again, then lay back in her prone position, apparently satisfied.

From that time onwards, we have exchanged the gesture on countless occasions. Sometimes I initiate it, and sometimes she does. It's not exactly a deep and meaningful piece of connecting, but I have the distinct impression it means something to her, and at the very least, I do believe we are communicating at a body language level.

Why do dogs feel the need to jump up at people, and is it wrong to let them?

The desire to connect and show emotion makes for a powerful motivator, but not necessarily a welcome one!

When a dog jumps up at you (and you're not a burglar or escaped convict they're trying to grab a hold of) it's a sure sign that they want to engage with you.

If you haven't realised by now, dogs are quite tactile creatures, if only out of necessity. Try seeing yourself from their perspective, and you will realise that (in most cases) you are a giant to your pet. This doesn't make you any less lovable, but it does mean that forming a connection that they regard as tangible, is challenging. They struggle to communicate with us, because we don't know how to listen to them, so they need to get physical. What could be more effective than jumping up and literally trying to get 'in your face'? They're trying to demonstrate that despite being small, they're significant.

A lot of the need for this literal 'facetime' has to do with the dog's standard canine greeting, which involves licking around another's mouth. This is a gesture both of deference and affection. But other jumping can be about the desire to communicate joy, love, pleasure, excitement or simple curiosity. They want to be close to you and many are just seeking eye contact or acknowledgement of their presence.

The desire to do this may be spontaneous, or it may be prompted by a verbal or visual cue that the dog learns. A gesture or a tone of voice can be an active indicator that a person *wants* them to jump up, at least in their belief. This is something that can only be learned from their people, so we may be quite culpable in our dog's jumping up.

Unfortunately, such unabashed desire for creating a link is not always restricted to those whom they know. A general bonhomie and love of life - all life - can cause the friendlier of dogs to want to jump up at anybody and everybody.

Dogs that repeatedly jump up, irrespective of any disincentives offered by humans, are as likely to be desperate in their desire to connect as they are to be stubborn. Humans can be plain fascinating for them, and it is something of a compliment if dogs want to get to know you in this way. Of course, some may just be 'trying it on', and seeing if they can force you to pay them attention. Occasionally, this evolves into a desire to dominate somebody who is not a part of their pack. Telling which behaviour is which may be tricky, and to dismiss it all as 'controlling' would be wrong.

When a dog jumps up at someone they don't know, it can be shocking and off-putting for the human. It may be all too easy to misinterpret good nature for aggression, or distinguish between aggression and enthusiasm. Some countries have even taken the outlandishly extreme measure of enacting legislation to give rights of legal action against the custodians of dogs that jump up at them, irrespective of the nature of the approach. Unfortunately, this may even result in the dog being destroyed.

So, whilst many guardians will be at least partially accepting, or even embrace (figuratively and literally) their dogs desire to demonstrate their sentiments, how to stop them doing it on a totally random basis presents a problem. If they are allowed to do it you, in their mind it will be OK to do it to whomsoever takes their fancy.

In many respects, although it should be highly flattering that a dog thinks we're worth the effort of this type of display, the 'rightness' or 'wrongness' of allowing it to continue is very much a matter for personal tolerance. And increasingly, preparedness to accept the consequences of highly damaging legal repercussions.

Most of our pack are classified as 'giant breed dogs', and the rest are 'large', with just a few 'mediums.' The jumping up thing is therefore not something we encourage, since it's all too easy to be knocked flying. We're not too bothered about visitors being surprised or upset, since everybody who comes to our house is very well briefed about what they will face. (We have one that will literally try to sit on the head of any newcomer!)

Recently, some have developed the idea that it's a status thing to jump up at me, the pack leader, when I return from any extended amount of time away from of the house (more than about four hours). It is particularly important for the alpha male dog to do this, whether the others see him do it or not. It is an expression of relief on his part that I have returned, and that the burden of responsibility is now off his shoulders. It is interesting to note that the others who try to follow suit tend to be the more dominant females, who are still unsettled as to which one of them holds true alpha status.

One of our very enthusiastic dancers!

Both Sharon and I also experience an on-rush of ecstatic energy if we make exaggerated dances moves around certain of the dogs. Several of them will jump up and try to join in, and their pleasure when they are allowed to do so is quite palpable. So, we let them!

How do dogs feel about us when we let bad things happen to them?

When something bad happens, humans tend to look for someone or something to blame for whatever has befallen them. Dogs do not.

It is a uniquely human failing that we seek to apportion blame when bad things befall us. We are seemingly unable to accept that bad things 'just happen' in life, and consequently dwell upon our negative experiences, or even remain trapped within them long after we could have moved on.

The need to hold someone or something responsible for our ills is not a facet of doggie mentality. Dogs are infinitely more fatalistic and accepting in their approach to life. It enables them to be far less encumbered than we are by troubling issues. This attitude even affects the quality of their sleep and dream states. Since they do not feel the need to reflect upon what is already passed, they are unlikely to have their either their waking hours or their slumbers impacted by ruminations over liability for what has occurred in their lives.

However, this does not mean to say that those negative experiences in which we are obviously the *intentional* perpetrators of harm (i.e. those situations where we *make* bad things happen and do things to dogs) are viewed in the same light.

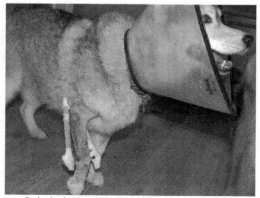

It looks bad, and it is bad; but she won't blame.

Chapter 11

DOGS, BABIES AND CHILDREN

"I'm not alone," said the boy. "I've got a puppy."

Jane Thayer, *The Puppy Who Wanted a Boy*

Do dogs know if their person is pregnant?

Yes, almost instantaneously.

Pregnancy causes responses in the female body that affect the individual's vibration and are immediately perceptible to a dog. If we could interpret their responses, dogs would be a more reliable indicator of impending birth than the expensive chemical tests so readily available in drug stores.

The altered vibration becomes noticeable within the human's auric field almost immediately after conception. The aura will change colour, have added depth, extending further away from the body than usual, and be more prone to rapid changes on its surface area than the dog has come to expect. Effectively, it is impossible for them to miss.

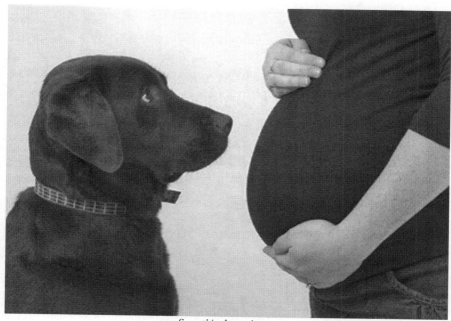

Something's coming...

How does a dog respond emotionally to the discovery that its person is pregnant?

With empathy and sensitivity; but the most common feeling is the desire to protect. Their feelings may also change as the pregnancy progresses.

Generally speaking, dogs regard pregnancy as perfectly normal and nothing particularly extraordinary. Whether it is another dog or their person that is pregnant, their response will be quite blasé in the early stages of pregnancy, and the discovery of it will not take them by surprise. They will likely respond to the mother-to-be with (perhaps unrecognised) empathy, and be concerned for their welfare, adapting their own behaviours to demonstrate genuine sensitivity and caring. Naturally, females are far better at this than the males!

For dogs that consider themselves to be alphas, the feeling that their person is ill equipped to take care of themselves, may cause them to become defensive during a pregnancy. Ironically, they are more likely to adopt this behaviour for a human than for one of their own kind. They know that pregnant bitches can be quite ferocious if threatened during pregnancy. Their desire to protect, even a pregnant human, is instinctive. However, it is proportionate to:

A. The dog's affection for their person. (The more they care, the more wary of threats they are likely to be).
B. The vulnerability it perceives in their person. (The more helpless the person appears to them, the more the dog will feel the need to guard them).
C. The number of lifetimes they have had experiencing being with a pregnant human. (The more they have had, the more laid back they will become; but never to the point where they are indifferent to the physiological changes that are occurring in their person. A dog that has no concern for their pregnant human is likely to have a very 'damaged' relationship with that individual)

The need to protect may or may not surface, depending upon what circumstances present themselves during the pregnancy and the dog may not need to step in to ward off threats. But in extreme cases, canines may become unusually aggressive to anything perceived as untoward. When a pregnant woman is out walking a dog, strangers or others of its kind may present as hostiles. Those visiting the home may seem dangerous undesirables. Normally placid and friendly companions may transform into something lethal. Such behaviours may continue until the child is born, and possibly thereafter.

As the pregnancy goes on, what has initially been accepted as something of little consequence could become a source of considerable trepidation. A dog will know that the pack order is due to change, and its own position may be under review. This is stressful for the dog, particularly if its people are paying it less attention; or the mother-to-be is unable to be as physically involved with their pet as they once were. In response, the dog may appear to become needier, in an attempt to assuage their troubled emotions. Anxiety levels inevitably increase as the pregnancy draws towards its conclusion, unless the guardians make efforts to make their dog feel as included in the event as they are themselves. Unfortunately, few may realise that from the dog's perspective, the impending birth is *a pack event*, in which the dog feels it has every right to be involved. Exclusion can be devastating for them.

Pregnant? It's all perfectly natural to a dog.

How do dogs feel about newborn babies?

Curious. Shocked. Awed. Confused. Horrified. Jealous. It could be any of these, and a great deal has to do with the way their people behave.

A newborn child will be the subject of great curiosity for a dog. Its sounds and smell may be quite unlike anything it has experienced before and its intrigue for the dog may be intense.

A dog will experience a child in a totally different way from its parents because it will see the baby's auric field and experience its vibration. A baby's vibration is substantially higher than that of an adult human. Immediately following and for quite some time after a birth, a newborn will literally pulse with the light energies that comprise its true being. Its auric field will extend many feet around its body. A dog may even find it difficult to be in the baby's presence for extended periods of time, simply because of the intensity it experiences.

If human parents are enrapt by a newborn, their pets may find the baby an object of awe and wonder, both of which might spark fascination or fear. Particularly when a baby is born at home, a pet is as likely to be as horrified as it is captivated by the new presence.

If a baby has been born in a hospital, when it is brought home it will already have its light energies somewhat dampened. This is because its 'inner light' quotient will have been affected by the vibrations in the hospital (which are the natural consequence of a place that primarily deals with sickness). Therefore, it will not present quite such a startling presence for a dog.

However, overall it will be a matter of what the dog must learn in their lifetime, as to what response they experience. The older the soul, the more likely it is to find the baby a thing of wonder and be wholly comfortable in its presence.

As the days pass, and once the initial shock is overcome, the dog has to become accustomed to the new life-form in its home. Adjusting may be every bit as challenging for the dog as it is for the parents.

A newborn baby can be a thing of wonder or a thing of fear. No prizes for guessing which it is in this photo.

From its perspective, a new pack member has joined. This will cause confusion about pack order and where the dog now stands relative to the child.

If the humans alter their approach to their pet even slightly, great upset may result. Changes in routine that affect walking, meals, play and petting cause stress and confusion for the dog. It was there first, and it will have no understanding of why it has suddenly been relegated to a lower standing in their affections. Jealousy is the most common result.

When faced with what (to them) appears as withdrawal of love, a dog will feel it has no option but to make its presence felt and force its people to take notice. The easiest way to achieve this is to draw attention to itself; or what humans generally will refer to as 'being naughty'.

People often report that their dogs undergo a personality change once a baby is born. All too often dogs find themselves thrown out of their homes following a birth. Yet it is not the dog but they themselves who have undergone the personality change. They are inconsiderate of their pet's needs, believing that the dog will be flexible in its expectations.

Why do some dogs hurt babies?

Not without reason, however awful it is.

Infrequently there are tragic stories reported of dogs attacking or even killing babies, and it is easy to assume that there is a dangerous incompatibility between infants and canines.

Were this to be the case generally, there would be far more reported incidents, and dogs would have a reputation that branded them as man's worst enemy rather than man's best friend. The incidents are mercifully so few and far between, that causes which have nothing to do with latent malevolence need to be examined.

A distressed and crying baby is greatly disturbing to a dog, not because the sound is frustrating, but because most dogs will feel concerned about the wellbeing of the infant.

Faced with situations when they are left alone with a baby, their instinct (particularly if they are females) is to intervene to assuage whatever upset is affecting a distraught child. The manner in which they will do this is as they would for their own puppies, which involves clasping their jaws around the skin at the back of the neck and gently shaking.

Unfortunately, the physical and circumstantial differences can create tragic results. Babies do not have the mass of fur and surplus skin tissue on their necks to both protect and be shaken by. The crying infant will most likely be on its back and the child's neck is therefore not nearly as long or accessible as a puppy's, and the throat is substituted. What constitutes gentle shaking for a puppy is hardly the same as it would be for a baby. So overall, the dog's ability to intervene without causing great harm is limited.

Because of the connection between young children and dogs (described below), young humans are often inexorably drawn to the household pet, wanting to experience them in as many ways as possible. It is not unusual for a baby to grab onto or even bite a dog in their efforts to sample this beguiling creature. They may all too easily grab hold of chunks of flesh, twisting and pulling, and inadvertently hurt the dog. The dog will respond in a reflex action to prevent the hurt and snap at the child. Even the most benign amongst the species are hard wired to defend themselves. The greater the hurt caused, the more aggressive the retaliation. A dog's jaws are very powerful and tragedy can all too easily result.

Since the baby is viewed as a new pack member, a dog with concerns about its position may feel beholden to demonstrate its predominance over the baby.

This will most often be the case where the arrival of the infant has caused its people to neglect the dog in favour of the child. As used here, 'neglect' is a relative term. In this case, the most obvious examples from a dog's perspective would include:

- An obvious change in the amount of attention paid to the dog.
- Excluding the dog.
- Forgetting or changing the dog's mealtimes.

The actions will be taken as symbolic of a change in pack order being imposed that the dog does not necessarily accept or agree with. If this is the case, it will wish to correct the situation.

Establishing position, as discussed earlier, can result in the necessity to 'teach a lesson' and physically dominate a lower level of pack member, which a dog will most certainly perceive a baby to be. Aggression is the dog's only option.

But to fully comprehend what is going on behind these (perhaps) understandable reasons, the reader should know that not a single tragic incident would have occurred were it not for the fact that a contract exists between either the dog and the child, or the parents of the baby and the dog. In other words, it has been agreed before all incarnated that the dog would do harm to the child to make some learning point apparent, or some opportunity for learning arise.

If this sounds dreadful and you are shocked by this, it is important to understand that when we transition through the etheric, planning our next lives, we are totally aware and accepting of the fact that all experience, good or bad, can result in the opportunity for learning and/or challenging ourselves to evidence our success in acquiring that learning. All types of beings will make contractual commitments to one another (out of loving kindness) that may involve hideous repercussions when they are earthbound and incarnate.

This is the way it is.

How a baby is introduced to a dog, and how its ongoing relationship with the canine is monitored can have a great deal of impact upon their compatibility.

Despite the contractual nature of injuring another being, the repercussions of hurting a baby or child will be dire for a dog. Few doing serious harm will walk away with their lives. Yet they will have been aware of the outcome of their actions before incarnating, and still elected to help us in our learning. But apart from dealing with their own outrage, or grief, there may be learning for both parents and child that requires them to empathise with the dog and forgive. But if there is, few will be able to keep to this part of the contract when their offspring are harmed. Emotions run high, and the parents will face societal pressures to do away with a canine so threatening. The fact that the dog has simply done what was intended is of no consequence.

Why do children form a bond with dogs?

The potential exists for all children to form an exceptional connection with dogs, or any other being for that matter. The fact that relatively few do, or lose the bond that they have created, is mainly circumstantial.

One of the unique qualities about a dog from a baby's perspective is that the dog may be the only thing in the household they have joined that can communicate with them!

Human babies are born with an 'intact' connection to the same chakra which allows dogs to use telepathic communication. But for the fact that we humans have evolved to use language to talk to one another (and thus lost the ability to use the chakra), a baby, after only a matter of hours, would begin to start recognisable conversation, telepathically, with its parents. (It does try to, but they seldom hear.) After a few weeks, it would be perfectly capable of holding a quite sophisticated conversation. Instead, it must start learning language because its attempts to communicate with its parents go unanswered.

A dog however, has the potential to hear everything a baby is trying to say, and *may* choose to open a dialogue with it. Dogs may often be observed sniffing around a baby's head, which is the equivalent of them trying to establish the 'butt telegraph' with another dog, since in humans the telepathy chakra is located a few inches over the crown of the head. This action may be repeated more often than they do it to other dogs. In part, this is because there is a level of disbelief they experience that this squirming human thing is talking, but also because the maintenance of the link is subject to what is best described as static-like interference. This is unwittingly introduced by the parents after the birth, by their immediate attempts to instigate (one-sided) spoken conversation with the baby. The infant is confused in where to focus its efforts at making a connection, and this presents itself as the equivalent of static.

Whilst it is wholly understandable that they wish to connect with their child, what they are doing from another perspective is distracting the child from what would otherwise be the development of its natural telepathic abilities and substituting a less sophisticated mode of communication. The newborn's brain is certainly aware of its parent's language-based attempts to connect, and will inevitably make efforts to overcome the dearth of communication that surrounds it by developing language skills. Consequently, a baby must divert its attention from its innate mind-based connection abilities.

This picture of innocence might well belie the deep connection and communication that is being developed between child and dog.

To a greater or lesser extent, a dog will have been aware of overtures of contact being made by the child (to its parents) from the outset. As the transition to use of language occurs, these will become progressively weaker. Even so, the baby does not necessarily abandon the use of its telepathy chakra immediately. If it receives no telepathic response whatsoever, it will rapidly give up and focus all its attentions on comprehending what its family are to trying to tell it via the spoken word. The chakra then falls into a state of complete disuse.

But if the dog persists in its own efforts, the baby may develop dual communication modes. Initially it will be able to have a more meaningful connection with the dog than it does with its parents. The effects of this kind of link are often seen in later life, manifesting themselves as an unusually strong bond between the child and the dog, an empathy with animals, a predisposition towards using what we usually think of as 'sixth sense', and sadly, an inconsolable sense of bereavement by the child when the dog passes over.

For its part, the dog will become totally enamoured of the child and be deeply devoted to, and protective of it.

Back track slightly and you will notice the words: *"If the dog persists in its efforts"*. Many will not and give up, largely because their telepathic efforts with humans have been unsuccessful up until that point. Again, the soul age of the dog will play a great part. A dog that has lived many lifetimes is far more likely to keep trying because deep down, even though it may not fully understand why, it senses the importance of establishing an inter-species link.

Once made, even though the child may ultimately abandon telepathy in favour of language and cease to talk with the dog, the loyalty of the animal to the child will be unending, and when such is bond is created, under no circumstances, whatever befalls it, will the dog ever do harm to the child. Somewhat tragically, even after it has long ceased to get any response and silence has fallen on their communications, it will try to talk to the child until the end of its days.

Readers may be aware of the legend of the dog Gelert, an Irish Wolfhound much beloved by its master, Prince Llewellyn of Wales.

The unfortunate dog was slain by the Prince, under the mistaken belief that the faithful hound had murdered his newborn son, when it had in fact risked its life to do battle with, and protect the child from a wolf, killing the beast and saving the child's life.

On discovering the truth and his overhasty error, the master was stricken with a terrible grief from which he never recovered. The story goes that after that time, he never smiled again.

The dog was buried with much grandeur, and despite all of this happening over nine hundred years ago, the grave is still a popular and well cared for tourist attraction.

The relevance?

If the dog had not already formed a bond with the baby it is unlikely that it would not have gone to such extraordinary lengths to protect it, and been prepared to lay down its own life.

It may be imagined that nine hundred years ago, attitudes towards child rearing were somewhat less 'enlightened' than they are now, and that perhaps the infant was not spoken to greatly by its carers.

In the absence of distracting spoken communication, the telepathic link the baby would have forged with the dog would therefore have been strong and powerful, and the dog's commitment to the baby without measure.

It may be a fanciful and romantic tale, but the grave exists and the bonds that dogs may form with children are certainly a matter of fact.

Beddgelert (whose name means "Gelert's Grave") is the village in Gwynedd, north-west Wales, which is the supposed site of Gellerts tomb. Two stone plaques relate the sad tale, one in Welsh, the other in English

Why do some dogs dislike children?

They look funny and they may be nasty!

The unusual aspects of a child's vibration may cause some dogs to be permanently fearful of children. Unless they have grown up in a household where they are present and become accustomed to them, there is no reason why they should not be constantly surprised when in their presence. Although they understand *what* it is, they will not necessarily understand *why* it is.

Despite not being as breathtaking as it is at birth, a child's auric field can remain palpable up until their teens. This is not a given, since children are increasingly subjected to negative input in the form of thoughts, ideas, images, experiences and foodstuffs that damage and erode their high vibrational qualities. These inputs effectively 'dampen' the field and reduce its output, power and visibility. A lower vibrational child may be less intimidating for dog, but depletion of the field is nonetheless an unfortunate devolution for the child.

It may also be the case that the dog has had unpleasant experiences with a child (or children) historically, and retains the memory. If this smacks of the antithesis of 'living in the moment', it should be borne in mind that there is more than a little practicality about remembering what has hurt you in the past. Avoiding contact with it in the future to prevent a repetition of the experience is just good sense.

No problem with disliking here!

How do dogs feel when they are displaced from their homes by babies?

Unsurprisingly, they never feel good about it.

You can almost guarantee that if you search the online pages of a dog rescue website, and read the reasons for dogs being surrendered, one of the top justifications for abandoning faithful canine companions will be related to a new baby.

The excuses proffered are usually one, or a combination of the following:

- When we got the dog, we didn't think we would be having children.
- We didn't expect the baby would take up so much time.
- We're not able to give the dog the attention it deserves anymore.
- We feel it would be better off with people who have time to devote to it.
- The dog's personality has changed. It's been acting strange.
- The dog doesn't seem to like the baby and we're afraid of what it might do.

The truths that underlie these seemingly credible and sympathetic concerns are usually one or a combination of the following:

- We love the baby so much we don't love the dog anymore.
- We can't be bothered to take care of the dog now.
- We don't have time/energy to give the dog the attention it wants.
- Having a dog and a baby is way too much work.
- Getting a dog was a rehearsal for having the baby, so we don't need it now.
- Having to look after the dog is just a pain in the butt.
- We didn't care about the dog that much in the first place.

Of course, there are those who genuinely wish that they could cope with both dog and baby, but for whatever reason simply can't. What is slightly surprising about these people is their unfortunate lack of foresight and failure to recognise when they got their dog, that they might at some stage in the foreseeable future also have children.

As for the rest, it is a woeful example of how disposable we regard our pets as being.

Seldom is consideration given to what the dog feels when it is displaced. The only appropriate word is 'devastated'.

You will have realised by now that the ultimate reason for their banishment may well have its source in the creation of a learning opportunity for human or dog. But in its incarnate form it will be incomprehensible to the dog that their beloved people could be so perfidious, that it is a cruelty from which they may never recover.

Abandoning the family pet for all the wrong reasons can mean wrecking many more lives and in many more ways than may be foreseen.

At least those that end up in rescue may have a chance of finding a new and truly loving home. Many more that are not summarily ejected, will find themselves exiled to the outdoors and have their companion privileges revoked. They may be destined to spend their remaining days as rueful observers of the happiness they perceive within, victims of the constant painful reminder of the way things were.

Those guardians who have the compassion and love for their pets to caringly and carefully integrate the new baby *and* the dog into their world, as equals, reap the benefits in more ways than they may imagine.

To me, as a confirmed and committed dog lover, the idea of shedding a pet, as if it were just so much dead hair, is as inconceivable as it is repugnant. Yet when Sharon was expecting our firstborn, my mother in law was adamant that we should "get rid of" our two Siamese cats because they were "a danger to the baby". Needless to say, we ignored her and both of our children grew up in a house with first cats, then shortly thereafter, cats and dogs. All coexisted happily and survived one another.

Dumping an animal we had invited into our lives? That's something I never could have forgiven myself for. What wonderful experiences and treasured relationships we would all have missed out on.

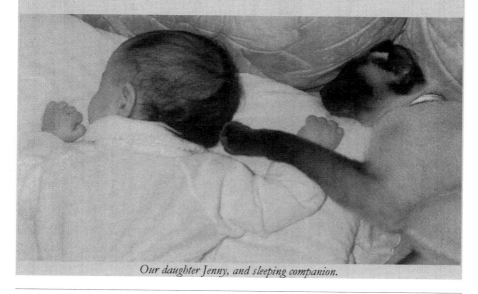

Our daughter Jenny, and sleeping companion.

Chapter 12

DOG PSYCHE

"Dogs are our link to paradise. They don't know evil or jealousy or discontent. To sit with a dog on a hillside on a glorious afternoon is to be back in Eden, where doing nothing was not boring--it was peace."

Milan Kundera

How intelligent is a dog?

How long is a piece of string?

Were we to consider the spectrum of human intelligence, it would incorporate everything from genius to the intellectually challenged, and anything in between. It is precisely the same in the dog world.

A dog's intelligence level may be thought of on a scale varying from 'great' to 'very little'. They may suffer from a range of mental drawbacks which, although not necessarily obvious to us, nonetheless impact upon their lives and impair conventional doggie intelligence and thinking.

Many dog breeders will swear, with great conviction, that their favoured breed is the most intelligent of all. And there may be an argument for the case that some breeds are more predisposed to possessing a higher level of intelligence than others.

But just as it does with humans, this should raise the question of precisely how we define intelligence. In humans, we still tend to defer to that which is based upon mathematical reasoning, despite extensive work being done that evidences at least seven separate forms of genius that have nothing whatsoever to do with numerical acuity.

In dogs, skill with numbers is a total irrelevance, so how are we defining intelligence?

Conventional wisdom has us believing that intelligence in dogs is evidenced by problem solving skills and the ability to follow instruction. It could easily be argued that all that these skills prove is an ability to respond to a human definition of what an intelligent dog should be.

Dogs themselves have a definition of intelligence which is somewhat different from ours. Amongst its fellows, an intelligent canine is one

one that travels through life as unencumbered by troublesome encounters and negative experiences as possible. True intellect is evidenced by the ability to make the most of any situation and circumstances that are faced, without faltering and without complaint. Genius is the ability to take pleasure in every moment, irrespective of whether it is a good or bad one, learn from it and grow as a result. Perhaps there is a message in there for us?

You wouldn't think it by looking at his face, but this — by any definition — is one of our most intelligent dogs.

The level of intelligence either humans or dogs arrive with is never a measure of what can be developed, and more than anything else, our self-limiting beliefs are what may hold us back in exploring the boundaries and possibilities of our intellectual potential.

Intelligence may be developed, or ignored and wasted. It is one of the challenges of learning that we may face repetitively across numerous lifetimes that we do not imprison ourselves within the boundaries of our own expectations (or indeed, those of others).

What makes dogs afraid?

Dogs are only naturally fearful of loud noises and falling. However, just like humans, they may easily learn new fears, some of which may terrify them.

The human source for learning to fear is those who are around us. Our integration of new concerns is relentless from quite early on in childhood. Whereas humans tend to accumulate fears based upon the almost infinite range of possibilities they may conjure up, dogs tend to restrict theirs to the actual things which are a threat to their wellbeing, and present a clear and present danger.

To us, the most obvious of these is probably physical violence. Since dogs routinely use negative reinforcement upon one another to assert precedence in all things, less confrontational dogs can easily grow to be fearful of their own kind. This is in spite of the fact that violence being used upon them is not an automatic consequence of encountering other canines hell bent on domination. Demonstrating passive behaviour is often enough to assuage the control oriented aspirations of all but the most belligerent of dogs.

Lack of what we might think of as 'normal' socialization for dogs can create a fear of the unknown. But by and large, they are not manufacturing reasons for concern, to anything like the extent that we do. Relatively speaking, they can live untroubled existences, particularly if they are loved and well looked after.

However, the greatest fear a dog may develop stems from the in-built pack mentality. Separation from the pack is a cause for anxiety which may be extreme in the way it is experienced. It may range from casual concern to blind terror if a dog when split from those they love. And as we have already explored, for so many canines their people are their packs.

I have a Yoda mask, used for Halloween parties in days gone by. When I put it on, the dogs get very upset and bark a LOT. However, I wouldn't go so far as to say that all dogs are afraid of funny looking Star Wars characters.

Why do dogs seem to be so scared of fireworks?

Because of more than just the loud noises we humans hear.

A reading of the previous answer gives what appears to be the biggest clue to this answer. However, the loud bang when the firework explodes is only part of the total experience for the dog. The entirety of the answer is made up of these components:

- Many fireworks, once launched (particularly rockets), make a peculiar 'whooshing' sound. We hear it briefly. Dogs hear it even after it fades from our range of auditory perception. It is an unusual and disturbing sound for them.

- All fireworks make noise that is out of the ordinary as far as a dog's expectation goes. If you observe your dogs at times when they hear a new sound, they are seemingly curious. What we don't realise is how unsettled they are by anything that is out of the ordinary.

- Humans start to behave peculiarly when fireworks are let off. Often, they will start watching them and ignore their pets. Conversely, if they realise that their pets are frightened, they will devote extraordinary attention to them, which might also cause an animal to believe something is wrong.

- Fireworks disrupt the ether (the vibration that is constantly in the air around us). They produce an unusual 'atmosphere' that is perceptible by dogs with an extraordinary palpability.

- The sulphurous smell produced by fireworks is unpleasant for them and infinitely more obvious to their noses with their very acute sense of smell.

- Bangs are evocative of gunshots. Deeply embedded within most dog's soul DNA is a fear of guns, because in previous lifetimes they have been shot. Depending upon how recent that last experience of this has been (in lifetime terms) the sound may easily conjure memories that are otherwise forgotten and dormant.

- The whole experience only happens a few times a year. It is not something dogs have the chance to become familiar or comfortable with, and since they are creatures of habit...

It is a torturous thing for any dog guardian to witness the terror that fireworks may evoke in their pets. But there is one more thing we blissfully disregard. Almost all wild animals go through similar agonies, and even blind terror, at the sounds these 'harmless' amusements make.

Some friends of ours decided to visit an annual firework extravaganza called 'Thunder in the Valley'. The title is apparently apt to describe the event, and it is one of the largest, and noisiest firework displays in the Province.

For reasons that I found unfathomable, they decided to take their newly acquired puppy with them.

I challenged them on the decision. Their logic was that the puppy would get used to the noise and not be afraid in future.

The rationale rendered me incredulous.

They lived in an area where fireworks were illegal and the puppy would *never* have to hear them.

The puppy survived the experience, but I dread to think what a totally nightmarish beginning it was for his relationship with them.

As a footnote: Although it is unlikely that it will catch on, I recently heard that one enterprising company had developed noise free fireworks. Whether this is true, I have no idea. However, it would take whole communities to be sensitive to the needs of pets for this sonic torture to no longer impact dogs

Why do some dogs kill sheep and chickens, seemingly for pleasure?

It's something they all go through, in one form or another.

Sheep 'worrying' and killing by dogs is not uncommon in rural areas where there are livestock populations. A similar thing may occur with chickens or other fowl. Canines getting access to these creatures may mercilessly slaughter them, seemingly without rhyme or reason. They do not eat those they murder, and the corpses are often torn to shreds. The acts appear to be those of a creature that is borderline 'crazed', and from our perspective, wholly unjustified.

In truth, the act of killing does bring them a pleasure of sorts. Aside from the thrill of the chase and the domination of prey, there is a peculiar sense of satisfaction for them about killing, albeit one that is possibly accompanied by puzzling and indecipherable emotions. The gratification stems from the fact that this is what they are *supposed* to do in their current lifetime.

Unfortunately, this is something all dogs must go through in at least one lifetime. These are the actions of those who are younger souls. They have not yet even begun to come to terms with an understanding of the value of life and the right of all living beings to make their progress upon their pathway, without harm or interference.

Older souls, dogs that have begun to 'get' this, but kill nonetheless if the opportunity presents itself, will experience a hollowness or disquiet that gnaws away at the pleasure.

Eventually, realisation that what they are doing is wrong and necessary will dawn upon them, and the harm will stop.

Humans go through the same thing. For some it is experienced through war, for others through illegal forms of killing. We *all* take lives at some point along our pathway. We must all come to terms with the implications of this wrongdoing, and by choice, refrain from participating.

Whilst some dogs will get away with their heinous crimes, others will find themselves summarily executed by a farmer's shotgun. Such an abrupt ending is not inappropriate for this type of lifetime. The act in itself is the essence of the learning experience they seek to achieve, and the current lifetime will hold little more that is of value to them. There is more to this than a mere 'live by the sword, die by the sword' philosophy.

Once a lifetime is embarked upon that is intended to incorporate murder, it can seldom be turned away from. Whereas a dog certainly possesses reasoning capacity, (as will be explained in the following pages), the application of the ability is unlikely to be applied to its own actions.

Humans, through realisation of the enormity of the implications of taking another's life, may feel remorse and consequently, change their ways. A 'moral compass' is evolved within us over numerous lifetimes of killing (as many as it takes to gain an understanding that it is wrong).

Our discernment then enables us to decide that such actions are wrong. During a particularly catalytic lifetime, we will have this realisation dawn upon us and change our actions accordingly, both in the current lifetime and those thereafter. The compass is embedded.

For a dog, the learning experience is somewhat different. Because of their naturally predatory nature, their 'Damascus moment' seldom comes within a lifetime, and is instead a piece of wisdom they glean in reviewing their lifetimes whilst transitioning from one lifetime to the next in the etheric. They become aware of the full cost of their actions and commit to work against type in their next lifetime. In this, they may or may not be successful.

Although it may take many lifetimes to learn the lesson, when the killing is prolific, it is a sure sign that the dog is a much younger soul who, unfortunately, will repeat the performance to some degree or another, in many lifetimes yet to come.

Do dogs understand that cars are dangerous?

No. Not unless one has already killed them.

In this case the perception of danger for a dog (that has not experienced physical contact with one) can only be based upon its ability to anticipate or envisage the likely outcome of physical contact with a machine of undetermined mass moving at unknown speed. Tricky!

Unlike humans, who have the advantage of being told about the repercussions of such an event at an early age, a dog must work out the potential danger for itself.

For many, it is not until they have been hit by one that they are truly able to understand just how lethal cars can be; and by that stage, it will be too late. However, once they have had the experience, it is a component of their soul DNA memory, brought with them in their subsequent incarnations. They will perpetually have access to this unfortunate memory and if it surfaces (as it is able to, in order to affect their decision making) the dog will receive subconscious input that chasing cars is not such a good idea. It will then be quite reticent to have any involvement with the outside of a motor vehicle.

So, whereas only a very limited few will be able to totally comprehend, and some will naturally err on the side of caution, a great many will require their fears to be based upon actual experience before they become real. And these apparently foolhardy canines will risk life and limb, facing oncoming traffic with reckless abandon, or even in hazardous pursuit of the death dealing tin boxes.

"Stupid dogs", we may think. But it's hardly their fault. Dogs are designed to live in a 'natural' world, not one that has become progressively man-made. The ever-increasing variety of lethal hazards that present their life-threatening challenges to all members of the animal kingdom (quite apart from the insidious presence of man himself), were simply not there as recently as one hundred and fifty years ago.

Dogs have managed to adapt and cope with comparative ease, but they do not arrive with built-in fears and a cautious mindset. Their remit is to embrace life and all it has to offer, as may be observed from the pleasure they take from the simplest of experiences. The fact that *all* animals must try to survive whilst living in a world that is increasingly fraught with dangers is our responsibility, not theirs.

Regarding the chasers, we might notice a curious anomaly. One of the dogs most frequently touted by humans as possessing the highest intelligence level amongst dog breeds, is the Border Collie. Yet the breed most renowned for perilously chasing motor vehicles is said same Border Collie. If nothing else, that must cause us to question our conventional definition of intelligence and do some reappraisal in the light of theirs!

Some dogs realise that cars aren't quite so dangerous if you're in them.

Why do some dogs love car rides so much?

Because it's addictive!

The image of a dog with its head sticking out of a car window, the wind carrying its ears aloft and tossing its hair wildly behind it, is almost iconic, bespeaking a hedonistic pleasure that most of us can only aspire to. It is easy to find hundreds of pictures of dogs apparently experiencing the joy of this activity. But by no means all dogs will be happy to get in a car, let alone stick their heads out of the window as it races along!

We associate the action with the belief that the dogs are enjoying the immense range of new and alluring aromas experienced as they go along. In actual fact, the rapid pace at which the vehicle travels does not allow them to savour the smells or even properly distinguish between them. Their intense sniffing may appear to be a desperate attempt to process the vast amount of sensory information that is coming their way; but they would never be successful. Instead they are more likely to be enjoying a kaleidoscopic overload, caused by synesthesia. It can be pleasurably (and harmlessly) 'mind-blowing' for them.

The head out of the window thing is a delight (almost) exclusively enjoyed by dogs who are younger souls. It is the equivalent of participating in an extreme sport designed for dogs. The rush that they achieve from the wind whooshing through their fur may be thought of as making them feel uniquely alive. The imagery created during the experience may be something akin to taking psychotropic drugs.

Older soul dogs may like to sniff the air and partially poke their heads beyond the (apparent) safety of the car, but they are more aware of the potential risks of this slightly foolhardy activity, and will not engage with such abandon.

The car ride itself is, in dog terms, the equivalent of the experience of flying for humans. It is something a little bit out of the ordinary, not experienced on an everyday basis, and thus exciting every time it is undertaken. The motion feels different from their accustomed self-impelled movement, and the sensation may be novel and even exhilarating on every occasion they experience it.

Raw pleasure or simple recklessness?

However, like humans who fear flying and dread getting on a plane, some dogs are terrified of being put in a car. The lack of being in control of their own progress, the speed, even the sense of potential danger in the mode of transport, may all feature as off-putting factors that make a dog a poor or unwilling car passenger. Some of these will undoubtedly have been involved in fatal car accidents in previous incarnations; for others, facing and mastering their feelings of fear will be part of the lifetime learning they have decided upon for themselves.

Of course, there are also those dogs who travel in cars every day and for them, like jaded businessmen for whom planes have become like buses, car rides hold no mystique.

Several of our pack love car rides and will go to extraordinary lengths to try and get in the car if I'm going out. But the majority are utterly indifferent to it. I have always liked the idea of (safe) doggy head-out-of-window hedonism, just because I want to see them experiencing the pleasure and thrill of it. To date, only one of our dogs, the Tibetan Mastiff, is even remotely interested in the experience.

Do dogs think, and if so, what about?

The rather obvious answer to the first part of this question is a most definite "Yes". But thought itself is a complex thing, and there are many thinking 'modes'.

The way in which we think on a spontaneous basis reflects many things including:

- Our innate natural tendencies
- How we are taught
- Our influences as we evolve as beings
- Circumstantial and environmental factors
- Opportunity.
- Personal preference

Some people are deep thinkers who take immense pleasure in intellectualisation and philosophising. Others prefer a lighter existence, taking everything at face value, and affording themselves little time for even the most superficial of reflections. The former might be described as intense, whilst the latter is probably more of the norm.

This is all a matter of choice, not of capability. Irrespective of the social conditioning that has brought the individual to the point where the choice is made, 'thinking' may be developed like any other skill.

Dogs are not prone to pondering and conjuring with possibilities. They do not speculate or conjecture. They are not interested in abstractions or fantasies. They certainly think rationally about issues that present themselves and they analyse, extrapolate and solve problems. They weigh choices and make decisions, form judgements and develop likes and dislikes. Intangibles do not commonly feature in their thinking, and they are not predisposed to introspection; although they may reflect upon themselves and their actions. Their thoughts tend to be of an immediate nature, and are concerned with the realities of their world and their unique dog perspectives. In other words, a dog's thinking capabilities are not dissimilar from our own; they simply choose to think about different things.

The principal difference is that humans tend to spend a considerable time preoccupied with forming and dwelling upon concerns about things that may or may not happen. We are troubled by matters over which we have precious little control, and indulge ourselves in fears about things that have no personal impact upon us whatsoever.

Can you see a dog thinking? If perchance you don't see intense thought being evidenced in this picture, what do you see?

In large part, this is due to the way in which we expose ourselves to mass media, which feeds a constant diet of negativity and fear. We incorporate huge amounts of this data into our reality when it is totally unreal for us. Even regarding 'light entertainment', rather than view what we watch on the television as fantasy, we make it part of lives, discussing situations and characters we have seen as if they were real. Soap operas are principal amongst the culprits here, since they seldom feature scenarios that are upbeat, majoring instead upon disaster, tragedy, grief and hurt. Reality TV puts us in the position of watching the lives of others rather than living our own. Manufactured and sensationalised events push up ratings and eat into the viewer's consciousness to the point where they allow it to become part of their reality.

Not being subject to the inconsequential leaves a dog's mind free and uncluttered. They are far more 'present' in their lives than we are, and not constantly wracked with pointless and unfounded fears.

Yet the subject of a dog's thinking capacity is a contentious one. We humans seem to automatically assume that animals are 'dumb' in all respects, and we throw doubt upon their thinking capacity.

Recently I came across the thoughts of one individual who is a dog trainer with a not inconsiderable following. They had the following to say about dogs thinking capabilities:

"Everything on planet earth is made of energy, and the heart is what governs and transmits that energy. Dogs have as much awareness as we do of things in terms of what they feel but they don't 'think' about them or judge. They live in the moment and so simply react to every single thing or situation with a new feeling. Essentially the flow of emotions is the factor in their behaviour choices, it's never the mind that's deciding."

Evidently the individual was trying to express their belief that dogs are purely spontaneous beings, reacting only from the heart and not the mind. This is not a wholly unpopular ideology, but it is wholly incorrect.

It presents our four legged friends as dumbed down versions of the beings we experience. By implication, it portrays them as utterly reactive and only capable of giving unreasoned responses (since reason, by definition, requires thought). I wonder if this person stopped to consider that without the capacity for, or exercise of thought, dogs are reduced to little more than the automatons that Rene Descartes declared them to be. (See later chapter!)

Doubtless, many of you have looked at your dogs and watched them thinking, observed their (often) astute and calculating minds, and seen them give carefully considered situational responses to what is going on around them?

Certainly, you will have seen countless examples of dogs being ruled by spontaneous outbursts of emotion, be that joy or fury, in much the same way that humans may allow their experience of an emotive situation to dominate their self-control. But what about in the majority downtime that comes between these events? Humans give pause for thought, consideration and reflection to determine their responses to what goes on around them. Does this person seriously believe that dogs don't? What base creatures they must be!

It could be that the statement *they don't 'think'* is meant to portray a notion that dogs are in some way sainted creatures that only act out of love. This would be an unfortunately demeaning way of assessing them, since it would rule out their capacity to act with discernment and experience their relationships as anything other than the blandest of superficialities. It would lay waste to any notion of the need to undergo and process a variety of experiences across lifetimes, or the need for consequent learning, and it would render the notion of the dog's life having purpose as obsolete.

Not thinking would remove their capacity for rationale, or informed decision. But with it too go caring, consideration, anticipation, sensitivity, and a whole host of other responses. Although they may be deemed emotional, they require thought and decision. And also swept away is intelligence. Reactive behaviour is spontaneous and in many respects, autonomic. It is not based upon thought, but upon accumulated experience that causes a 'gut' reaction. Emotional intelligence stems from innate or learned consideration of the needs of others; or in other words, the ability to demonstrate empathy. And this, of course, is something you need to think about before you can exhibit it.

But there's a further more disturbing and off-putting part of this limited line of thinking about dogs:

Dogs are considered high up the pecking order in terms of their ability to relate to humans and form relationships. We value them for their loyalty, perhaps their malleability, and their connection with us. But if creatures we respect are as unthinking as the comments suggest, then what worth is there in those we consider less intelligent? To claim that dogs do not think is an indictment of the whole animal kingdom that, in common with the flawed science of centuries before us, places us firmly at the top of evolutionary scale, and everything else far below.

With ideas like this being touted, it is small wonder that we have such precious little regard for the animal kingdom. I understand the desire to pretend that the world revolves around a 'peace and love' philosophy. It should indeed be that way. But we also lack both compassion and humility if we try to deal with any creature without attempting to empathise with its state of being and accept that like us, it has a mind that it uses. If we do not or cannot do this, we simply evolve a series of reactive responses to whatever creature it is. Our own human history has already amply demonstrated that this is a pathway to ruin.

Just don't try and tell me that this animal is not thinking and reasoning.

Is there any truth in the saying 'If your dog doesn't like someone, you probably shouldn't either'?

A dog can recognise things in others that we can only begin to guess at.

A dog can make a wholly reliable evaluation of another being that has no parallel with the way humans scrutinise one another. This assessment is not based upon appearance, body language, what a person says, or the way they say it; but upon the vibration that is coming from that individual.

At a superficial level an individual's vibration reflects their state of being in the moment; but at a deeper level, it reflects who that person is, or to be more accurate, what they have become. We are all born with pure and high vibrations, but they may quickly become sullied by anything from what we think about and do, to what we eat. Although a personal vibration is effectively fluid, and the superficial aspects of it can be affected by mood swings or something as apparently innocuous as the impact of a TV show upon us, its deeper aspects are more fixed and have been defined by the person you have evolved into since childhood.

Our human senses do not commonly allow us to perceive this information in any way we are used to accepting. We *do* register 'disturbances' or unexpected 'irregularities' about people and we most often describe as 'having a feeling about somebody'; but we do not readily identify a person's vibration as its source. Yet this is precisely where it comes from. We are as likely to dismiss such feelings as foolish as we are to accept them.

Dogs register and process information that they receive in this manner without a second thought. If your dog reacts oddly towards somebody, it *may* be because they sense something is unusual about their vibration that they adjudge to be incongruous. They are particularly adept at spotting malicious intent and disingenuous behaviours. If a person is 'up to no good' they will know, and some will telegraph warning barks before the person has even had a chance to begin whatever mischief they have in mind. Guardians are advised to be cautious if their pet starts issuing them with warning signals.

There are exceptions to every rule. Despite being in possession of this ability, not all dogs choose to use it, apparently preferring to see the good in all. Some will allow their (genuinely) better judgement to be distorted by visual triggers. For instance:

- The most benevolent of individuals could arrive at your door with a crash helmet on and your dog may go crazy. The strange and unexpected headgear causes the reaction.

- A dog may develop an intense dislike just because they are reminded of someone from their past with whom they have had a bad experience. If the memory in not fully embedded, anyone who seems vaguely similar is tarred with the same brush, irrespective of contradictory vibrational information.

- Some dogs, particularly guardian breeds, will start barking at anyone. Shoot first, ask questions later.

- Even vibrations can trip your dog up. A particularly high or strongly positive vibration can catch them totally by surprise and cause a negative reaction, a bit like a baby's.

Although having a bad person detector can be very useful in weeding out associates you should disconnect from, it is important to differentiate between your dog's active dislike, and that which is an unusual/short term reaction they are giving to the strange and unfamiliar.

Whereas we may take time to express our reactions to somebody (or more likely mask them completely), a dog just lets it all out. As such, what you witness from them may be a response to an impression gained in the moment.

The only way you can truly tell if your dog dislikes someone is if they have time to get accustomed to that person. If, after an hour or two, the dog is still actively hostile, then it may well be advisable to consider severing the connections with that person. Whether you recognise it or not, their impact upon you is likely to be negative in the long term.

At a time that now seems long passed, when we only had four dogs, our home was visited by some friends who brought with them another individual who we had not met before.

One of our four dogs, who was the epitome of gentleness and accepted and loved every being she ever met, shocked us with her response to this stranger. She snarled, curled her lips and bared her teeth with a ferocity the likes of which we would not have previously believed her capable of. For the duration of the visit she maintained her hostility, so much so that we had to shut her away until the hapless individual had left. As our friends departed they averred their intention to return, and the newcomer made a point of saying that they too would visit us again.

It was, of course, the last time they were ever allowed to visit our house. We had found this person every bit as disturbing and unwelcome as our dog.

Dogs are pretty good at telegraphing their perceptions about others, even with just a simple facial expression.

What emotions do dogs experience?

It would be easier to ask "What emotions do dogs not experience?"

When we consider animals there always seems to be an immediate and unwarranted supposition that they do not have feelings. It is a staggeringly short sighted assumption based upon such flawed reasoning as:

"Animals do not cry"

(They do. Several species including elephants and cows are regularly witnessed shedding tears that can be directly attributed to fear or grief. Many species do not have tear ducts. This could be a reason why it is not universally common!)

or

"Animals do not laugh".

(I know people who I have never heard laugh, but I've never suggested to them that they have no emotions. There are other animal specific considerations. Animal vocal cords do not necessarily allow for laughter. How do we know the meaning of all the sounds animals produce? Perhaps some of them *are* laughter? If you communicate primarily via telepathy as most animals do, wouldn't your expressions of mirth most likely be inside your head too?)

Sometimes we rely on 'scientific thinking' and proof way too much at the cost of ignoring what instinctively we should know. Every sentient being has emotions. It's essential for experiencing incarnate life. Perhaps it's just convenient for us to pretend that animals don't have emotions so that we don't feel bad as we destroy billions of their lives every year.

Dogs may have a slightly different array of emotions from us, or perceive their experiences differently, but a very full range of emotive experiences is available to them. For the average well cared for dog, the most common amongst these are love, joy, excitement and jealousy. However, depending upon the circumstances of their people and the depth of connection the dog has with them, they may well experience anxiety or even depression as equally dominant emotions if they are left alone.

Are you quite sure dogs don't laugh?

The spectrum alters very quickly for a dog that finds itself in a rescue situation; and some of the positive emotions listed above may never be sustainably experienced by street dogs who live rough.

At this moment in human history (and perhaps it has always been this way for humans) a preponderance of our emotional experiences are negative and fear based. The same cannot be said for dogs, for all of the reasons you have read elsewhere.

Before you jump to the conclusion that they have less to worry about than we do (so of course they're not as fearful as humans) ask yourself why we have so many fears, and how they have been created?

WARNING. If you enjoy thinking and intellectualising and work this one through, you may not be wholly comfortable with the answer.

Is that an attempt at a smile? Or is he just stupid looking?

Do dogs hold grudges?

They can certainly maintain anger for short periods of time, but dogs do not hold grudges per se.

Dogs are far more accepting that actions taken by others that impact them negatively, and experiences that are not pleasant, are all part of life. They do not apportion blame or hold on to resentments if the individual who has harmed them amends their behaviour. If they do, grudges are neither necessary nor worthwhile. Life is too short.

This does not mean that they do not remember those who have wronged them. These people they will regard with caution and a certain amount of mistrust.

Interestingly, our Grey Wolf definitely *does* hold grudges.

She's sweet really. She just has a long memory!

When dogs are 'faithful' in human terms, what is motivating them to behave in such a way?

There are levels of faithfulness ranging from loving attachment, to excessive and unwarranted devotion. Invariably the extremes will be motivated by the learning opportunities such attitudes may offer. The rest is just love.

Readers will probably be familiar with the story of Greyfriars Bobby, the Skye Terrier in nineteenth century Edinburgh, Scotland, who spent fourteen years guarding the grave of his dearly departed person, before he himself died. Or Hachiko, the legendary Japanese Akita who spent the last nine years of his life returning every day to Shibuya train station to wait for his person to disembark. He was there at the same time without fail, unaware that his person had died whilst at work.

A photo of the actual Greyfriars Bobby.

Both these exceptional examples of fathomless loyalty are commemorated by statues of the dogs and (multiple) movies. But most custodians who prove themselves worthy of it will find themselves the recipients of selfless and 'faithful' behaviour from their pets, if they but look for it. The motivation is perfectly simple to explain: Love.

Guardians can sometimes fail to realise how deeply their dogs can love them, and how utterly devoted they may become. If worthiness were the criteria for what they will give to their humans, it is fairly obvious that many of us humans would fail miserably. But their motivation is worth exploring in some detail, since it provides another example of the learning a dog must achieve, and puts Bobby and (maybe) Hachiko in a slightly different light.

It is part of all our journeys that we experience a multiplicity of relationships. Over the course of many lifetimes we do this with varying degrees of intensity. Some connections are hugely significant in what we learn from them. Others are relatively inconsequential. Not all are meant to be enjoyed! Some result in suffering and hardship. Others are nurturing and supportive. Throughout all of them, no matter how cherished they are to us, we must arrive at the conclusion that another being does not 'complete us'. They may serve to complement us, be learning partners with us, assist us on our individual journeys, be guides for us, or us for them. But ultimately, we learn and we move on as separate individuals.

We do not have 'soul mates' in the romantic sense. There is not only one other person meant for us. This romanticised notion is responsible for more distress, dissatisfaction and unhappiness than it is bliss and contentment. A soul mate is simply someone who we are vibrationally compatible with and who will be, for us, all the positive things just alluded to. But they are not our be all and end all; we do not exist exclusively for them and they do not validate our existence. And when we lose them as we inevitably will, it is not the end of the relationship. Someone with whom we share such a close bond is almost certainly a member of our soul family and we *will* see them again. We will *always* see them again.

Lifetimes are embarked upon in full knowledge of those with whom we are intended to have relationships. Our connections with them do not always come about as we had specified, so a lifetime is also underpinned by any number of contingency plans. Relationships in all their varieties and forms are inevitable. The learning that we aspire to from our relationships is accumulated across many lifetimes. In some lifetimes, we may come very close to achieving our goals; in others, we might meet with hopeless failure.

You may have concluded that this refers to human to human relationships, but this is not exclusively the case. The relationships we have with *all* life forms are important; none more so than those with whom we have chosen to share our lives. Neither should we arrogantly conclude that it's all about us. As already indicated, learning can flow two ways. Our relationship with a pet dog is as likely to be about its learning opportunities as our own. They too must accept the wisdoms outlined above, and opportunities to do so may come from dog-dog, dog-human, or even dog-other species relationships.

Perversely, once we have learned the lessons we need to, we then create colossal challenges for ourselves to prove our ability to apply that learning.

Greyfriars Bobby found himself in a lifetime where he was faced with experiencing overwhelming love for his person. It presented as a wonderful, possibly unique experience, but also a huge challenge. Once the object of his adoration, John Gray, was no more, could he master his own emotions, come to terms with his grief, and continue to find meaning for his life without his master? Or would he be emotionally crippled by his loss and unable to continue his journey alone? On face value, he totally messed it up. Fourteen years playing sentinel at a graveside does not imply success.

But what if he wasn't grieving? What if instead he chose to spend that time reflecting, like Buddha under the Bodhi tree, demonstrating his devotion to his dearly departed master, but content in himself and still participating fully in life, just restricting its scope to the confines of the churchyard, raising the spirits of mourners and evoking compassion?

I don't know the answer. I'd like to think it was this way.

The newer, and one of two statues depicting the legendary Hachiko that can be visited in Japan.

And Hachiko, now a Japanese by-word for the noble virtues of loyalty and faithfulness. Was he misguided in his loyalty, or simply a prisoner of the routine that delineated the days of his life? He would only appear at the station at the precise time that his former master's train was due, suggesting he did get on with his life, since he wasn't there all the time.

Again, I'd like to think so. If you want to break your heart, watch the Richard Gere movie, Hachi: A Dog's Tale, which is based on Hachiko's story.

Dogs are faithful to those whom they love, and the extent of that faithfulness will undoubtedly be in direct proportion to the depth of that love, and how much they receive in return. Sometimes those they love are wholly unworthy, and often their devotion is unrequited. But it is not foolish, pointless, blind faithfulness. There is always a purpose behind their commitment. Learning, or evidencing their ability to apply that learning is the real goal.

One of our dogs, for whom I felt a greater than usual affection, reciprocated my love in a way I did not feel I deserved.

Relatively early on, he developed an attachment to me and always seemed to feel the need to be where I was.

He would want to come with me on even the most unrewarding car journeys, and in accumulated time, must have spent days of his life waiting patiently outside grocery stores while I was inside shopping.

He would always sleep where he could see me; but when it got too hot, he would go outside, only to wake us up several times during the night, desperate to come in, just to check that I was alright, before going out again.

In his youth, we hiked possibly hundreds of miles together, conquering mountains and appreciating the wonders of the Canadian wilderness.

When age crept up on him, he was no longer able to join me on my great treks, and had to be content with pottering about on the land we live on, following me as quickly as his age would allow, and sometimes not catching me up until I had been back in the house for a full five minutes or more.

The most heartbreaking element of this behaviour was his evident distress when I had to go out and simply could not take him with me. If he were outside when I was departing, he would try to chase the car, and even if kept indoors, if let out too soon, he would still try to follow.

There were several occasions when I returned home after a short trip to find him searching for me in the road, a long way from our house.

Eventually we wised up to the need to keep him indoors for at least fifteen minutes after my departure. Then he would wait patiently for me on the doorstep, interested in nothing else but my return. And when he would hear the car engine start up our nearly half mile-long driveway, he would come racing as fast as his legs would carry him to greet me. When I got out, he was unfailingly ecstatic to see me, and he developed a little dance that he would do to demonstrate his pleasure.

It was both funny and a little tragic to me that he could be so devoted.

A 'selfie' with my perpetually loyal friend and hiking companion.

He's gone now, only having had the relatively short life giant breed dogs so often do. Coming home is never quite the same without his massive presence to greet me, and there's an emptiness when I get out of the car. Sometimes I wish he hadn't been quite so faithful, then he wouldn't have felt so bereft on those many occasions when I had to abandon him. And I wouldn't feel quite so bereft without him now.

Why do dogs love humans?

Frankly - almost by chance

It's easy to suppose that dogs must be hard wired to love people, so strong does the human/canine bond appear to be. It might also be an ego thing for us to imagine that the love we experience flowing from our dogs to us is not only warranted, but somehow prompted by our individual uniqueness. In part, this may be true, but more than this, it reflects a dog's psyche.

It is the case that as a species, dogs have evolved to the point where those incarnating come with an expectation of having a close relationship with people, for at least most their lifetimes. But the source of the loving relationship that may develop is not based upon spiritual imperative. It grows because of them experiencing liking, tolerance, acceptance, and trust of us; although for a truly strong bond to build, it must be accompanied by reciprocity.

If this sounds a little like the way in which love between humans blossoms, that's because it is similar. As for reciprocity, as any true dog person will tell you, they may have stronger feelings of love for their dogs than they do for most of those humans who are closest to them.

There are however, key differences in the way dogs experience the emotions of love, which affect both their receipt and delivery of it.

- What a dog is prepared to give in a relationship is delivered without condition or reservation.
- Dogs begin from a position of non-judgemental acceptance. Their expectations of outcomes are positive, and although they may change their initial responses to align with what happens, they go into all their relationships with an optimistic view point.
- Once they give their liking/tolerance/acceptance/trust, dogs tend not to be fickle in their devotion and will remain loyal to the objects of their affection through thick and thin.

- They are fully prepared and willing to extend their liking/tolerance/acceptance/trust to many (even though their greatest devotion may be to a single individual).
- Their expectations of what they will receive in return for their giving are almost insignificant when compared with a human's.
- A dog likes/tolerates/accepts/trusts you for what they know to be inside you, not what you display in your behaviours.
- Their ability to sense what is going on within us takes precedence over all else. This allows them to ignore any incongruities between what they perceive and the behaviours we outwardly demonstrate towards them.
- Consequently, even though they may take huge amounts of pleasure in being the recipients of our affections, their attitude towards us will not waver, even when we don't let them see that we feel the same way about them.
- The capacity a dog has to like/tolerate/accept/trust is not limited by gender or species.

The almost throwaway nature of the last point should not be dismissed lightly. This answer should lead us to understand that there is no particular reason, other than the circumstantial, for why dogs *should* love humans above all others.

Instead, we should recognise that they are naturally liking/tolerating/accepting/trusting creatures that seek out connections with other beings. They may develop equally strong relationships with any other species, even those we might suppose to be their prey.

Were it not for the hundreds of years of evolutionary connection that has led us to develop a proprietorial relationship with them, and claim them as our own, the whole fabric of their existence, and ours, would bear no resemblance to our present state of affairs. The plain truth is that if humans were not present on the planet, dogs would be out there, liking/tolerating/accepting/trusting other species every bit as much as they do us.

Should we feel slighted by this? Not in the least. We should feel privileged that we can share our lives with this species, rather than vice versa.

However, within the answer lies another thought to ponder:

If dogs are capable of the experiences and emotional output outlined above, how many other species do you think we could also have such a close relationship with?

Here's a clue: the answer would be disturbing for anyone who *really* cares about animals. It would change every aspect of the human relationship with those we share the planet with.

"You are the sun in my day, the wind in my sky, the waves in my ocean, and the beat in my heart"

When dogs see us go out the door do they know we are going to come back?

No.

Stanley Coren, the psychology professor, neuropsychological researcher and author, renowned for his books about the intelligence, mental abilities and history of dogs observed:

"The greatest fear dogs know is the fear that you will not come back when you go out the door without them."

He was probably right.

Even though you may have a routine and they have ample evidence to suggest that you will return, when you leave a dog, it will never be one hundred percent certain that you are coming back.

A dog's perception of time is very different from our own and the absence of their human may appear to be extraordinarily long, even if it has only been a few minutes.

Quite how a dog reacts to separation is very often an issue of their soul age and how much mastery they have managed to gain over their own emotions. Learning not to overreact, not feel unduly concerned, avoid a sense of depression or take on feelings of abandonment, are all issues that present a serious struggle. Overcoming anxieties in this situation may be a real lifetime challenge for them, which many fail.

As you might anticipate, how concerned they become about the separation is directly proportionate to the strength of feeling they have about their person. The greeting we receive upon our return may be more about relief from boredom and anxiety if our dogs do not hold us in high esteem. The more effusive and emotional the reaction, the more likely it is that your dog adores you! The sad part is, that if this is the case, your absence will have seemed like an eternity. What's more, your dog may now be living in dread fear of your next departure and their next bout of heartache.

What most frustrates dogs and what are their utmost dislikes?

The greatest cause of frustration for a dog is inconsistency on the part of their humans; and their dislikes totally depend upon the individual dog!

Dogs appreciate routine because it gives them a certain feeling of security and they unconsciously develop habits which create expectations for the way things will be. When frequent change by their people dashes their assumptions about the way their day will be, dogs can experience a variety of emotions, most common amongst which would be frustration.

Note the word frustration implies mild irritation or annoyance, not necessarily full blown anger. A dog will soon forgive their person's shortcomings provided they are not a frequent offender. However, it is a short step from inconsistent, to unreliable; and from unreliable to uncaring; and thence, to (at least from a dog's perspective) abusive.

Dislikes can only be relevant for individual dogs, and it would be wrong to try to provide a definitive, all-encompassing generic answer. It would deny their individuality. What many hate, one will like, and vice versa.

Some dislikes are obvious!

It is said dogs have no concept of time – is this true?

Totally false! Dogs have a very acute sense of time, but what it means to them and how they let it affect them bears little resemblance to the human experience.

They have what is best described as an 'internalised body clock' which gives them a constant sense of one moment, relative to another. This is not anchored to any notion of a twenty-four-hour time period, but simply to a sense of what is happening in the natural world; but this is not as simplistic as when the sun rises and sets.

They are perfectly aware of the constantly variable amount of daylight in any given day, and are not 'fooled' into altering their divisions of time on this basis. They are instead mindful of continuously evolving cyclical patterns or routines in the framework of their lives which allow them to understand one point and its happenings in reference to others. They are especially aware of repeated events and can anticipate their coming with a precision that would surprise any clock-watcher.

A dog's use of this internalised timekeeping system does not give them cause for stress as it does humans, since it seldom implies that they must do a certain thing at or by a certain time. Its sole function is to allow them to anticipate those things which they deem to be important such as meals being due, or the return of a loved one. They may certainly become agitated if an event they are expecting does not happen per schedule, but time and timekeeping is far less of an issue for them than us.

If nothing else, the Hachiko story referred to above amply demonstrates a dog's sense of timekeeping.

Vendors at the station reportedly never needed to look at the station clock to tell the time in the afternoons, because Hachiko's timekeeping was so impeccable.

Do dogs 'live in the moment'?

Yes, sort of…

The claim that dogs 'live in the moment has become a much-vaunted phrase. Indeed, many of things already written suggest that this is likely to be the case.

It is certainly true to say that dogs are nothing like as encumbered by regrets from their past, or concerns about their future, as humans are. Their thought processes do not extend far beyond the immediate future and they have no concept of time being pressuring or limiting.

However, this does not imply a lack of memory, automatic and immediate forgiveness of unpleasant acts perpetrated against them, or an inability to relate to historical events as indicators of future events (all of which has already been alluded to).

'The moment' for a dog, in most matters, is a timespan of no more than a few hours. There are very few issues that will trouble them on a basis that would extend beyond this timeframe.

Living in the moment?

Do dogs recognise their own reflections?

No, and they are so much the better for it.

Mirror images may prompt interest when first seen, but only because for an instant, a dog might believe that it is another dog. Most are quickly dispossessed of this belief when they realise that the image before them omits no vibration whatsoever, and so they dismiss it as unreal. The occasional dog may continue to be fascinated by what they see and when this happens, it is cute and amusing. However, it could be symptomatic of their sensory array being damaged in some way.

The reason they do not recognise themselves is because a dog does not have the same sense of self that we do. From a very early age we are introduced to images from photos and videos as well as mirrors, and told that this is *who we are.*

We quickly come to identify totally with our appearances to give us a sense of self, and all too easily become fixated upon the outward look of our bodies as a way of defining ourselves, rather than who or what we are inside.

To many, this way of regarding ourselves becomes an inescapable prison that determines worth and influences personality. Our self-image can literally be based upon an image, leaving too many preoccupied with such illusory concepts as beauty, size, shape and colour.

A dog may see itself, but since it is not told "*This is who you are*" it never characterises itself in this way, never judges itself for its appearance or becomes a victim of a meaningless comparative designation, based upon irrelevant societal norms.

Consequently, a dog is never troubled by its appearance or concerned with looking its best. (That latter one is left up to us to impose upon them.) It is free to live a life without the concerns and hang ups that can erode the confidence of humans, and we should envy them this.

And even if they were to discover at some stage that the dog in the mirror was them, their society is such that it simply wouldn't matter.

If it's not another dog, it's not real!

How do dogs feel when they're put in boarding kennels?

Going into kennels is seldom a happy experience for dogs. Aside from possible issues related to the accommodations in which they find themselves, the biggest issue they face relates to their separation from their people.

It is all too easy to imagine that dogs are indifferent to their immediate surroundings, and it is certainly true that they will have little concern with, or respect for your decorating scheme or the aesthetic value of your furnishings.

It is the familiarity of their environs that is the issue for them, and once whatever type of living space they are accustomed to is substituted for another, a dog will almost inevitably begin to experience stress.

How long their disquiet lasts will be somewhat proportionate to how intimidating an environment they are presented with. Simply by viewing a few comparative examples of different boarding establishments online, you will quickly find evidence that not all kennels are equal!

Local authority guidelines for size and standard of care are often enacted on a retrospective basis (since it tends to be the case that only recently has society developed a concern for the welfare of those occupying these facilities) and not necessarily enforced in established businesses that were in operation prior to controls being imposed. But even complying regulation pen sizes (despite veterinary and SPCA recommendations) vary enormously depending upon local authority conventions.

Confinement, strange smells, the presence of other strange canines and an unknown routine, can affect dogs enormously. The more resilient amongst them may exhibit great bravado when being escorted to their temporary residences, and even demonstrate a degree of enthusiasm; but the sad truth is that the excitement is nervous, and the swagger is seldom a true response to how they are feeling.

Although we might offer platitudes, assuring them (and ourselves) that they will be having a wonderful holiday, you might well have been consigning your beloved pet to the doggie equivalent of Stalag Luft III.

If you refer to the earlier question regarding a dog's awareness of the likelihood of your return when you leave the house, imagine that response multiplied cumulatively by the total time you are 'missing' for, coupled with the strange and possibly off-putting environment, and the extent of the potential emotional trauma starts to sink in.

Of greatest importance to your dog will not be the facility itself, but the manner and attitude of the owner and staff. However unsettling the accommodations, if there are caring people to look after your dog, this will go a great distance towards alleviating the emotional suffering. The most unfortunate thing for the dog will always be that their human interface time will inevitably be limited, and their ability to connect with those around them of their own kind will hampered by a combination of shared fear and potential hostility

However, if all this presents a positively grim portrait, it is worth considering that the separation, hard as it may be, can form useful learning experience for any dog. They may well grow as a result of confronting the demons the experience might present.

Although I have encountered many boarding kennels, after writing the response to this question I decided to explore images of kenneling facilities online. In general, I was disappointed, or even appalled by the quality of residential options. There were some desperately bad 'vacation' homes for dogs.

But amidst the depressing mire of small pens, tiny runs, questionable cleanliness and unengaging environments, I came across a shining example of what must be near perfection as far as boarding kennels go.

Clean, spacious, well-kept and in a beautiful setting, the *Kennel Club USA* facility seems remarkable in many respects. It was specifically intended by its owners to be as stress free as possible for its occupants, and every aspect of the operation seems to have been given a great deal of thought and attention. And remarkably, even the prices are reasonable.

None of this should be of any surprise to you once you learn that the proprietor is Mark Jeremias, who was once a senior member of the Ralph Lauren fashion retailing organisation, at one time managing Ralph's pride and joy flagship store on Bond Street, London, England.

The experience of walking into that store was without parallel, and the same loving attention to detail that Mark applied to create a remarkable customer experience for humans has obviously been applied to Kennel Club USA on behalf of dogs.

Unfortunately, it's unlikely to be of any use to you unless you live in the Johnstown Ohio area, or are prepared to travel to give your pet as pleasurable an experience of separation as possible. Nonetheless, it is a role model for how all kennels would be in an ideal world.

NOT a kennel at Kennel Club USA, but sadly one of the better examples of 'holiday' accommodation dogs are subjected to!

Why do some dogs run away from home, or disappear while on a walk?

Sometimes because they need to, sometimes because they have to.

Simplistically, there are two basic reasons why a dog will run away. It's either because it's been mistreated and doesn't want to be with you; or because the allure of the great wide world is too intoxicating to resist.

In the former case, a mistreated animal can hardly be blamed for wanting to escape. Since many dogs are exposed to home situations where their lives are miserable, it shouldn't surprise the reader that this is the cause for countless canines ending up in dog pounds and rescues. It's a reasonable assumption that if their people are found, those who mistreat won't want their pets back. Shelters see this kind of response to tracing a custodian all the time: indifference, apathy and even hostility. It's a sure sign of an unhappy home life for the dog.

Unfortunately, many dogs must go through this experience because of contractual agreements made before incarnating. Most often these favour the human, since they are the ones who are meant to be learning the error of their ways; whereas the dogs are suffering because of them.

Mistreatment doesn't just constitute violence or abuse towards the animal in the way we might think of it. From their uniquely personal perspective, a dog will feel itself mistreated if it is:

- Ignored (not spoken to or given any affection)
- Not sufficiently exercised (as per the needs of the breed, which vary greatly)
- Underfed
- Not psychologically stimulated
- Kept in a confined space

(NB. If you are reading this and feel concerned that perhaps you are guilty of mistreating your dog, it should be borne in mind that pretty much all of the factors listed have to be present in some combination before they will feel aggrieved.)

Some dogs will flee because they are treated badly by children behind their parent's backs, often under the guise of 'playing with the dog'. When they can tolerate it no longer, they will be off.

If opportunities for escape present themselves, they will likely run for the sheer joy of running, and not feel drawn to return to their homes. Why would they wish to? They are offered precious little that is of value to them other than food. (Shelter will be a secondary factor if the weather is clement.) Many dogs with unhappy lives that do return, do so for this need only, feeling that they have nowhere else to go.

Again, it is usually the case that a contract of learning exists between the unhappy dog and the mistreating custodian. The former may have to learn to cope with their feelings of not being valued; the latter needs to recognise the full extent of their responsibilities towards another being in their care.

However, running away is not necessarily all about the desire to escape. For all the reasons discussed a few chapters back, the outdoors, and particularly the natural world, is the equivalent of an endless theme park, as far as dogs are concerned. They are drawn to it like moths to a flame. (Any that aren't are likely to still be struggling with self-development issues.) For a balanced dog, the harmony it feels with the great wide 'out there', is seductive in the extreme. Any opportunity presented to experience it has an addictive effect. If spontaneous chances don't arise to be out there, they may become hell-bent on creating them.

Many guardians can feel themselves slighted or even inadequate in their provision for their dog's needs if their pets then run away. Usually, this is far from the case. To begin with, the addiction can only develop due to experience. In other words, if their people well-meaningly introduce them to the joys of forests, lake shores, mountains and beaches, they may well get hooked. This is especially the case if they are allowed to run off-leash and gain a sense of true freedom.

When this happens, all other considerations tend to go 'out of the window'. Despite the apparent indifference to their people in the moment, the last thing the dog wants is to say 'goodbye' to them; they'd rather share it with them! But humans can't keep up, and what's out there is simply too good to resist! After all, dogs are, in their essence, wild creatures living alongside us. This is *their* world and they want to be in it.

A dog that is not mistreated, by any of the definitions given above, will try to get back to their people. Unfortunately, it is only the myth that all dogs have a great sense of smell that enables them to find their way back home, that causes us to disbelieve that they may (easily) become totally lost. They can, and they do.

A dog that loves its people will, when the euphoria of the freedom wears off, (probably due to time, fatigue, distance travelled, bad weather, or maybe frightening incident) suddenly find themselves wishing desperately that they were back in their homes and missing their loved ones with a painful sense of regret and anguish. The lucky ones will somehow find their way home safely, and their people will experience their rapture at being back in the pack. But some will never manage it, as fate and circumstance intervenes; but that does not mean that they ever intended to sever their relationships with those they love.

The huge irony is that even having gone through an experience that has caused them to be fearful or doubt the good sense of running away, the next time an opening arises, they will most likely be off again. Dogs have no appreciation of the danger they place themselves in as runaways, and the drug of the big wide world is too powerful to resist.

It should also be noted that if another dog is with them, a false sense of security arises. They will feed off one another's apparent confidence, neither wanting to show fear or reservation about going exploring. One potential miscreant will almost inadvertently egg on the other, so that the wariest of canines may become runaways. Even those dogs who are normally obedient to their recall, or prefer staying loyally by their guardian's side, will find themselves seduced by the call to adventure. It's nothing personal.

Chapter 13

HEALTH, ILLNESS AND DYING

"When you have dogs, you witness their uncomplaining acceptance of suffering, their bright desire to make the most of life in spite of the limitations of age and disease, their calm awareness of the approaching end when their final hours come. They accept death with a grace that I hope I will one day be brave enough to muster.'

Dean Koontz, *A Big Little Life: A Memoir of a Joyful Dog*

It is said dogs are colour blind – is this true?

No. Rubbish!

The assertion that dogs are colour blind is made on the basis that they only have two colour detecting cells within their retinas instead of the three that humans have. The extrapolation from this is that although they do not see in black and white, they must experience the same thing as humans who have red-green colour blindness. This is a conclusion based upon our belief that what we can see is *only* the result of what is apparent on the visual spectrum. It does not take into account the impact that vibratory information received olfactorily, translated via synesthesia to imagery, will have upon perception.

It does not occur in humans. It does in dogs. Not only are they far from colour blind, they can perceive a range of colours that significantly extends those available to the human eye. But what they see is quite different from what we see.

Intense, piercing, watchful, knowing? Yes. Colour blind? No.

Colour is not a definite. We have no way of knowing precisely what others see. All we may agree upon is that what we are looking at, at the same time as others, is a colour that we agree we will call by whatever name is chosen. Thus, what one person sees as yellow, another person could be seeing as blue, but because they have both learnt the same name for that colour, they would agree on what it is.

Is it OK to leave dogs outside all the time?

Sure, if you're cruel, heartless and want them to suffer. It is a threat to their health in ways you may not have considered...

There is a whole tranche of the dog owning population that never lets their dogs come indoors, and believe that the point of getting a dog is:

1. For the dog to live outside to provide 'protection' for those who are supposed to be their guardians.
2. For the dog to live outside because that's where dogs live, isn't it?

There's something asinine in either of these trains of thought, although undoubtedly, a biddable dog will come to accept being banished outdoors (for either reason) as their lot.

The former attitude tends to stem from a deeply embedded psychology not within dogs, but in us. This mindset defines canines as servile appendages, whose only purpose is to be of service to humans. Unfortunately, it's a limiting and vaguely Neanderthal mode of thinking. It clouds our judgement about all beings that are not human. But we like it because it conveniently allows us to control, manipulate, dominate, take advantage of, and generally use/abuse them to our own peculiar advantage or whim, without conscience. Simply put, it allows us to indenture all creatures, including dogs, into different forms of servitude.

Were we to explore its origins, we might well discover that our forebears (who faced more immediate threats to their physical wellbeing than we do), observed the propensity of dogs to 'sound the alarm' in the presence of intruders. This response would strike primitives as not only useful, but potentially lifesaving. Thus, they recognised that a useful partnership could be formed: A dog, if (meagerly) rewarded, would stay in human proximity and provide an advanced warning service.

After countless generations, there are still those amongst us who have never paused to consider the 'rightness' of this pigeon-holing about their purpose, or moved on in their thinking. Rather than seeing our four legged friends as beings who may have value to add to us in other ways, some of us expel them to the periphery of our lives. We only consider the animal worthwhile whilst it is useful/necessary as an organic burglar alarm and quasi-intelligent deterrent.

Since a dog's range of needs are so much more sophisticated than the mere exchange of their presence for food, keeping a dog outside just for 'protection' may be thought of as a form of oppression, and a long way from what the dog itself *wants* to do with their lives.

As for those who believe that a dog's natural place is outside (along with all 'inferior' creatures), there are, of course, many who would question whether it can be harmful for a dog to be outside? Surely that's where they would live, if their lives to be lived 'normally'?

Physically, a dog may be equipped to cope with the rigours of an unforgiving climate. Thick fur and a dense undercoat may see off snow and rain, and a single coat may allow body heat to be dispelled in warmer climes. But hardships most certainly occur when a breed type is found in an inappropriate geographic location. A heavy coated dog living in the tropics is a travesty; and frailer dogs like Chihuahuas constantly need protection from harsher weather. But even the hardiest dog's health can suffer if they must constantly cope with the ever-changing weather, whatever the kind, unprotected in any way.

It is the case that millions of dogs literally do live their lives on the streets, never seeing the inside of a building. We must also accept that dogs do not need to live indoors all the time, and would suffer greatly without the opportunity to experience the outdoors.

However, there are more aspects to be considered in this argument than the merely physical:

Dogs can and do suffer greatly from emotional hardship if left alone and excluded. Their need for companionship should not be forgotten. Many 'yard dogs' that are not allowed to be with their people are kept as 'only animals'. They quickly experience loneliness and depression, or develop psychological issues affecting their temperament.

Ironically, outdoor dogs frequently lack exercise and stimulation. Because of the mind-body connection that causes us all to be affected physically by our emotional state, illness and disease can follow.

As for street dogs and their apparent resilience, it is what they intend for that lifetime, and their lot is not the same thing as being bought by a human, apparently offering a lifetime of companionship, only to deny it.

Ignoring the desire for (significant) interaction is thoughtless at best. At worst, it is a form of emotional torture. There are a variety of common explanations to rationalise a pet being denied a space in a home.

Many such attitudes have their genesis in the experiences individuals were brought up with, or the value set that was imposed upon them by their immediate family members. I have met many who bar the door to their dogs because "that's what my parents did". Curiously few seem able to think for themselves and break with such an exclusionist precedent. Conversely, I have yet to meet an individual whose parents allowed a pet indoors, but they do not do so themselves.

Perhaps the saddest of this second category of 'dogs should live outside' exponents, are those who have previously allowed their dogs indoors, but now expel them. The usual cause for this phenomenon is the birth of a new baby, and the emotional torments suffered by these dogs are already documented on previous pages.

Then there are those who are so house-proud that they cannot abide having a 'dirty creature' within the walls of their domain, afraid that they will do damage to their treasured environment or cause them embarrassment amongst their friends. Perhaps these people would have been wise to be honest with themselves about their anally retentive natures before they got a dog, and thus avoid the hardship and heartache they will likely cause to a sentient being they have invited into their lives.

If any of the above reasoning could provide justification for causing a dog to live in exile, there is a final fundamental that we are overlooking:

Today, our evolved relationship with dogs is not the same one as that which was experienced by the cave dwellers and nomads who first forged bonds with the species. We have consciously and intentionally selected dogs as companions; a status quo that has now been maintained for millennia. Their expectations, before ever incarnating, have adjusted correspondingly. It now becomes of greater value and desirability to

a. their overall purpose
b. the range of experiences they intend to sample

that they dwell in close proximity with us, and don't get stuck outside, where they are largely ignored and taken for granted.

Only if we humans can adjust our thinking about *all* non-human beings, will this juxtapositioning of our lives with our dog's become redundant. In the meantime, it serves *us* that we have as close a relationship with them as possible. If we can start to see and respect the value in *their* lives, we might start to see the value in *all* life. And this is crucial learning.

He has a house of sorts, but is it a home?

Do dogs experience pain like we do?

Why would anyone imagine that they do not?

It may seem incredible to the reader, but human acceptance that dogs can experience pain is not a given. Our steadfast belief in the supremacy of the human has led us to explore not the similarities, but the differences between humans and animals, as if we needed to reassure ourselves of the validity of the supposition of human pre-eminence. As an almost coincidental aspect of this, it was long proclaimed and accepted that animals did not suffer pain as we do.

Absolute nonsense.

Dogs most certainly experience pain; but to say that they experience it as we do would be as misleading as saying that one human being experiences pain in exactly the same way as another.

Pain comes in various forms from the sharp and fleeting to the gnawing and sustained, and dogs may experience the whole range. Frequently they will evidence their discomfort through their various vocalised responses which would include a brief yelp, and continuous whining.

As with us, pain thresholds vary greatly. One may instantaneously respond to the slightest twinge or smarting, whereas another may be oblivious to anything inflicted upon them until the effect is excruciating.

Generally speaking, a dog's pain threshold will be considerably higher than a human's. And like humans, there is a great deal of physical pain that once we become accustomed to, we no longer register outwardly.

In fact, dogs are exceptional at bearing their discomfort without complaint or sign of the agonies it may be causing them; but it certainly does not mean that they are not going through every bit as much of a living hell as we might. Unfortunately, this can seem to support our misguided and erroneous belief that they do not feel pain at all.

In part, their tolerance is sheer fortitude; in part a fear of demonstrating weakness because of the way it may impact upon their standing in the rest of the pack; in part our inability to easily recognise non-verbal cues given by any species other than our own.

Revealing aches is also an issue of how the source of the anguish has come about. Dogs master gradually encroaching pain with ease. Guardians are far more likely to be able to spot the relatively short lived than they are those that creep up upon their pets slowly and affect them over long periods of time. Stomach cramps, bites, physically evident injuries, and even headaches may present themselves with an inescapable obviousness. But a dog is just as prone to crippling joint pain and aching muscles as humans are; to say nothing of cancers and other insidious diseases. We are likely to miss the symptoms of the physical repercussions as they will be masked by stalwart behaviour and an apparent enthusiasm for physical activity that belies what is really going on.

There is also a custodian's preferred self-deception. None of us like to think our loved ones are suffering. It can be easier for us to dismiss the evidence of our own eyes than face up to the fact that our pet is not as healthy as it once was. Furthermore, we should not allow our definition of pain to encompass only the physical. Dogs experience emotional pain that will cause them every bit as much anguish as its physical counterpart. Regrettably, this may be even more difficult to spot, and even more difficult to address.

Rene Descartes, the seventeenth century French philosopher averred that all animals were "thoughtless brutes". He referred to them as being "complex automata that can mimic human behaviour and sounds in response to specific stimuli". Because he claimed to know that they were lacking souls, he considered it perfectly accurate to say they were merely machines. As such, they could not possibly feel pain, and could only act as if they did.

To prove it, he reputedly spread-eagled a dog and nailed it down by its paws, whereupon he proceeded to dissect the animal whilst it was still alive, unaffected by the 'appearance' of pain, since it could not possibly be experiencing it. It was a 'proof' he was to repeat many times over.

Descartes was so highly regarded as a thinker, he has gone on to be dubbed 'The Father of Modern Philosophy'. His influence has lasted for centuries, impacting almost every element of society. Scientists in particular based both their thinking and methods upon his supposedly 'profound' observations, developing what is known as the 'Cartesian Method', i.e. one which follows Descartes' philosophies. First amongst his principles (and the probable reason why Descartes could happily be the deliverer of excruciating pain without remorse - other than being a sadist) was to: "Never to accept anything as true unless I recognised it to be evidently such". For this, read: "If I don't believe it, it can't possibly be right."

We did not move on quickly. As recently as the end of nineteenth century, and more than two hundred and fifty years after Decartes death, similarly 'learned' men were still expounding upon human predominance. In attempting to both illustrate and highlight the dissimilarities between human and animal physiology and response, they were still indulging in presenting similar barbarity to audiences of enrapt spectators, claiming that a key difference between the preeminent species on the planet and animals, was that the former experienced pain both physically and mentally, producing an emotional response; whereas the latter felt nothing.

Astoundingly, to this day the debate continues about how just much pain a dog experiences, if any at all.

Frans Hals portrait of the blameworthy and not so charming Rene Descartes

Why do dogs seem to hide their pain?

For reasons that might strike humans as unnecessary.

When pain is an instant thing, catching them off guard, even the most stoic of canines will be unable to mask the discomfort that courses through their body. A sudden yelp or even something approaching a scream is a sure sign of an uncontrollable urge to give vent to what ails them. But given a choice, most dogs will not betray their physical experiences with anything nearly so obvious. Within their 'natural' world, crying out in pain is to evidence weakness. To do so in front of others is a potentially dangerous thing to do.

Puppies learn at a very early age that showing anguish is a sure pathway to alienation from their siblings and a short walk from an existence plagued by bullying or rejection. In a wild pack environment, weakness of a physical kind can represent a threat to survival, revealing frailty and drawing unwelcome predatory attention to the group. Therefore, dogs come hardwired with the instinct to eliminate infirmity amongst their own kind. Every dog knows at some level that palpable registration of suffering may result in attacks from their own pack, intended to eradicate that risk. Even if they are not in a canine pack, they try to avoid showing their anguish at all costs. This tells you that if a dog cries out, it's pain is sudden and unexpected, or quite serious.

Cries of pain may be misinterpreted as signs of aggression that can cause other dogs to respond aggressively. Unlike most canine vocal communications, pain related noises merely indicate suffering, without any further explanation or nuance. Like humans, dogs learn at an early stage to interpret what they mean. But whereas human scenarios for understanding what these (otherwise incomprehensible) sounds mean tend to take place in controlled environments, dogs first experience them through direct or peripheral involvement in puppyhood confrontation. In the melee of a fracas, sounds of pain are intermingled with those of belligerence. In the minds of participating and observing dogs, both noises become associated with the violence that is transpiring,

Thus, when they hear a pain sound, even if it is made in the absence of hostility, the association is made with the fighting scenario in which they have previously heard the noise. Their likely response is therefore one of instinctive and defensive antagonism towards the one emitting the noise.

Irrespective of the cause, dogs intuitively try to mask pain. If the above explanation makes them sound heartless and vindictive, it is only because we have lost touch with the fact that they are, in essence, wild animals, like any other. It is only through chance that we have domesticated them. Despite innumerable generations of adaptation on their part, primal instincts remain.

It should also be noted that given different circumstances, behaviour is very different. Pain that does not elicit an immediate and alarming outburst is recognised vibrationally, and dealt with by other dogs far more sympathetically. Dogs are neither callous nor oblivious to each other's sufferings, and if no threat is perceived, they will often respond with sensitivity and respect.

Of course, the downside of such a stoic mentality is that many humans watching their dogs age can be oblivious to those tell-tale signs that their dogs might let slip. For some, it may be convenient to ignore suffering, using the rationale that 'if they don't show it, it can't be that bad'. Others may conclude that their pet's apparent bravado as a response to themselves, concluding that their dogs do not wish to disappoint them by showing suffering, and there may be some truth in this. However, there is little that dogs may do to adequately convey what they go through and their suffering in silence is seldom just about us. The uncomfortable irony for any caring guardian is that because of all that is written above, they may believe it is necessary to mask their misery. We are after all, their pack.

In short, if you can tell that your dog is in pain, you may be confident that what they are experiencing, on a pain scale comparable with a human one, is something way worse than most of us will ever have to go through.

Can dogs tell if they are ill?

Of course. They are acutely aware of their own physicality.

Not only can dogs tell when they are ill, they are remarkably adept at recognising whether they may do anything about what ails them.

Within every dog exists an instinctive knowledge of herbal remedies, or at least a basic understanding of the power of plants to bring about reactions within the physical body. Unfortunately, these 'curatives' may not be freely available to them, perhaps due to their living environment, and so their ability to self-medicate is by no means unlimited. Even if illness is not a factor, they are sensitive enough to their own needs to recognise when their bodies are suffering from deficiencies or imbalances and in a somewhat similar fashion to humans taking vitamin pills, they will actively seek out sources of nutrients crucial to their wellbeing.

Most guardians will, over time, observe their dogs eating anything from grass to soil. But they may also note that certain types of grasses are preferred, and realise that there is more to these behaviours than quirk or habit. Although by no means infallible in their choice of prescription, dogs could tell us humans a thing or two about what we have forgotten is available to us in nature.

Self-awareness of ailment, and possible cures, is a feature of every dog's consciousness.

Do dogs get ill for the same reasons as humans?

To understand the answer to this, it is necessary to understand why, broadly speaking, humans get ill.

All humans are prone to experiencing minor ailments such as colds, headaches, muscle strains etc., but these are temporary and of little consequence to our learning. Significant illness presents learning opportunities for us, and may be part of our contractual purpose whilst we are within any one lifetime.

Although choosing to have a disease, especially a terminal one, may seem like a bad choice, the experience of having that illness may be of great benefit to the individual, or members of their family who are affected by it. Coming to terms with, accepting and even embracing physical difficulties and the emotions they create can provide huge leaps forward in our personal learning. Although the circumstances at the time may seem painful in so many ways, in the long run, deciding to go through illness is always a good thing and something we *must* do.

However, we can also acquire illness during our lifetime because of what we create in our own bodies. Our minds have the ability to control every aspect of our physical being and we can bring about disease through stress, negativity, anger and all sorts of other 'less than healthy' emotions.

It is no different for dogs. They also need to experience serious illness during some lifetimes, simply because of the learning this will bring to themselves, or their people. However, the likelihood of dogs creating illness for themselves is considerably less than ours because dogs do not encumber themselves with the same emotional baggage that we do.

Some people speculate that dogs can (voluntarily) take on the illnesses of their guardians. This is not the case. To do so would be to deprive their person of their learning opportunities and interfere with what was intended. However, they may well be affected, albeit temporarily, by the vibrations a disease in their person will inevitably cause.

Can dogs tell if something is wrong with one another, and if so, what do they feel about it?

Whilst a dog is no diagnostician, their perceptions about illness are acutely observed. But responses are not so sophisticated.

The same traits utilised by dogs that are employed to detect illnesses in humans, apply equally to their perceptions of one another. Simply in passing by another dog, they may detect a vibration that is not as it should be; one that is unbalanced or symptomatic of disease (i.e. literally not at ease). A good butt sniffing will confirm almost all suspicions, but their ability to sense precisely what is wrong comes with a fair number of flaws. Their experience does not allow them to amass and maintain a comprehensive database of ailments; although over time it is possible that they may come to understand more through experience and association. From their perspective, it is the knowledge that a dis-ease is present that is more important than knowing precisely what it is. They can determine if it is serious, or merely passing and relatively trivial.

How they respond is an issue of their own development.

For the most part, dogs are powerless to assist one another (although licking may be observed as a method of trying to correct gaps in an auric field which are also symptomatic of dis-ease). Therefore, sensitivity to what is affecting another may vary from responses that suggest sadness and empathy, through to gung ho chivvying along. And this is because these are precisely what their responses are.

Dogs are not ignorant of their own inadequacy in being able to help one another. But they are more fatalistic in their outlook. If the dis-ease is serious, the sufferer will be treated with according respect and a somewhat resigned approach. If the illness is passing, encouragement is the better support strategy.

They also have a heightened awareness of the nature of disease and the role it can play in all our lives. Thus, they accept it, and whatever it may bring, with far more ease than we might.

Can dogs suffer from mental health issues?

Although the causes are somewhat different, a dog's state of mind is every bit as prone to circumstantially induced mental health issues as a human's.

It may strike us as strange that other beings can suffer psychologically, but a failing to accept or recognise this point is missing a whole level of understanding of animals. Any sentient being has the potential to have its thought processes and emotional state disrupted so as to cause what we would recognise as mental health issues.

Dogs may suffer from depression, anxiety attacks, emotional breakdowns, bi-polar disorders, and even psychological disorders that parallel schizophrenia or total mental imbalance.

Like humans, these issues present themselves as challenges for the individual that they may or may not be able to overcome. They are no less challenging for dogs than they are for humans.

Just as an unbalancing response in a human's psyche may be caused by circumstantial events and pressures, self-imposed or otherwise, so it is for dogs. The difference is that *we* are often the catalyst for what unbalances them. Our actions and treatment of our dogs are far and away the greatest single cause of mental health disorders in our pets.

Many years ago, I worked with an individual who owned a Red Setter.

She was a beautiful creature, extremely affectionate, gentle and sensitive, and utterly devoted to my colleague and his wife. They took her everywhere with them, and they frequently referred to her as their 'child'.

After some time, the marriage ran into problems. Inevitably, this resulted in extended arguments and a very altered atmosphere in their home. Both 'parents' would be intermittently either too angry to have time for the Setter, or desperately needy of its unquestioning and relentlessly loving ministrations.

Over time, the dog began to undergo subtle personality changes, constantly seeming to be ill at ease. She became, in their terms, quite 'needy' and unpredictable.

Eventually they separated, and prior to their divorce, they agreed upon shared custody of the dog. Unfortunately, the exchanges of the animal were bitter and often accompanied by accusations and recrimination. During these times the dog palpably registered great stress and confusion, and irrespective of which partner it then found itself with, it cried piteously. This was not met with sympathy.

After only a few weeks of this new status quo, the Setter had what they termed a 'complete nervous breakdown'. It would not settle at all, refused food, whined or howled 'at nothing', and was in a constant state of apparent torment. So they mutually agreed to have their pet put to sleep.

It's easy for us humans to be concerned about the harm that we do to other beings of our kind with our own issues, but if we are closed to the intelligence and sensitivity of all beings, we can easily wreak havoc on the lives of *all* of those who care about us.

Not a dog with mental health issues (it's not a laughing matter).
Just one pulling a face to fill in the space!

Does spaying or neutering affect dogs mentally?

It certainly has the potential to do so, but will most likely not because of pre-incarnation expectations.

From many perspectives, including protecting dogs from themselves and the population explosion they are capable of producing, spaying and neutering is not only a necessity, but a very good thing.

When dogs incarnate it is with planned intention and awareness of the likelihood of them experiencing parenthood during their lifetimes. It is an accepted fact that not every incarnation presents the opportunity, and that steps will be taken to ensure that this is not the case. Memory of intended experiences and planned events in a lifetime are seldom recalled at a conscious level, but during the neutering procedure, if anesthesia is administered, the subconscious mind where such data is stored and accessible, takes over. Thus, the dog has access to the knowledge of what was intended and to the extent that it is possible (bearing in mind the uncomfortable physical repercussions of the surgery), will not 'mind' that they have been rendered barren.

There are of course exceptions.

Because they are so subject to what humans require of them, what a dog has planned and intended for its life, even with the pre-agreement and collaboration of their people, may be swept aside in an instant. The same being that had agreed to cooperate in allowing them to experience parenthood may deny them that chance on a whim, since they are also unlikely to be mindful of pre-incarnation agreements.

A dog that then undergoes unanticipated sterilization may awake from the procedure experiencing mental repercussions, most commonly depression. How long this is sustained for becomes an issue of mastery for the dog. Whether they can overcome potentially overwhelming emotions that can create a personality alteration, will be a matter for their own strength of character. They may or may not exercise their ability to understand that the outcome of the surgery will ultimately be a matter of how they respond to it.

Are dogs aware of it when they are dying?

Almost certainly "Yes".

A dog's awareness of its own physicality (and that of other beings) far exceeds that of a human.

We have already seen that dogs can be trained to indicate when a human has cancer or is about to have an epileptic fit; but you will have noted that recognition of the condition is not something that they are taught, it is a capability that they have to begin with. And this ability to identify physical imbalances and understand their repercussions is something they may apply to themselves as well.

As a result, they are most certainly aware of the imminence of their own death, and that of others. It enables them to prepare themselves psychologically and goes some way towards explaining why their response to death may be more balanced and accepting than that of their people. Only a sudden death precipitated by an accident or instantaneous physical malfunction will prevent this awareness. Nonetheless, the manner and time of death is predetermined for all beings.

If physically capable, a dog that is aware of its impending demise may use its remaining time to demonstrate particular and unusual affection towards its people. Naturally enough, the desire to do this will be dependent upon the strength of the bond that exists between them. The humans may notice the display, but likely be blissfully oblivious to the import it carries.

A few dogs, aware of their imminent passing, will prefer to be isolated from their pack and loved ones. If the opportunity presents itself, they will wander away to die. The behaviour is a mirror of what wolves may choose to do in the wild, and is not uncommon amongst other species too. Choosing to leave this world as they came in, alone, may be a learning choice for them; but it may present some heartbreaking challenges for caring guardians. This is best met with acceptance and should be viewed as a learning opportunity the dog provides.

Why do some dogs just seem to give up when they are dying?

Why not? It makes things a lot easier for them.

Because of their heightened level of physical awareness, a dog can pretty much tell when the end is near, or when there's no point struggling against the inevitable. Under these circumstances, some will refuse to eat, be reluctant to move, and eventually not drink, thus guaranteeing their demise. They know what is coming, so why fight it? Why not embrace it?

We humans spend countless dollars, endless amounts of time, and bucket loads of emotional energy, desperately trying to prolong our lives. Sometimes we may be rewarded by extra time that we might regard as 'precious', but medical science can work against what we have intended for ourselves before incarnating. A part of our learning can be about letting go, and not being fearful about what is to come. When we resist the inevitable, we may be doing ourselves a great disservice.

Dogs are not beleaguered by fears about dying. They have an instinctive knowledge that passing is not the end, and thus they may accept their fate. They take heed of its call and are less apt to struggle. It makes the transition easier and far less fraught for them. They can pass with grace and emotional ease, prepared, and on their terms.

Of course, for their people, seeing their beloved pets giving up is a bitter pill to swallow; but only because so few guardians understand that this is their choice, which *should* be honoured every bit as much as a DNR order. If we forcibly try to cling onto their lives (ostensibly on their behalf, but in reality, because we cannot bear to let them go), we do them no favours, and may even be consigning them to a repeat lifetime.

The opposite reaction is probably worse. When we see rapidly failing health in our pets, it is most frequently taken as a cue to euthanise them. It's time to get a new one!

Deciding whether to fight for the life of a pet is a gut-wrenching decision for most guardians, if they will even give it a second thought. So many of us rush in to try and save them, simply because of our great love for them.

One of my most powerful memories of childhood is of my parent's Siamese cat, who in later life suffered from a dis-ease of his liver. I vividly recollect my mother's determination that he should not be *allowed* to die, and since he refused all food and water, this involved force feeding the animal concentrated liquid beef essence, along with extensive chemical medications.

After several weeks of this 'treatment', he rallied and lived for a while longer before a second round of the dis-ease kicked in. This was met with the same response. A third finally claimed his life. The overall effect was to prolong his life by perhaps as many as two or three years.

At the time, it never struck me as anything but the 'right' thing to do. The cat was loved by all and none of us wanted to lose him. But even today, although he passed nearly forty years ago, I can still recall his wretchedness during his 'treatment'. I still wonder if he was in pain during the intervals between the bouts of obvious suffering; and I cannot help but feel that perhaps it would have been kinder to let him go when he had so obviously chosen to do so.

The only way I can reconcile my feelings about the issue is with the knowledge that perhaps in the actions of our family to 'save' him, there was learning for both us and him.

However, with our dogs, having taken so many that are riddled with dis-ease when they arrive, we have tended to take an approach to their care that alleviates pain and suffering, but does not attempt to fight the inevitable.

This does NOT mean automatically euthanising them, for reasons which will become clear later in this chapter.

Why do some dogs respond positively to the introduction of another, perhaps younger dog, if they are old or sick?

For some pretty good reasons, but not necessarily the ones you might imagine…

A new and unfamiliar presence in a home can be a tonic for an old and ailing dog. Guardians who bring a fresh member into their pack often report that the new dog has given their old dog a 'new lease of life'. Although not always the case, a dog's interest in all that is around them may seem to return; their activity levels increase; their eating improves; and they may even rise from their sick beds! We joyfully see what we would wish to see, and credit the turnaround to the pleasure the old dog takes in the company of the younger one.

If the incumbent dog is thrilled to have new and stimulating canine company, this tends to occur if a companion has already been lost, or if the dog has been ignored by its people for most of their time together.

But most often, the older dog's reactions are not evidence being overcome with excitement or enthusiasm for their new companion. The spur to an improvement in health is caused by simple rivalry. The incumbent is unwilling to have their place usurped by a young upstart, and so they make a special effort to evidence to their guardians that they are still very much 'alive and kicking'.

Sadly, the effort this takes may eventually take its toll. Aching limbs that were being rested must now be brought into action again. The desire to simply sleep must be put aside in favour of play. Food must be forced down, despite a lack of appetite, just to stop the newcomer stealing it. The upturn in health is seldom long lived, and the old dog may eventually 'crash'.

However, bringing a new dog to the home as an older one ails is *not* something to be discouraged. Whatever the reasons, the old dog may experience all the positive outcomes outlined above, and those fleeting moments of forcibly reliving their glory days may be worthwhile experiences, whatever the ultimate outcome. Who is to say they may not form a bond with the new dog, however the relationship begins? If nothing else, it provides companionship of their own kind. And the presence of a new dog may be great consolation to guardians when their old pet passes.

It would be remiss to not add a final cautionary note: There is also a possibility that the arrival of a new dog may alienate the incumbent from its guardians, if their attentions are now lavished upon the 'new model'. The 'sanctity' of their relationship may be breached and the old dog may feel rejected unless its people are careful to ensure that it still feels loved and wanted. Uncertainty about being loved may even cause a dog to be jealous and hostile towards a newcomer.

Unfortunately, many people seem unable to empathise with their older pet's needs. All too often, bringing in a new dog seems to provide justification for custodians to euthanise their old dog; or perhaps worse, surrender it to a 'shelter'.

If you think this sounds cruel and heartless, it is. If you don't think it happens, please take my word that this is a fate that befalls huge numbers of dogs every year.

A few years ago, we took in an old St Bernard who had been surrendered to a shelter by her custodians. Their story upon giving her up was that they had gotten a new dog (a younger male St Bernard) to be company for her. Unfortunately, she had *"attacked the young dog and done significant damage to him."* They claimed that she *"could not be trusted around younger dogs"*. They also expressed their concern that she *"was very old and would not make it through another winter in their climate"* and felt that she should *"go to a home where she can die in peace!"*

Her forelegs, face and nose were a mass of deep bite wounds that took a considerable time to heal. It seemed fairly evident that she had been attacked and that 'significant damage' had been done to her. When she joined our large pack, it was quite clear from the outset that she was actually a gentle and non-confrontational soul. We also brought her to a physical environment with a climate at least as bad, or even considerably harsher than the one which she had come from. And we brought her to a home wherein she would have to cope with several younger males. Funnily enough, she has now been with us for nearly 4 years and survived 4 hard winters. She has never attacked, or been attacked.

If she truly responded so badly to having another dog introduced into her pack environment, there is no doubt in my mind that it was because her people were thoughtless, stupid and insensitive in their introduction.

Or it could have been that they were barefaced liars with an alternative, self-interested agenda, that had precious little to do with her welfare.

What do you think?

Struggling to cope with climate and youth?

How do I know when it's time to euthanize my dog?

Why on earth would you assume that there will be such a time?

Inherent in this question there lurks the implication of a belief that dogs should be euthanised as a matter of course and that there is an onus upon us to decide when it becomes appropriate to end their lives. In other words, it is perfectly acceptable for us to play a godlike role and determine their fates, at our whim.

Even though the question may have been intended to be a caring one, based perhaps on a belief that all canine lives are ended in pain and suffering, from which any caring guardian must surely save them. Such thinking is plain wrong.

There may indeed be situations where euthanasia is justifiable because it ends great suffering and pain. But the power over life and death is something we should not take lightly, since it brings repercussions for both the animal and ourselves.

All too often decisions to end a life are based on 'convenient' kindness. Impaired sight or hearing, joint issues or immobility, loss of memory or degrees of dementia, susceptibility to all manner of illnesses, and potentially embarrassing personal issues such as incontinence are NOT reasons to have a dog put to sleep.

Dogs value their lives every bit as much as we do. Just because we consider that their quality of life has gone downhill does not mean that we should have them killed. Just like humans, they would rather endure the torments of physical decay than miss one more day that is available to them; one more meeting with loved ones; one more chance to look at the sky, and be glad to be alive. Dogs cherish every single living moment; every kind word; every loving touch of their person's hand; every poorly sensed scent; every experience that has made them relish their lives.

And even if they have been unfortunate in the circumstances their lives have thrown at them; even if they have lived harsh lives on the street being shown no kindness or compassion; even if they have been mistreated and abused; even if they have faced continuous cold and hunger; even if they have lacked freedom and experienced constant oppression; even when their lives seem unappealing and lacking in worth to us, this does not mean that every second has not been important and worthwhile from their perspective, or that they would for one second gladly give up their right to live, as we all too readily and easily suppose.

An individual who truly values their pet and honours the relationship they have with them, will only ever elect to terminate their lives where there are genuinely extenuating circumstances, where real suffering will be ended. People can tell us about their suffering. Animals cannot. But to assume that every dog's life ends in suffering so traumatic that we should automatically alleviate it, is folly.

Every dog would prefer to die on its own terms and the intervention of humans in precipitating the event may not only be highly unwelcome, but also damaging for them and their learning needs. How we cope with dying is as much of a learning point as how we cope with life. If the opportunity to go through the experience is curtailed by human intervention, there exists the possibility that we consign them to another lifetime, just so that they may go through the opportunity we have robbed them of.

Caring pet owners and those who have ended their pet's lives (and I am amongst the many millions to have done so) will be upset by these comments. Don't be if you can answer this question truthfully and be left with a clear conscience.

"Did you have your dog put to sleep for their benefit, or yours?"

At the time of writing this, we have lost seventeen dogs. Of these, only eight died of natural causes at home. We chose to have nine euthanized. All nine were rescue dogs whose lives before they came to us were in some way coloured by trauma and/or abuse. Many had been through multiple homes. One had lived with six families before arriving at our door. One had never had a home in the thirteen years of her life before we took her in. All suffered from cancers or some form of systemic collapse or breakdown.

If we felt we could, we would have let nature take its course and allowed the dogs the full learning that the experience of physical illness can provide.

With every single one, we waited until *we* were unable to bear their suffering, even though they bore it with strength and dignity.

Yet I know that in the case of at least two of them, helping them on their way was totally contrary to their express wishes and intentions, and I am always troubled by that knowledge.

Of the eight who have died at home with us, five had spent their whole lives in our home, having come to us as puppies. They slipped away in their own time, on their own terms.

It was by no means easy to watch them go and the temptation to intervene was great. Unlike the rescues, they were not in unbearable pain. They were not facing unimaginable agony. They did have to confront the ravages of old age and discomfort, but all faced their end with resignation and ultimately, ease.

It is only in writing this that I have come to realise the startling statistic the data above presents.

It must surely beg the question in the mind of the reader "What were the root causes of the illnesses that ensured the untimely ends of the rescue dogs?" The answer perhaps, is rather obvious.

If a dog is about to be euthanised are they aware of what is going to happen?

In most cases, they will have no idea. But it's a difficult thing to hide from them.

The ambience that surrounds having a pet euthanised is seldom a happy one. The stress experienced by the guardian, the probable venue of a veterinary clinic, the presence of a relative stranger, and the possibly negative associations from previous visits, will all combine to give a dog a clear indication that something bad is afoot.

Yet none of this will lead them to conclude that they are about to be terminated. Generally speaking, any expectations they may have will be drawn from their previous lifetime's experiences. Being euthanised may be something they have been through many times before and thus, their understanding of the situation is an instinctive one.

However, a dog that has developed and maintained the ability to read its person's mind may well have full knowledge of what is to come. This is particularly heartbreaking for them, since they are then powerless to do anything about it. Most will not even be able to believe it.

In some respects, the best that can be hoped for in a situation where a dog is about to be euthanised is that it has such an awareness of its imminent natural demise, that it will forgive those who choose to deprive it of its life; or is in so much pain, that premature termination will be welcomed as a relief from suffering and greeted without regret or desire to continue living. Unfortunately, this is very frequently not the case, as the previous question unintentionally implied.

How do dogs feel about the loss of a companion?

Potentially devastated; but everything is relative.

Almost irrespective of issues of liking one another, a pair of dogs provide company for each other and an opportunity to communicate with one of their own kind, on an almost constant basis. The loss of this can be a crushing blow, leaving the remaining dog potentially shattered. Feelings of grief, loneliness and isolation, possibly resulting in depression (or worse) are likely outcomes. Whilst popular thinking might have us believe that dogs 'live in the moment', their memories of a lost companion pass no more quickly than they would for a human.

However, there are several provisos one must place around this answer. These would include:

- The strength of the dog's response to their companion's loss will be in direct proportion to the strength of the bond that existed between the animals.

- If the dogs were a closely 'bonded pair' in the sense described earlier, the loss will always be tragic for the remaining animal.

- If the dogs were not 'close', the remaining animal's focus upon its guardians may be enough to fill any void it might experience.

- If the dog's guardians are unsympathetic to the loss, or are not physically present enough to provide substitute companionship, the remaining dog will feel loss, irrespective of their relationship with the dog that has passed.

- If there is another dog or animal in the house, it is possible that the grieving dog's focus for attention will switch to this one, substantially assuaging feelings of anguish.

- If the companionship was not a long term one, the remaining dog may not experience any sense of loss at all.

- The soul age of the remaining dog will affect their response and the extent of the sense of loss experienced. Older souls will have an innate understanding and acceptance that the parting is temporary, and be able to master their grief, overcoming it in a shorter amount of time.

- The introduction of a new companion may have the effect of distracting the remaining dog from its unhappiness if the newcomer is well chosen. But an incompatible dog may simply serve to exacerbate the sense of loss.

These two were always great, if somewhat unlikely, friends.

Do dogs understand death?

Probably a lot better than we do!

Perhaps much more than humans, dogs accept the inevitability of death. More importantly, they have an innate awareness of its lack of finality, and consequently, they don't tend to fear 'the end' in the same way that we do.

As with so many things, this can make their experience of life as a whole somewhat easier. None are fixated with 'leaving their mark' or the somewhat vain notion of having 'made a difference'. A statue erected in their honour, a building named after them, or a plaque on a house to commemorate their existence, would mean nothing to them.

This is not to say that they don't value their lives! Far from it. Many will want to cling on to the last precious seconds of their incarnate experience (which is one that we all too often deprive them of because it suits us). Others will totally understand that death is not the end for them, and even find some contentment in slipping away.

What is more important to dogs is:

-   That they have lived.
-   That they could take advantage of those opportunities that presented themselves.
-   That they have not lived lives full of disappointment, lack of connection, confinement and unrequited love.

When satisfied with their experiences of their lives, a dog may not only understand death, but also see the value in it, since it heralds the beginning of the next phase of their development.

Is it important for a dog see a deceased companion?

Not really.

Frankly, believing that seeing the body of a dead companion can bring closure for a dog *is* anthropomorphising. Even for humans, seeing the empty shell of a departed loved one can be a traumatic experience that distresses and haunts them. Dogs can be every bit as sensitive as we are about this issue.

Providing evidence of passing may offer certainty of what has become of a friend/companion. It will underline the finality of their passing. But since dogs have an innate understanding of death, it is not a useful healing opportunity for them.

Their awareness of their companion's passing, (if they are within reasonable proximity) will already be quite apparent to them. The sight of a dead body will be relatively meaningless. They know they've gone because they can no longer maintain telepathic communication or sense their vibration.

Unlike us, they know with confidence that they will see them again. If they feel any grief or sense of loss, seeing the body will neither assuage the emotions or make them any easier. But it might make them worse.

One of our dogs collapsed and died of a heart attack quite suddenly. It was shocking and upsetting, doubly so because he was the father of a litter that is still with us. But it was before I wrote this book and became aware of the issues; so at the time, it seemed to be the 'right thing' to let his mate, the mother of his children, see his body before Tristan and I buried him. We led her outside to where he still lay and she sniffed him for the briefest of moments. Then she looked up at us as if to say "Why are you showing me this?", and wandered away. If she was upset, she displayed no grief then or subsequently; or maybe that was her way of coping. I have no answers but am quite certain she was aware of the insignificance of death.

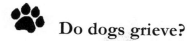 # Do dogs grieve?

Most certainly.

Anybody who has seen a grieving dog surely cannot have failed to notice their general state of withdrawal, accompanied by sorrowful body language, muted levels of (all aspects of) communication, and the distinct absence of zest. They may even have heard the piteous whining and seen the pain so evident in the dog's eyes. If you miss the symptoms, there is something significantly wrong with your ability to empathise.

But not all dogs are riddled with angst or an all-pervasive mournfulness. Some may seem perfectly normal following the passing of a friend. The danger for us would be to assume that they do not feel sad, or lament the bereavement.

Like humans, all dogs tend to grieve somewhat differently. Following a normal routine and not showing their feelings may be just as much of a coping mechanism as 'wearing their hearts on their sleeves'. The challenge for us as their guardians, is to have enough sensitivity to allow them to experience what they are going through, whilst treating them in a supportive and nurturing manner, and not discounting the fact that if they experience a loss, they may need us more than ever.

Grief is also a feature of soul age. The older the soul of the dog, the easier coping with grief and loss is likely to be for them.

The grief captured in this photo followed the passing of our alpha male, whom this dog adored. His mournful state lasted weeks.

Chapter 14

THE
SPIRITUAL
DOG

"My dog doesn't worry about the meaning of life. She may worry if she doesn't get her breakfast, but she doesn't sit around worrying about whether she will get fulfilled or liberated or enlightened. As long as she gets some food and a little affection, her life is fine."

Charlotte Joko Beck, Everyday Zen

Why do dogs live such a short time?

A short life may be all a dog needs to experience what they have determined their lives will contain. But irrespective, a lifetime can only be as long as its time may usefully be filled.

As a (very broad) general rule, the longevity which may be experienced by any being is in direct proportion to the range of experience which may be available to it during a lifetime. In other words, the more a being can go through, the longer its life is likely to be.

This is a generic measure and does not relate to the ability of the individual to take advantage of the potential that exists in any one lifetime. This may be limited by so many other factors.

The notional lifespan available to all beings (of any type) may be curtailed because of the need to include experiences that directly impact upon longevity, such as accident or illness. This is agreed upon before incarnation.

A dog's lifespan may be limited or extended by the choice of breed which they go through life inhabiting. Some breeds have considerably shorter lives than others; mixed breeds tend to live longer than pure-bred dogs. Because different breeds present different challenges and learning opportunities, all souls incarnating as canines must experience a wide variety of breeds (though not all), without the opportunity (or the desire) to elect for incarnation as only the longer-lived ones.

Also, factored into the equation must be the fact that many of the lifetimes dogs face will not be as they intended for themselves. A lengthy duration spent incarnated in the wrong place, having the wrong experiences with the wrong people, is not conducive to fulfilling intended purposes. Therefore, briefer lifetimes can be of some benefit, if only because they allow another 'shot at it' (i.e. life) with a chance of getting the right circumstances, sooner.

Although we humans may suffer greatly from the aftermath of their always too short lives with us, dogs do not.

Are dogs able to see ghosts?

A dog is certainly able to sense vibrational anomalies, and may see presences with more clarity than humans can.

Before this question can be answered properly, it's important to understand precisely what a ghost is. I cannot describe this is any way which is better than I have previously in my book *Tails and Tribulations*, so here are a few borrowed paragraphs.

A ghost is simply the residual energetic vibration of an individual that has been left behind in a certain place. It's not the actual person. It is an emanation of their energy that is trapped by its own inability to completely remove itself through the blue light tunnel that was made available to it upon its passing.

The reasons for this always relate to the free will of the individual and the selection of choices that go against that which is for their highest good. In an earth-bound soul, this freedom is so sacrosanct that we may even contradict our higher selves (even though it knows a lot better than we do what is best for us!). Thus, we may, in our dying moments, choose not to go, for whatever reason.

Unfortunately, our bodies are scheduled for departure, regardless. This leaves the vibration of the being in a state something akin to being shipwrecked on a desert island with little cognisance of their state of being, and no way of getting off the island until they themselves realize that they can float away!

Stranded, they can remain almost in perpetuity, their own energy sustaining the vibration that maintains their presence. It is not totally limitless and may be thought of as having the equivalence of a radio-active half-life, dissipating over (potentially) thousands of years. The longevity of its presence is a feature of the conviction to remain earthbound at the moment of passing. The stronger the desire, the longer it remains. However, the energy may be fed by the vibration of others:

When earthbound beings become aware of the presence of a ghost, their thoughts about this 'entity', which emanate from them (irrespective of their intentions) add to its energy and may by themselves sustain its presence. In certain cases, they may substantially add to it and even fundamentally alter its nature.

Since the ghost is largely unaware of its state of being i.e. it doesn't really know that it's dead, it tends to get frustrated and may seek contact with the living. When it is able to do so, the upsurge of energy it experiences reinforces its sense of self and therefore, it seeks more connection. We tend to call this a haunting.

Some living beings emanate far more energy than others. Children in particular, being closer to their point of entry into incarnation from the etheric, are much more vibrationally powerful. Therefore, many residual vibrations of this nature are attracted to them. This does not mean that they are harmful; simply that they feel more alive when around children.

Energy may be witnessed. Thus ghosts can be seen, if only for the most fleeting of moments. (Since children experience far greater ease in seeing them, this also helps to perpetuate their presence.) We are surprised if we see them and we have an alarming tendency to fear what we do not understand. A ghost is therefore generally regarded as a thing of fear, when in many respects it is quite a natural (if rather unfortunate) phenomenon.

A haunting begins when a vibration has been able to make itself known or has been perceived. The fact that it now exists in a state of awareness not only increases its energy, but also furthers other's awareness of it in the living world by word of mouth communication. In essence, the more people who know about something, the more the vibration gains in energy.

However, if people think about it negatively, the more negative energy is transferred to it. And so it may become something that it was not originally. This is also known as a 'construct', something that is the product of collective consciousness that has actually given it life.

Distortions of its energies may arise from the expectations that the living have of its purpose; in other words, we endow it with something other than that which it would naturally possess, most commonly, evil intent. We tend to do this because our collective consciousness, fed by the media, relishes the salacious and finds that fear sells. We have learned to fear ghosts and assume that they are bad. Movies that intentionally play upon fears, like The Exorcist, create an expectation that becomes its own self-fulfilling prophecy.

Many hauntings that would otherwise be quite innocent and harmless assume proportions that are based upon our fear, not upon the original intentions of the being that has not properly transitioned. That is not to say that the intentions of the departed being were automatically good; simply that we may, by our own devices, alter what is there.

A residual vibration cannot in itself be harmful. It can certainly affect our own vibration and cause a cascade of emotional and consequent physical response, but this in turn is a matter of our own choosing. If we are in mastery of our own thoughts, it can have little effect.

The more fear based responses that 'feed' a haunting, the greater its ability to impact the vibrations of others becomes, giving it the semblance of something that may be capable of intentionally performing harmful acts.

In truth, a residual vibration or ghost, is to be pitied not feared. It needs help in getting to where it should be as its progress has been waylaid by an unfortunate mistake in the exercise of its freedom of choice.

So, can dogs see them? Yes. They can certainly sense their vibration with utmost ease. And synesthesia will enable them to observe 'the unseen' with more clarity than humans, even though they might not believe or understand what they see!

Seeing ghosts is just plain disturbing for them. Spectral presence will cause a sensation quite unlike any they commonly experience. Dogs have no more comprehension of them than we might, and their reaction to seeing one (which will usually be very obvious to us) evidences a predictably alarming and unsettling experience.

However, in the light of all that is written above, you might well understand why there is no real need for people to be alarmed if they see their dogs behaving strangely in response to an invisible presence.

Can dogs actually be ghosts?

Dogs may become ghosts in the same way that humans can.

A dog ghost is a relatively rare thing, primarily because dogs do not experience the type of emotions that can cause humans to resist their passage through the 'blue light tunnel'. Nonetheless, a sudden or shocking transition can cause them to become 'trapped'.

They may be assisted in moving on in the same manner as humans (this does not mean via exorcism!), but will have far more difficulty in doing so because of their lack of comprehension of anyone trying to assist.

Dogs are not the only creatures that may find themselves consigned to a virtual netherworld. The potential exists for any animal species to become an incorporeal being, although relatively speaking, very few do.

An amusing picture, but ghost dogs can and do exist

Many years ago, I was driving down a very narrow, single track country lane in the English countryside, in the dead of night. Steep banks bordered the road on both sides, topped by dense hedges.
At one point, I slowed down to read a partially obscured road sign when suddenly, out of nowhere, a pure white dog appeared and ran across the road directly in front of me, narrowly avoiding being hit.

As it passed it was caught in the car headlights, but did not pause for an instant. In fact, it seemed totally oblivious to my vehicle. It simply dashed from one side to the other.

I thought little of it except to wonder where the house was that it had come from (or was going to) in such an isolated spot.

I drove on, but fifteen minutes later, I was retracing the same treacherously constricted section of road, and noted as I approached a signpost that I was in the precise place where the dog had previously appeared.

Then once again, the dog dashed across the road in front of me, this time causing me to brake hard. Again, it seemed totally oblivious to my vehicle. Again, a collision was barely avoided.

As I accelerated away, I mused that dog must have been returning from whence it came.

Then it suddenly dawned on me that it was going in the same direction as when I had first encountered it.

In that instant, I knew with absolute certainty that I had witnessed the ghost of a dog.

I reasoned that most likely, it had been killed by a car on that precise spot, and was now perpetually present in that place until released.

I was a young man at the time, without the knowledge and 'connections' I have now. I have often wished I had the opportunity to go back and help the stranded soul move on

.

What is the 'Rainbow Bridge'?

It's a lovely concept, but it's one which is simultaneously accurate and inaccurate.

The Rainbow Bridge is a concept embraced and beloved by many dog people. It is most easily explained as the holding place between our incarnate reality and what has been calling the etheric throughout this book (but many will think of as Heaven).

The notion is that our departed dogs wait for us in the grassy meadows at the Rainbow Bridge, where we joyously reunite with them, before crossing the Rainbow Bridge, presumably to then spend an eternity together.

The concept of the Rainbow Bridge is accurate in that when a being transitions from one lifetime to another and passes through the etheric, they certainly encounter all those beings with whom they've shared their incarnate lifetime (if they choose to do so).

Those who we meet are first recognisable in the form which we knew them, and then as the beings of light that they really are. Our reunification with our most beloved pets is guaranteed. For the most part, they will be members of your soul family, who you are destined to 'go around' with lifetime after lifetime. Not only will you see them again, you can't get away from them! By that definition, you are destined to spend an eternity with them.

Those dogs who have come to us unintentionally and are not members of our soul family, may also be present if they choose to reunite with us. However, that meeting may be the last we experience with them. This contact will be an expression of gratitude for the life you have shared together.

The Rainbow Bridge concept is inaccurate because the etheric is not Heaven. The etheric may be 'heaven like' in our conceptual understanding of it, but it is not a place of permanent residence for beings who pass over. It is merely a place through which we transition, although it may be thought of as a home we are temporarily visiting before setting out on further adventures.

Heaven in the way that we commonly perceive of it does not exist. Unfortunately, it is a convenient concept created as an aspirational reality: a place into which we have to earn entry by being 'worthy'. This is good way to try and motivate us to be good whilst we are here, but is ultimately a controlling mechanism. Everybody and everything returns to the etheric, only to move on again.

The Rainbow Bridge is a beautiful if slightly inaccurate concept.
(The conversion to B&W unfortunately loses the rainbow, but you get the idea!)

It has always struck me as somewhat odd that people might prefer to think that both theirs' and their pet's lives are permanently over, rather than consider the idea that the much-vaunted concept of 'everlasting life' means reincarnation.

Surely spending an eternity doing the same thing, however enjoyable it may be for a while, would be an actual purgatory?

When they die, do dogs go through the same process of evaluation as we do?

The process that all beings go through upon returning to the etheric is pretty much identical.

Following their passing, dogs are greeted by all those members of their soul family with whom they have shared a particular connection in their lifetime and basically party!

When they are ready, they will review their lifetime without judgement, rancour or distress of any kind. They will be able to be clinical observers of all that has transpired and observe both the cause and effects of all their actions, with particular attention paid to the ripple effects of their life choices.

They will then spend the remainder of their time before incarnation involved in the extremely detailed planning for their future lifetime.

Despite this sounding like a long and onerous task, it is a most pleasurable experience and in earth terms, may feel like it takes as little as a few minutes to achieve.

This is in part due to the fact the period of reflection that dogs go through begins before they pass. Elderly dogs may be observed as becoming increasingly withdrawn in their dotage. Were we to endow them with human qualities, we might suggest that they appear to be contemplative. This is precisely what they are. In their final days, extended periods of sleep and quiet may be evidence of the onset of absorption in a search for understanding of the truths of their lives.

This phenomenon is by no means unique to dogs. It assists in the process of transition and is undertaken by all those beings aware of the impending implications of their mortality.

This is not morbid or morose. It is a peaceful reconciliation.

Do dogs incarnate with the same soul family each time?

In the same time space, yes, but...

All beings perpetually incarnate with members of their soul family.

However, as we have already seen, intentions to connect with these individuals may not be successful and the dog may spend its lifetime with those whom it has no connection with whatsoever.

This phenomenon is not restricted just to dogs. Humans may be born into families that create blood ties for them, even though they may have no soul family connection.

For humans, this is usually intentional, since all by itself it creates another dimension of experience and learning opportunity. And when it does occur, it may be almost guaranteed that across the course of that lifetime, they will still encounter multiple members of their soul family.

The same is not guaranteed for dogs at all.

This one is on his second time with us.

What are a dog's purposes in life?

They are many and diverse, but probably incomprehensible to us.

When we discuss or hear the word 'purpose' when applied to a lifetime, we automatically seem to assume that it means having a task to perform that is highly significant and impactful. It is almost as if we feel a need to add the dimension of 'a purpose' to our existence in order for it to be meaningful. But irrespective of whether we are aware of it or understand it, all lifetimes are chock full of purpose!

Like us, dogs come with an agenda for what they desire to achieve. Each is unique and different. For a great many sentient beings, life's purposes may be briefly explained as fitting within three broad categories. Those which are about:

- Experience
- Relationships
- Service

Purposes relating to experience are about those things we go through on both major and minor levels. The way in which a dog perceives and responds to an event will define their learning from their experiences and the benefit that accrues. They will encompass everything from the minutiae of everyday events, such as playing with a frisbee, eating a meal, walking in a forest; through to major happenings or circumstances that affect whole lifetimes such as living rough on the streets, contracting a debilitating dis-ease, having puppies etc. The possibilities are almost endless.

All of our experiences inevitably change our outlook and thinking. Via a range that spans from miniscule steps through to giant leaps, our mindsets adjust. They are constantly evolving. As they do so, our motivations, choices and actions alter. The more experiences we have, the more we evolve.

Whole lifetimes are devoted to gaining new and different experiences. But as they evolve as souls, dogs arrive at a point where it becomes more relevant to their development to participate in exploring the ways in which those formative experiences shape their relationships with other beings; and not just those of their own kind.

There are countless permutations of what is possible in relationship terms, but when these have been examined to the extent that is deemed necessary, relationships evolve so that one being, who is more advanced upon their pathway, may be of assistance or service to others.

Dogs may be of service to one another, or to another species. The service may be overt, such as a lifetime as a Seeing Eye Dog, or less obvious, such as being the companion of another elderly pet. Again, the permutations of the possible are almost without boundaries.

Service is a new form of experience, and as much for the benefit of the soul living through this level of being, as it is for those whom they may assist. It is a total change in life focus.

It should be understood that this is a brief and rudimentary explanation of a dog's purpose. But if you were to now go back through the book and consider the questions and their answers in the light of what's written here, a great deal about what components of a dog's life contribute to their purpose then starts to become evident.

I am sure that there are many reading this now who already recognise that there is much more to dogs than meets the eye. You will doubtless have no problems accepting much of what is written in this book.

However, I have come across many who believe wholeheartedly that our four legged friends are 'put here' to help us on our journeys through life. It seems quite natural for us to assume that dogs are only here for our benefit. Surely, if other creatures have purposes, theirs are at best ancillary to ours; or even inconsequential when compared with our own. Framing a dog's purpose in terms of the roles they play in our lives is therefore a logical extension.

I unreservedly concur that dogs *do* help us on our pathway, but to imagine that this is their sole purpose for being cheapens their existence as the sentient and purposeful beings they are.

We humans may like to perpetuate a belief about our existence that is based upon absolute human supremacy and total domination over the other beings on the planet. We may prefer to reason that all others are here to serve our needs because we're the only thing that is important. But this is very definitely NOT the case!

We are *all* here with purpose. Our lives interact with, and even integrate with other species for (notional) mutual benefit. Their purpose and existence is every bit as valid as our own.

If the reader takes anything away from this book, it would be my profound hope that they fully understand that the importance of all life does not stem from our ability to control it.

There's more to life than just having a blast?

Are dogs aware of their purpose in life?

No more than we are.

Imagine how you would feel if you grew up knowing that you had arrived in this lifetime having already established for yourself a route map or plan of the life you intended to live, complete with complex and challenging learning and experience criteria, that are vitally important for you to fulfil.

Envisage that you are fully aware of your self-imposed objectives and the implications of not achieving those goals that you have set yourself; of realising that if you fail to succeed with any of them, you add to an almost perpetual 'to do' list, and that you automatically consign yourself to at least one further lifetime wherein you try once again to fulfil those purposes.

How do you feel about that? Do you believe you would be able to live your life freely, without care or concern? What other emotions might affect you? Are you:

Tense?
Pressured?
Resentful?
Frustrated?
Angry?

When we transition through the etheric, we have a laissez faire attitude towards what we will face in our upcoming lifetimes. We realise that in the 'big picture', intimate knowledge of our purpose is by no means a good thing. We know that when we are incarnate, our perspective will change substantially, and if we are cognoscent of what is intended for us, by us, we could all too easily (literally) freak out!

Thus, when we arrived, we are like clean slates. Our memories are blank and the only knowledge of purpose that we carry with us is embedded deep within our 'soul DNA', perhaps surfacing at some stage, but only when we're ready for it. We may be prompted into recollection by the beings that remain behind in the etheric, but only if we have asked that they do this for us. More likely, we may experience people, or events, or situations that provoke us to remember, and we may undergo something best described as a 'spiritual awakening' (although we are unlikely to recognise it as such at the time). Such happenings may change the course of our lifetimes and alter our pathways irrevocably. But only if we want to open our eyes to the truths of our existence and accept that we all have a purpose.

As it is for humans, so it is for dogs, and every other sentient being on the planet. We are all subject to the same protective rules for our existence and like us, dogs only develop a sense of purpose when their deepest instincts cause them to reappraise their lives. The slight difference is that the circumstances they intended for themselves in order to achieve their purposes, are so often dependent upon getting to the right home in the first place. Since this always presents a degree of difficulty, it accounts for why a dog's list of purposes may be far less complicated (but no less important or valid) than our own.

Upon a blank slate, great wisdom may be written.

Do dogs become aware that they are on a journey of multiple lifetimes, as humans might?

Yes, sort of. They couldn't progress without something 'clicking'.

A spiritual awakening within a dog cannot accurately be said to parallel that of a human. There are too many differences in the lives that we lead to expect they could come upon a dawning of understanding quite as we would. Nonetheless, through the experiences of their life, the connections they make, the processing they undertake and conclusions they arrive at, they most certainly do become aware of the need to make certain choices within their lives.

Whether this understanding incorporates knowledge of the entirety of the process is a matter for the individual dog; but progress in total ignorance is an unknown thing. A dog's arrival at such awareness would not likely be a thing we might notice, or could observe and be wholly confident in what we were seeing; at least not without comparative referencing of that same being's behaviour across numerous lifetimes. But just like us, they do get there.

Would we even be able to recognize awareness if we saw it?

Are dogs fulfilling their original purpose in being here, as a species?

Judge for yourself.

The purposes of a dog's life are as manyfold as our own. Overall, in the broadest possible terms, it may be stated that a dog's purpose is to live synergistic and supportive lives with another species, wherein one or both may help the other on their journey.

Dogs are not dependent upon us for their progression, although a high level of necessary collaboration exists. We are supposed to learn every bit as much from them as they do from us; in some lifetimes, more so.

Are they fulfilling that purpose? I think so.

A dog who taught me a great deal.

Chapter 15

DOGS IN AND FROM RESCUE

"Saving one dog will not change the world, but surely for that one dog, the world will change forever."

Karen Davison, The Perfect Companion

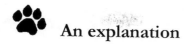

An explanation

This chapter is a little different from the others, because I didn't receive any questions about dogs in need of rescue.

Because of our personal experiences with rescue dogs, I know a great deal about the issues of dogs that find themselves displaced. Naturally, if you are not exposed to this world, there is no particular reason why you should have any knowledge of it; but I am still shocked by how little awareness there is.

I shouldn't be. It is only as recently as ten years ago that I started to gain an appreciation for the suffering of dogs in need of rescue. So, I thought it would be a good idea to include this section about some of the issues they face and the impact the experience has upon them.

What follows is an unashamedly blunt exploration of what becomes of dogs that find their way into rescue situations. Whilst it may appear critical in tone, it is certainly not intended to be a condemnation of anyone. The situations faced by individuals who work in the types of establishment discussed herein are egregious to say the least. This is simply a frank assessment of the way things are. It is a cold hard look at a problem that most of society would prefer to turn its face away from.

It should be noted that the references made are to common practices in North America, and the statistics are derived from the United States, simply because they are easier to access. The situation in Canada is somewhat less harsh (particularly regarding shelters having no-kill policies, which are much more common north of the border), perhaps because the dog population is so much smaller. However, US policies and practices are by no means untypical of any country, apart from the fact that they are *significantly better* than in most countries.

It is also worth understanding that these figures only relate to dogs, because of the subject matter of this book. The statistics for cats are worse, and it must be noted that countless other species are affected by the same issues.

What is the purpose of a life where the dog is in need of rescue?

Tragically, it's valid and often necessary.

Sad to say, going through several lifetimes where they lose their homes is standard stuff for dogs; as are lifetimes spent living (at least in part) 'wild' or 'rough' on the streets.

In many respects, never having had a home shared with a human is better than having one and losing it, if only because you don't miss what you've never known.

The experience of being separated from a beloved family and all that is familiar, is a deeply painful and upsetting one for any dog. Although it presents trials and challenges which, if successfully endured, lead to great learning and development, it is a grim experience that all too seldom has a happy ending.

 ## How big is the problem?

It's major.

Estimates vary enormously, but it may be concluded with certainty that the total dog population on the planet is more than 500 million and as many as 900 million. However, it is likely that of these, only about 300 million are 'companion' dogs and the remainder are strays (from birth) or unwanted pets that have been displaced from their homes. This means that there may be as many as 600 million unwanted dogs.

Whilst the majority of strays from birth are thought to be mixed breed dogs, displacement of dogs effects purebreds also.

Two of an incredible (possible) 600 million.

 ## Defining the term 'rescue'

The way the term is used here is not as you might expect.

In this context, I am using the term 'rescues' generically to cover those places in which dogs find themselves if they are lost or surrendered, from which rescue becomes necessary if they are to survive. Be they dog pounds, shelters, humane societies or animal control establishments, these publicly funded 'rescues' seldom offer the safety their names might imply, and are not in themselves, places of permanent refuge, or anything close to 'homes'.

I am *not* using the term to describe the great many independent and safe 'rescues' that do provide a safe refuge for those who come into their care. These operate on a voluntary basis and most often utilise foster homes to place their charges, whilst seeking permanent or forever homes for them. These rescues tend to take their dogs from the above-mentioned establishments, and without them, countless unnecessary deaths would occur. This is because when a stray is found, or when somebody surrenders their dog for rehoming, if they are not handed over to one of these genuine safe havens, the chances of the animal ever finding its way to another home are 50/50 at best.

Terms like 'shelter', and sometimes even 'humane society', belie what the place may be there for. The descriptors are comfortable platitudes that allow people discarding their pets to convince themselves that they are doing 'the right thing' by their animal, and giving them the opportunity for a better life. After all, it sounds so much better than 'the dog pound' or 'animal control'. ('Animal Welfare Services' is also a popular misnomer).

 ## What happens in 'shelters'?

Standard procedures are followed.

There are approximately 13,600 publicly funded, community animal shelters in the USA.

Where the named organisation is local authority controlled and funded, they usually have responsibility for 'animal control' (catching strays etc.) as well as accepting animals brought in for surrender by their custodians.

A typical sight in a shelter.

Full time staff are paid, but many shelters will have volunteer workers too.

The number of animals which may be admitted will be limited by the size of the facility.

Conditions vary enormously depending upon the age of the property and the amount of financial resources that have been allocated for the building.

Frequently, new arrivals will require medical examination and possibly extensive treatment.

Mandatory spaying/neutering of unclaimed dogs is standard policy before adoption.

Commonly, any stray dog arriving through its door will have a limited period of opportunity to be claimed by its people before it is put up for adoption. This is usually days; sometimes as few as two.

Surrenders are automatically put if for adoption, if they fulfil certain criteria.

Being put up for adoption is by no means guaranteed, because all dogs are submitted for a behavioural assessment intended to determine whether or not they are suitable for adoption.

If they do not pass the assessment, they will be euthanised.

Depending upon the extent of the overcrowding problem faced by the organisation, dogs passing assessment may have as little as two weeks in which to be adopted out to a new family; sometimes less.

After that time, they will be euthanised.

The greater the number of pets arriving through the door, the less likelihood there is of them surviving. Shelters in areas with the highest arrivals rates or those with very limited resources become what are referred to as 'high kill' shelters.

Survival time in these may be less than one week.

In many respects, taking a pet to one of these organisations can be little better than taking an old refrigerator to a recycling centre. Unless it is in very good condition and a newer model, the chances are it will immediately go for scrap.

There are 'no-kill shelters' where there is a policy that no animal that enters through their door will be euthanized, except in cases of great suffering.

These may be few and far between.

 ## What happens in a behavioural assessment?

Boxes get ticked or crossed and lives hang in the balance.

Assessments of a dog entering a shelter are made very early on, usually within the first 24 hours.

Largely because of the volume and frequency with which they occur (to say nothing of the financial implications), behavioural assessments are almost certainly not conducted by dog behavioural experts, or even veterinarians. There is no legal mandate for the qualifications of those who should conduct the assessment in many jurisdictions, and the task falls to staff who must follow a standard format, involving scales of measurement, or simple yes/no answers.

The assessment is intended to explore the animal's responses to 'key factors' such as behaviour towards other dogs, responsiveness to commands, attitude towards food (removal of), leash malleability etc.

Responses require subjective judgement on the part of the assessor, although those completing the forms may get input from their colleagues.

A part of the assessment is the breed 'desirability factor'. Purebred dogs are favoured over mixed. Certain breeds are more appealing than

others and therefore more likely to be rehomed. Some, even purebreds, may be considered unadoptable. Mostly this will affect the stereotypically 'aggressive' breeds.

It is estimated that as many as 93% of all dogs of a Pitbull type that find their way into shelters will be leaving in black sacks. Irrespective of any positive and friendly behaviours they may demonstrate during their incarceration, they may not even be given a behavioural assessment. Their breed alone is enough to mark them for death, so fixed have we become in our belief in the danger they present.

If a dog fails to make the pass grade in the assessment, it is almost certain to be done away with. But even if it passes, there is no guarantee that it will survive.

If there are too many dogs that pass assessment for the available space, the shelter may practice a strict 'first in, first out' policy; so those animals that have been in the shelter for the longest without being adopted are terminated first. Others may select those with the greatest perceived potential for adoption, to stay alive.

How this latter assessment is made is a matter of subjective choice by the staff of the particular organisation.

Nonetheless, certain selection criteria may come into play. For instance, although unproven, 'black dog syndrome' is a term used by shelters to describe the fact that black dogs are, statistically, far less likely to be selected by potential adopters, and therefore spend far more time in shelters.

The inevitable breed preferences or prejudices of assessors may come in to play. A dog that is noisy or has rambunctious tendencies, irrespective of its friendliness, is less likely to be on the positive side of a selection.

Consider the experience of being in that situation from the dog's perspective:

The sense of fear will be overpowering in many kill shelters, particularly in those that are crowded and terminate their inmates. Quite apart from the fact that an abandoned dog is usually terrified, confused, miserable and depressed, if it responds to the atmosphere in a manner that reflects the emotions therein, it is likely to display many negative qualities that have very little to do with its true personality, and a lot to do with the stress of the circumstances.

Disorientation and fear will inevitably colour a dog's behaviour, and prompt unusual reactions. Inaccurate assessments unavoidably account for many deaths. Dogs that have been, and would still make the most wonderful pets, die in vast numbers.

The desperation in the eyes cannot be hidden.

Several of our rescue dogs have been saved from euthanasia after having failed behavioural assessments. They have not been problem free, and initially struggled to cope with the trauma they have experienced. Nonetheless, all have gone on to be wonderful dogs.

How many dogs survive the shelter experience?

Far less than you might hope.

Some authorities claim that of the dogs entering shelters, approximately 35% are adopted, 31% are euthanised and 26% of dogs who came in as strays are returned to their custodian. The remainder are in too bad condition to survive, but are not counted in the euthanised figure.

Statistics may be used to tell any story desired, but even those of the (possibly optimistic) ASPCA acknowledge that at least fifty percent of those dogs who enter such establishments do not come out again and end their lives on the tip of a needle, or even in gas chambers.

At least things are improving. Last year it is claimed that only 1.4 million of the dogs that found their way into these places were euthanised. In recent years, when the financial crunch first hit, the figure was as high as 4 million put to death. But if we were to go back to the 1970s, up to 15 million per year were being executed. And these are the figures for the United States alone.

Shelter accommodations.

Sadly, despite extensive efforts to educate the public about the plight of rescued animals (carried out over many years), a study conducted by Best Friends Animal Society revealed that nearly forty percent of the public still believe that shelters are safe places for their occupants.

 ## Why do dogs find their way into rescue situations?

For some good reasons, and a lot of bad ones.

Per the latest available statistics for the USA, approximately 3.9 million dogs enter animal shelters nationwide every year. About twice as many animals enter shelters as strays (lost, abandoned, thrown out of their homes or otherwise living rough) compared to the number that are relinquished by their custodians.

Without delving into the arguments about puppy farms, irresponsible breeding practices or careless attitudes towards spaying/neutering, there are many reasons why a custodian may wish to surrender their pet. These may be categorised as genuine reasons, fault on the part of the custodians, and excuses for dumping the dog.

Of course, how 'genuine' a reason is has a lot more to do with the person giving it, than A part of the assessment is the breed 'desirability factor'. Purebred dogs are favoured over mixed. Certain breeds are more appealing than others and therefore more likely to be rehomed. Some, even purebreds, may be considered unadoptable. Mostly this will affect the the explanation itself.

Per the American Humane Association, the most common reasons why people surrender their dogs are as follows:

- Place of residence does not allow pets (29%)
- Not enough time (10%)
- Divorce/death (10%)
- Behaviour issues (10%)

The remaining 41% is not accounted for.

Cesar Milan's website has a top ten list of reasons for dogs needing rescue that is a little different.

- Lack of training
- Lifestyle changes
- Moving (new place doesn't allow pets)
- Not enough time for pet
- Cost of dog guardianship
- Health issues
- Biting
- Too many animals in the home
- Allergies within household
- Straying

This is all very civilised, but let me posit some more reasons. (NB. There are some overlaps with Cesar's list, I'm just not being that polite.)

- Can't cope with the dog.
- Bored with dog.
- Dog is too old.
- Can't spare the time to look after the dog.
- Dog is ill.
- Baby issues (already covered in a previous chapter).
- Got a new, younger model.
- Dog's personality has suddenly changed.
- Somebody suddenly (almost miraculously) developed an allergy.
- Somebody died and nobody will take their beloved pet in.

I could go on. Speak to people who work in rescues, and you will discover a general level of cynicism about the excuses people give for abandoning their pets. Every day they face the lies they are told by those who wish to exonerate themselves from responsibility for their own shortcomings; but despite efforts to hide them, the reasons are pretty transparent.

The ASPCA list is rather sanitised, Cesar's is more honest and explains the first one on my list; but what neither seems prepared to face is the fact that large numbers of people will treat dogs as disposable items.

Co-existence with a canine is not an easy thing. We struggle with it at least as much as we do with our fellow human beings, the principal difference being that we can't (notionally) just throw people out if they get too much for us.

The plain truth is that countless people enter dog custodianship in a gung ho and ill-considered fashion. They research what they will face poorly, subscribe to 'dog mythology' all too easily, and aren't prepared to live with the consequences of their own choices.

A great deal of the outcome of the decision to take in a dog will be of their own making (Cesar's 'lack of training' item), and yet it is the dogs that suffer. Our society attaches very little stigma to giving up on a dog, and there is no chance of the dog contradicting the distortions of truth custodians will utilise to try to make themselves appear blameless.

Irrespective of how the animal arrived at its place of confinement, the one thing that all of these dogs now have in common is that they are in need of rescue.

What sort of dogs find themselves in rescue situations?

Any dog may find itself in a rescue situation irrespective of age, breed, gender, size, or personality. Shelters are often replete with older dogs that have been cast-off by their owners; many puppies begin their lives in shelters, either because their mother was a street dog or because custodians have decided to rid themselves of the dog once its pregnancy became evident.

It's a very common misconception that only mixed breed dogs are abandoned by their people. In fact, between twenty-five and thirty percent of dogs found as strays or surrendered to shelter facilities are purebred.

Certain breeds are more likely to be in rescue than others. At the time of writing, the top ten are:

1.   Pit Bull Terrier
2.   Chihuahua
3.   Labrador Retreiver
4.   German Shepherd
5.   American Staffordshire Terrier
6.   Dachshund
7.   Boxer
8.   Beagle
9.   Border Collie
10.   American Bulldog

The primary reason for there being do many more mixed breeds in rescues is quite simply because they are the progeny of unplanned matings of unsprayed and unneutered dogs.

Purebreds may not be any more likely to be adopted than mixed breed dogs. They are indeed more likely to be claimed, simply because they have typically been bought from a breeder and therefore their custodians have invested in them. (Mixed breeds, often given away from unwanted litters, are generally seen as more disposable.) But surveys indicate that potential adopters have a general perception that purebreds will cost more. They are associated with higher levels of post-acquisition expense due to their greater potential for health issues. Their usually shorter lifespan is also an off-putting factor for many.

Additionally, for adopters, many purebred dogs, with their specific looks and claimed personality traits, do not have the mass appeal and popular regard as mixed breeds. Surveys indicate that the majority of people seeking to adopt from shelters arrive with an expectation of taking home a 'mutt'; and some potential owners may feel that 'privileged' purebreds are not as sympathetic or worthy of rescue as crossbreeds

The notion that only dogs with behavioural issues (more commonly described as mean or bad dogs) find their way into rescue, is ridiculous. On a relative basis, only a tiny percentage of all dogs have what may be termed undesirable personality traits, and these are as likely to have been engendered and developed by their humans as they are to be part of their psychological make up.

Uncertainty can all too easily lead to misery.

How do dogs feel when they're surrendered to rescue?

Devastated. Plain and simple.

For dogs living rough or lost, it is possible that being taken to a shelter presents the illusion of safety and a return to something approaching the normality they might have known. For the worst off, it may offer a glimmer of hope for them that they will be returned to the home they loved. But as the statistics indicate, it's a 1:3 chance of a happy ending.

For dogs who have lived with people and are being surrendered, there are few experiences in their life that can come close to the emotional agony of being placed in a rescue. From their perspective, it is a betrayal from which some never fully recover. The act of abandonment by their custodians is distressing beyond anything we may be able to imagine. They are being discarded by those they trusted, removed from everything that is familiar, handed over to strangers, deprived of their freedom, and probably being separated from those they loved. The cruelty of the action, irrespective of the reasons, will always be incomprehensible to the dog.

Just like being put in kennels, the dog may adapt, or the dog may spiral into hurt and depression. In the case of latter, the emotional range they will go through will be something like this.

- CONFUSION, followed by
- ANGUISH that rapidly develops into
- FEAR, leading to
- PANIC, overtaken by a wave of
- EMOTIONAL PAIN that quickly turns to
- PSYCHOLOGICAL AGONY subsequently replaced by
- HELPLESSNESS and feelings of
- FUTILITY, growing into a gnawing
- MISERY that becomes
- GRIEF AND HEARTACHE, finally displaced by
- DEVASTATING DEPRESSON.

Those that are psychologically robust will stand a better chance of not being broken by the experience. They will still be in turmoil and hurt, but if they can hold on to hope, they may come out unscathed.

The experience is truly one that presents a challenge for a dog on its journey.

It may not be there yet, but depression is a common factor for many of those who are discarded.

Perhaps one of the most shattering situations which will result when a pet is put in a shelter occurs because their much-loved person has died and the deceased individual's family is either unwilling or unable to take in their relative's beloved companion.

I always find this particularly heartrending for two reasons:

Firstly, I can all too easily imagine that it might have been the dead individual's fondest wish that their pet would be taken care of. In my observations, canine companionship can be a blessing for the elderly, the sick, and the dying.

But in equal measure it must be terribly distressing to know that there will be no one to care for and love the animal you have cherished after you are gone. I recognise that I am endowing everyone with the same feelings I would have myself, but I do believe that it would be a person with a very hard heart who could ignore an uncertain fate for their pet.

Secondly, the dog must cope with the grief of losing its person, then its home, then being displaced and imprisoned, and then it might not even survive.

The trauma must be horrendous.

 ## What is the experience of a dog in rescue?

However kind and compassionate the staff may be, it's still not a good one.

Depending upon the age of the facility and the wealth of the authority that runs it, dogs will find themselves in small, usually windowless enclosures that seldom do more that comply with statutory requirements imposed by local authorities. These are usually established in conjunction with veterinary or animal welfare bodies. However, a very large number of older facilities may have considerably smaller kennels and a lack of funding to upgrade them. The floor will be concrete, or some other surface that can be easily hosed down. One end of the enclosure may have a lockable door that gives access to an outdoor exercise area into which the dogs will only be released for a certain part of the day. The other end gives access to the main facility and may be barred, meshed, wired or even solid.

The enclosures may have single occupancy if the facility is not overcrowded. Dogs that do better with company may find themselves sharing with others. Unsociable animals will be left alone.

Modern buildings, purpose built for animal welfare, will be considerably lighter, having better accommodation and possibly facilities such as an infirmary/assessment room, and an isolation room (which must inevitably double as termination rooms in kill shelters), and large outdoor exercise/toileting areas.

The routine for dogs will consist of long days spent in isolation in their (very limited) 'cells'. These are punctuated by kibble meals, and an exercise period which will vary enormously in length and substance based upon policy, facilities and availability of staff members and volunteers.

Exercise may be as little as 15 minutes in a grassless and confined area that is only a little bigger than their cage. Only very well-funded facilities have larger grassed areas. It may be a communal or individual exercise period, depending upon shelter policies (which may come down hoe risk averse they are) or the temperament of the dog, and others in the facility. Aggressive dogs or those responding badly to confinement will find themselves alone.

The enclosures are usually hosed out once per day, during an exercise period.

Excitement may present itself if a prospective adopter visits the facility.

When visitors leave, hopes are dashed. The prevailing air of excitement and anticipation dies down and anticlimax and disappointment set in.

Daytime bravado may give way to nighttime fears.

Staff who are sensitive to the despondency will try to encourage the dogs and give them as much love, encouragement and personal attention as time allows for. But as those caring individuals would sorrowfully concede, the environment can never replicate a loving home.

At night when the dogs are completely alone, the silence is often punctuated by pitiful whimpering or occasional mournful howling.

 ## How do shelters attract adopters?

By relying on walk-ins, coupled with the power of the internet age.

Historically, rescues have had to rely upon public awareness of their existence to encourage potential adopters to come through their doors. However, social media has greatly assisted in spreading awareness of the plight of many helpless creatures, and many shelters have their own websites, as well as listing their 'inmates' on public sites such as Petfinder.

The quality of input and information on these sites varies enormously. It usually (but not always) includes a photo of the animal, and a description. Photos, often taken in a rush or under difficult circumstances, may be of very poor quality, and unflattering to the dog. This can make the animal seem lees unappealing than it is in real life. Descriptions of them can be unrevealing and impersonal, or even be so perfunctory as to only contain a supposition regarding the breed.

It may be supposed that the dearth of information provided is down to staff shortages or a lack of time on the part of staff members; or that in some rescues it is possible that the staff lack the motivation or creativity to describe their charges fully. Or perhaps they have not made the connection that the more fulsome the online description is, the more potential adopters they are likely to attract.

Somebody. Anybody. Please.

However, there is also the possibility that their staff have been specifically instructed not to publish too much information about an animal. This would be a precautionary measure taken to protect themselves against litigious adopters who might sue, claiming that they suffered disappointment because they relied upon information given to them by a shelter and their adoption did not work out. Whilst it is farcical that this should be the case, it is certainly a possibility.

Some shelters and rescue groups partner with pet supply stores like Petsmart, who have an in-store adoption program that has now been in operation for more than ten years. These should NOT be confused with other large stores that still sell dogs, mostly sourced from puppy mills. This perpetuates endless suffering, hardship and (per research carried out by the University of Pennsylvania School of Veterinary Medicine) potential behavioural problems.

Others may organise adoption events held in parking lots of local malls or other open areas, where the public may come and meet the dogs in neutral, open areas, where the dogs may feel more at ease.

How do dogs in rescue react to potential adopters?

Each according to their own.

Reactions may be greatly circumstantially dependent. Those dogs that are greeting prospective adopters in the type of events listed immediately above will likely be able to conjure an optimistic state of mind. If they have been confined for extended periods in the limited spaces and caged runs of a shelter environment, the opportunity presented by such 'day release' will engender excitement and anticipation. The responses to those who visit with them will be correspondingly upbeat. The danger is that they may appear overly excitable. Only those who have attended several such events will realise that they are no guarantee of rescue.

The situation may be somewhat different with those who are not afforded the chance to put themselves on show at such an event.

If you walk around a dog shelter and comparatively observe the occupants, it is relatively easy to spot those who are managing the experience, and those who are sinking into the mire of misery that might engulf all eventually. Their reactions may be broadly categorised as follows:

- Those who will come to the bars of their cage with smiley, grinning faces, a furiously wagging tail, and a panting tongue that is eager to lick. They exude enthusiasm and will befriend you in an instant. If you leave, they may bark as if trying to call you back. That's exactly what they're trying to do. These are the dogs who still have faith that if they put on a good enough show, somebody will love them again. What the visitor seldom sees is the complete transformation that can occur once the prospective guardians have left, and the all-pervasive sadness that sets in when the light goes out.

- Those who appear aloof or diffident. They will be alert and watchful, but wary and cautious. You may catch them watching you intently, although if you do so, they will feign disinterest. It will take some considerable coaxing to get them to engage with you and if they do, they may be either skittish or shyly demonstrative. These are the ones who hardly dare believe that there is a chance for them. Their initial reserve is their way of putting on a brave face. They have experienced too many disappointments already and do not wish to build themselves up with false hopes. They are going downhill.

- Those that are unable to cope. The easiest to recognise, these are the ones huddled in a corner, faces turned away, heads hung low. They are seemingly uninterested and unresponsive to attempts to gain their attention and (unintentionally) make themselves unappealing to prospective guardians. These are the ones who are crippled by their grief, or unable to get over the sense of betrayal that plagues them. Often the older ones, they have already lost hope or cannot master the devastation the experience has wrought upon them. They are broken and at the bottom. A happy ending of any sort is a slim possibility.

Dare I hope?

From everything you have read in this book, you may realise that their behaviour is a matter of their own freewill, and a challenge they must overcome to move forward. Those who have felt the most for their people will feel the pain the greatest and struggle the most.

 ## How do shelters select adopters?

With varying degrees of care.

This will vary greatly depending upon the shelter in question. But generally speaking, anyone can turn up, provide proof that they are not underage, furnish the shelter with an address and an assurance that pets are allowed, and then take the dog away.

However, it is being increasingly recognised that shelters are a potentially easy source for the cruel and unscrupulous individuals who want to obtain animals for use as 'bait dogs' in dog fighting rings. If you don't understand the term, you are probably best not to.

Consequently, more searching measures are being implemented to try and provide some protection for these most vulnerable creatures.

 ## How does a rescue dog feel when it gets adopted?

A dog may be ecstatic that it is being freed from a shelter; but it is equally likely to be cautious and concerned.

Even those that display the most crowd-pleasing antics to draw attention to themselves may not be able to live up to the perpetually enthusiastic promise they offer to all-comers whilst incarcerated.

The longer a dog has been 'inside', the more institutionalised it may have become and consequently, the more intimidated it will be by another change to what has become familiar.

The pleasure of contact and receiving attention is obvious.

A flooding sense of relief and disbelief may be displaced by growing trepidation, caused by massive uncertainty and a rising tide of doubts and fears.

A dog that has been previously owned and discarded will inevitably have been considering the reasons why it was abandoned in the first place and be anxious not to repeat the experience.

A dog that has never had a home will simply not know how to react to anything it now experiences.

For a period, any dog may mask its true self every bit as much as humans do when meeting somebody new.

Adopters expecting instant love and gratitude may be disappointed. These will come later, but in the meantime, the dog is still at risk.

What is the success rate for adoptions?

Less than might be expected.

The image and notion of dogs who, once rescued from a shelter are instantly comfortable with their new people and are bundles of pure joy is an easy one to conceive of. So, it is all too easy and comfortable to assume that everyone lives happily ever after. Sadly, this is not the case.

The fail rate for adoptions is upwards of 10%, and there are estimates as high as 40%. Of that number, over 70% fail within the first few days following the adoption. The figure may be massaged somewhat by not including in the failure figures dogs that get adopted, then returned, but subsequently have successful adoptions thereafter.

These are not good statistics to broadcast because they are potentially off-putting for prospective custodians; but if more people understood why there are so many failures, the circumstances might not arise with anything like the same frequency.

Expectations are high.

Why do adoptions fail?

The reasons for returning a dog almost always come down to one of two things.

It might be imagined that there are a whole host of reasons for an adoption failing, but basically all the reasons given tend to come down to one or the other of these two:

1. "The dog's temperament was unsuitable"

or

2. "(I/my partner/my child) discovered (I/he or she/son or daughter) have/has a dog allergy. (For this one, just pick whatever is appropriate.)

For reason two, read reason one 9 out of 10 times; and for reason one, read "The dog didn't live up to expectations."

Expectations for a dog that has been rescued are high.

Stories of dogs liberated from shelters often extol the sainted virtues of the animals, including their remarkable loyalty, great affection and obvious gratitude.

But whilst it is certainly the case that these attributes are the features one may commonly expect, they may take a little time to develop.

For many rescued dogs, particularly those that have been imprisoned for a long time, or come through an especially unpleasant time, adoption results in tremendous anxiety because of their desperate desire for the whole episode to be behind them.

Despite the freedom and the potentially loving family, they have no automatic reason to trust or feel secure.

Those from certain backgrounds (particularly puppy mill rejects or lifelong strays) are unlikely to *ever* have been:

- played with
- had a toy
- been fussed with
- been loved by a child
- been inside a house
- ascended or descended stairs
- walked on (or not on) a leash
- slept on a bed
- have had grass beneath their feet (in some extreme cases)

Although circumstances are obviously not quite this bad for all dogs, I could fill another book with stories about what dogs *do* face that would sicken the compassionate reader.

Release is not without anxieties.

Why do some rescue dogs have difficulty adapting to new homes?

For all sorts of totally understandable, but apparently unforgivable reasons.

Whilst we might expect them to instantly recognise the benevolence of an adopter and anticipate a seamless transition, for the dog, the 'jury is out'. Although some may feel instantly at home and adapt, appearing as if they are finally in the 'right place' (which they might well be) there are some dogs that will need a considerable period of adjustment to get used to (what for them will be) a wholly new situation.

As a result a rescued dog might:

- Withhold and shun affection
- Be suspicious and on edge
- Be standoffish
- Seem uninterested
- Appear antisocial
- Be hostile to existing pets
- Be food protective (particularly if they have been living on the streets)
- Be unresponsive to calls
- Not be playful
- Act fearful of the new family
- Be picky about food and water
- Obsessively mark territory (even their own beds)
- Bark at the slightest provocation
- Appear wholly ungrateful

There will be very good reasons for these behaviours (most which are fear based) which you may be able to work out for yourself.

It may take weeks, months, or even years to get over what has happened to them in the past. Some never do completely. Sadly, dogs do not live in the moment in some respects. They *can* be emotionally scarred for life.

Excitement and eager anticipation on the part of adopters may not take into account the extent of the horrors that the dog has been through.

People can find themselves faced with a new dog that dramatically defies their expectations. It may seem as miserable, if not more so, than they appeared in the shelter. It may exhibit behavioural traits that prompt profound disappointment. Lack of understanding, empathy, patience and tolerance all too often result in dogs being returned.

Conversely, the dog may be so totally thrilled and joyous at its release, and so ecstatic to have found a new home and people, that its ebullience will be beyond anything the adopters had anticipated.

Thus, a rescued dog might:

- Constantly want to interact
- Have apparently boundless energy
- Be extremely playful
- Run around wildly
- Be invasive towards existing pets
- Pull overly-enthusiastically on a leash
- Demonstrate seemingly perpetual excitability
- Be excitedly demanding of food
- Obsessively mark territory (even their own beds)
- Bark animatedly
- Be apparently domineering

Again, there will be very good reasons for these behaviours, which you may also be able to work out for yourself.

The unbridled joy and pleasure a dog feels at receiving a reprieve from death or unending uncertainty, may come spilling out in cascades of spontaneous delight that its new people receive as overpowering and unnecessary. It is difficult to appreciate the release from tension that the dog may be undergoing. Dogs develop an awareness of their potential fate when in rescue. They know that they have had a close call. Yet their zest for life, and their overwhelming desire to demonstrate their happiness can all too easily be their undoing.

Even when it is on its way to a new home, a rescue dog may be uneasy and fearful. It does not know what is to come.

A further reason for these types of behaviours being demonstrated stems from a simple attempt by the dog to be accepted and please their new people. They act based on what they *think* will please and in so doing, essentially present themselves as being 'over the top'. They have no way of knowing that from a human perspective, they are trying too hard.

So, when the dog is returned to the rescue and that excuse "The dog's temperament was unsuitable" is trotted out, in all its many forms and permutations, the greater likelihood is that the dog, under the immense pressure it felt, was unable to relax and be itself any more than some dogs are at their behavioural assessments. Thus, it has been rejected and ejected once more.

Although somewhere between 10-40% may seem like a small number to go through this experience, it still accounts for a huge number of adoption failures that could otherwise be avoided with a little understanding and patience.

 ## What happens to rejected dogs?

A rejected dog that is returned to a shelter will basically be starting all over again.

Unfortunately, adopters are often inclined to embellish how the dog was in their home, to provide justification for the return of the animal and ensure that they are allowed to adopt again. If they are convincing, the staff will not spot the deception and the dog will now have a black mark against it. If conditions in the shelter are pressured, the returned dog is now more likely to be in consideration for euthanising.

However, if circumstances are favourable, the process begins all over again, the only problem being that the dog is now more uncertain than ever about its future, and even more temperamentally vulnerable. Repeated rejections may ensure a dog's apparent lack of adoptability.

 ## Do dogs know when they're in their forever home?

With an insight that should by now come as no surprise to the reader.

One further reason why dogs experience unease in their new homes relates to how their adopters have approached the process: Shelters will often have a policy that insists on the dog being returned if circumstances in the new home do not work out. This is a very good policy for the rescues to adopt for a whole variety of reasons that are ultimately in the dog's interests.

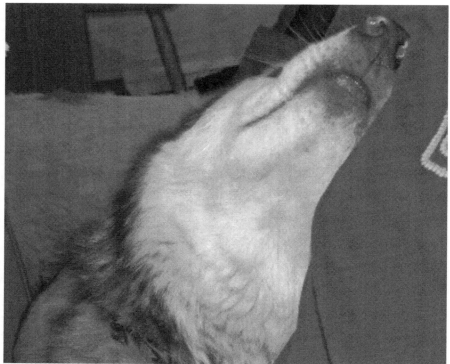

A dog will instinctively know when it is home for good, and respond accordingly.

However, many people will approach adoption as if they were taking the dog out for a test drive, and if it is not totally to their satisfaction, they will have no qualms about returning it and looking for another model. Unfortunately, the dog will sense the uncertain and unresolved nature of their predicament and know at a deeply instinctive level, on a moment by moment basis, whether or not they're being accepted in their new home.

There is a major difference in the vibrational responses of those who have taken the dog and are committed to sticking with it, come hell or high water, and those who are just taking the no-risk, free, home trial. Knowing that they are under assessment, their ability to relax is severely hampered and although not necessarily the cause of all of the new home responses outlined above, certainly a factor in whether or not they are able to get over them. A dog that senses commitment and the genuine intention to offer them a forever home will make the adjustment to that place with far more ease than if they do not.

How do real/safe 'rescues' work?

Diligently and strictly.

Real rescues, in the truest sense of the word, are safe havens that do not euthanise. Some will take all-comers; some only purebreds; some only specific breeds; some only dogs of a certain size; and others only those over or under a certain age.

Privately operated, they function through networks of volunteers, (although many are just run by one or two individuals) and commonly instigate many fund-raising initiatives to support their activities. Their dogs are often placed in foster homes. This is a far more comfortable situation for them, allowing the dogs to maintain a certain level of continuity in their relations with humans. It makes the transition to a forever home a much easier thing.

They seldom suffer from the same limitations regarding attracting adopters as their public counterparts. They may be better resourced, and their volunteers often take publication of information very seriously. Multiple photographs, video footage and comprehensive descriptions of their animals are quite common. Forthright analyses of a dog's shortcomings and strengths are published, utilising private/public sites.

Of course, there are no guarantees for adopters, and even with these dogs, the expectation for a dog might not match the actuality of the experience; However, if they are returned, they will go back to another foster home and not be at risk.

The rescues are generally very aware of the stress multiple rehomings will cause a dog, and as a consequence, they are often extremely strict in their adoption processes. Unlike their public counterparts, they have the luxury of not being under so much pressure to move the animal on so as to create space. Therefore, their objective is to make sure that the right dog goes to the right home, first time out. An application to adopt may require completion of a very detailed questionnaire, telephone interview, home inspection, and the taking of veterinary and personal references.

If this seems extreme, think again. The sole purpose is to do as much as possible to ensure the welfare of the dog. If it were a human that was being adopted, we would think this amount of research deficient and would expect far more personal details (such as means testing), along with police references, to be taken. But because it is only the fate of a dog in question, we would consider more complex procedures 'over the top'.

If anything, what is described above represents the ideal. But these processes are not always applied. Some are every bit as lax as shelters, others even stricter than outlined. Breed specific rescues (for instance) are particularly renowned for the desire of those running them to protect 'their' breed, which they do with considerable vigour. It is common for them to insist on adopters already having had previous experience of the breed, or other strictly applied criteria. If anything, their own ferocity in protecting 'their' breed may damage a dog's chances of finding a good home. We're not ready to be challenged when deciding something as 'trivial' as getting a dog.

It would not be appropriate to end this answer without mention of an alternative model that exists outside of North America, where large scale successful rescues operate on a more professional basis, complete with full time staff and facilities.

Perhaps most notable amongst these is the world renown Battersea Dogs and Cats Home, which has been in existence since 1860. Spread across three different locations around London, England, it is a shining beacon of what is possible with a commitment and determination to protect, by combining a business mentality with genuine caring and dedication to animals. They may boast of excellent facilities and a history that has ensured an almost unparalleled understanding of the problems involved in their work, for both humans and animals alike.

Operating like a well-oiled corporate machine with a sophisticated management structure, BDCH has a large full-time staff contingent that includes a team of veterinary surgeons and assistants that would be the envy of any shelter. They may also rely upon a substantial volunteer pool, and a publicity/marketing function to rival any private company, that enables their continued success.

Most significantly, the Home offers a truly safe refuge for thousands of animals every year. They have a policy that whilst physical circumstances permit, they will never turn away an animal in need. Moreover, they will keep that animal safe and well cared for until a good home is found for it.

But what is truly remarkable is that all of this is achieved without any Government funding whatsoever. They have attained a reputation that is second to none, and the mere name is enough to engender goodwill and public support, which has ensured their survival and growth even in times of economic hardship.

It is interesting that the success of this model has not been emulated in cities on the other side of the Atlantic. The far more decentralised proliferation of pet welfare solutions has meant that some areas are well provided for, whilst others struggle. Whereas these smaller rescues must rely upon very localised support for their survival, the Battersea Home may call upon a catchment area that extends across the whole country.

 ## What is the prognosis for dogs from rescue?

If given the time, and treated with the patience, sensitivity, tolerance and acceptance that they deserve, a dog from a rescue situation has a more than excellent chance of developing into the loyal and devoted companion, typified by the dog mythology.

Only those who are too scarred by the bitterness of their experience to regain their trust in humans; or are dysfunctional because of the choices they have made for their lives, will not be able to adapt to new homes.

Many people who adopt will ultimately report the sense of gratitude that their dogs seem to convey to them, and form bonds with their new charges that they may come to regard as unparalleled.

There are a whole host of reasons why rescue dogs should not be excluded from an individual's thinking when they are looking for a companion. Not least amongst these is that for some dogs, it is the only way they might be able to get to the 'right' person.

 ## Why do dogs elect to have these sorts of lives?

They have no choice.

It is a sad and unfortunate truth that across the possible spectrum of lifetime opportunities that are available for a dog, going through the whole rescue experience, with all its potential horrors, is basically an essential.

A lifetime allied with a human that is consistent, secure and cruelty free is a surprising rarity. However, if you consider that at any one time there are at least 500,000,000 dogs on the planet, perhaps it's not so surprising.

 ## An acknowledgement

It is important to acknowledge the wonderful work done by those who work in rescue – public 'shelters' or otherwise.

Every day they may face heartbreaking experiences and sights that have a blistering effect on their souls.

Individuals who care deeply find themselves making choices that eat away at them a little more each day, sometimes up until the point where they can no longer bear their work.

They make our lives easier. We should be grateful for them. Thank you, whoever and wherever you are.

Chapter 16

A FINAL TRUTH ABOUT DOGS

"Mankind's true moral test, its fundamental test (which lies deeply buried from view), consists of its attitude towards those who are at its mercy: animals. And in this respect mankind has suffered a fundamental debacle, a debacle so fundamental that all others stem from it."

Milan Kundera, The Unbearable Lightness of Being

Dogs are the lucky ones.

Dogs have evolved their preferred animal companion status by chance. But the privileged position they occupy in the hearts of those who are likely to read this book is by no means global.

There are surely few readers who will not be aware that eating dogs is practiced in some Far Eastern countries, and even celebrated in festivals that involve rounding up stray dogs, or kidnapping pets.

I have no doubt that many readers will be shocked and appalled by this practice, disgusted that anybody could treat 'man's best friend' so dreadfully. If you feel this way, you are rightly indignant. Dogs are amazing creatures with a level of sentience beyond anything our society typically gives them credit for. I've just spent over 400 pages explaining it. They deserve better.

But let's just pause to think about that.

We decry what happens to dogs in other places, yet we happily participate in, and are knowingly complicit in the slaughter of 160,000,000 other animals *per day*. This we consider acceptable, because we call them food, whereas dogs are pets.

It is only through fortuity that dogs are not considered the stuff of meals all over the world. The decision wherein the lucky ones became our companions, and the rest merely fodder, happened eons ago and was taken in ignorance of the understanding that ALL creatures go through the same process of progression during their lifetimes of journeying, just as humans do, and just as dogs do.

The information outlined in this book is not exclusive to humans and dogs. It is relevant to all creatures. They are not here for us to subjugate or use as we please; and they are certainly not here to be our foodstuffs.

Were we to see them in the etheric in their true form, we would be unable to distinguish between what was human, and what was dog, lion pig, cow, chicken, elephant, sheep or whatever.

Dogs are no more 'worthy' of companion status than any other being; and all beings *could* be our companions. In adopting dogs, we are persuaded by matters of convenience such as size or level of food consumption, and beliefs (often ill-founded) about cleanliness or ferocity.

Perhaps above all else, we do not believe that we can have a nurturing relationship with non-traditional pets that is reciprocated; that some animals are naturally more closely allied with who we are than others; that they do not all share the ability to give the love and devotion to us that we would wish from our pets. Or perhaps we just don't want to look at the fact that others might.

Deep down, inside every living human, there lurks the knowledge that all animals are the same as us. All creatures, be they two legged, four or none, think, feel, have emotions, and are on their own journey.

They are every bit as capable of having meaningful, loving and companionable relationships with humans as any 'domesticated' pet. They weren't put here for us to eat. They treasure their lives. They are devoted to their young. They don't want to die prematurely so that another creature can have a meal.

It seems that the vast majority of society is happy to wait for science and accepted thinking to catch up with the knowledge of what some people already experience. Do we really need tangible proof of the soulful nature of other creatures, rather than trusting in what we instinctively know to be right? Are we happy to ignore our instincts about them, or turn a blind eye to how we make them suffer?

While we are content to allow excuses like taste, tradition habit and convenience to seemingly exonerate us from the horrors that are perpetrated against so many benign and gentle beings, we might do well to reflect on the fact that our beloved pet dogs, who although eminently suited to their role as companions, are no different from any other animal soul out there.

They're just the lucky ones.

You may well have realised by now that the information within this book has been delivered with a purpose that is only partly about helping us understand dogs better. It has been just as much about you as it has been about them.

As you have read and (hopefully) paused to consider the implications of what is written, you may have discovered broader insights. They are not radical or earth shattering, but if you have allowed it, you will have come to a subtle understanding of a great many things about the world around us, and gained insights into human kind, and maybe yourself.

As I have gone through the process of being the conduit for writing it, I have learned every bit as much as the reader might. When I began, I knew virtually nothing of the answers that have come spilling out. But in writing the answers to the questions posed, one thing has become abundantly clear to me: There is a great deal more truth in Kafka's quotation *"All knowledge, the totality of all questions and all answers is contained in the dog"*, than we may possibly imagine.

If you wish to learn more or explore the issues raised in this book in more detail, you may be interested in the books on the following pages, written by the same author. (Available on Amazon, worldwide.)

You may also enjoy visiting our websites:

www.somedogsareangels.com

and

www.angelsincanada.com

CONTENTS

FROM DOGS TO YOU

INFANCY

FEEDING

COMMUNICATION

THE PACK

homes by babies?

DOG PSYCHE

HEALTH, ILLNESS AND DYING

THE SPIRITUAL DOG

DOGS IN AND FROM RESCUE

MORE BOOKS BY THE SAME AUTHOR

SOME DOGS ARE ANGELS

The most extraordinary true story you will ever read

Mark Starmer

Some dogs *really* are angels

This true story about dogs and a voyage of spiritual discovery follows the rollercoaster journey that results when a perfectly 'normal' businessman discovers that he has the ability to hear and speak to angels.

As his family struggles to come to terms with a perplexing new version of the realities around them, not least amongst their discoveries is the revelation that some dogs literally are angels and that they have been living with one. An unstoppable chain of events is put in motion that uproots the family and culminates in their guardianship of nineteen dogs.

Their tale is warming, amusing, heart wrenching and occasionally, downright bizarre. It is the most extraordinary true story you will ever read.

290 Pages
ISBN 978-1460922316

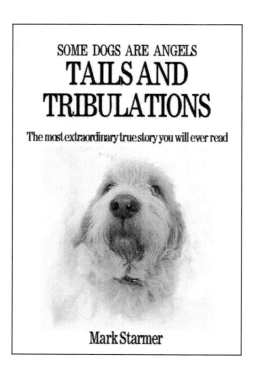

SOME DOGS ARE ANGELS

TAILS AND TRIBULATIONS

The most extraordinary true story you will ever read

Mark Starmer

This world is not as you see it.

Already sharing their lives with nineteen dogs, the author and his family are committed to helping those whom the etheric guide them to assist, and the number of incoming dogs continues apace. But life is getting harder by the day, and just around the corner awaits a devastating turn of events that will throw the lives of all, humans and dogs, into complete disarray.

This is a *true* story that has already captivated the hearts and minds of both dog lovers and those who know that there is a lot more to life than we think! The continuing tale is heart-warming and deeply moving. Readers will find it a difficult book to put down.

372 Pages
ISBN 978-1460974353

There are more things in Heaven and Earth...

With their world rocked by the occurrences at the end of *Tales and Tribulations*, the author and his family are left reeling. What happens next? How can the etheric's intentions for their future and the avatar sanctuary ever come to fruition?

In this final installment of the *Some Dogs are Angels* trilogy, the angels take us to an even greater depth of understanding about their role in our lives, sharing more detailed wisdom and insights than ever before.

388 Pages
ISBN 978-1503036383

Made in the USA
Middletown, DE
30 September 2017